JOB SATISFACTION OF COLLEGE TEACHERS

JOB SATISFACTION OF COLLEGE TEACHERS

Dr. D. Ramakrishnaiah
M.Sc., M.A., M.Ed., M.Phil., Ph.D.
Department of Education
Sri Venkateswara University
Tirupati - 517502
Andhra Pradesh
Editor :
Dr. Digumarti Bhaskara Rao
M.Sc., M.A., M. Ed., Ph.D.
R.V.R. College of Education
D - 43, S.V.N. Colony
Guntur - 522006
India

Discovery Publishing House
New Delhi - 110 002

First Published - 1998

Reprinted - 2018

ISBN: 978-81-7141-427-7

Job Satisfaction of College Teachers

Published by:

DISCOVERY PUBLISHING HOUSE PVT. LTD.
4383/4B, Ansari Road, Darya Ganj
New Delhi-110 002 (India)
Phone: +91-11-23279245, 43596064-65
Fax: +91-11-23253475
E-mail: discoverypublishinghouse@gmail.com
sales@discoverypublishinggroup.com
web: www.discoverypublishinggroup.com

Printed at:
Infinity Imaging Systems
Delhi

PREFACE

Every profession has got certain aspects conducive for job satisfaction, and at the same time it has other aspects too that lead to dissatisfaction. Teaching profession has no exception. Under this situation, it was decided to study the job satisfaction of college teachers.

In this study, the college teachers were satisfied with their job in general and in particular the college teachers were satisfied with the job factors such as principal, physical facilities, self esteem, fringe benefits, entertainment, prestige and courses and girl students, personal activities and place of work. The college teachers were dissatisfied with the job factors such as parents and students, academic policies and co-teachers. The service length, sex, size of the family, attitude towards teaching profession, personality design, etc., have played their legitimate role in deciding the job satisfaction.

As job satisfaction plays a major role in moulding the students, this study will help many a people in conducting many such studies in different parts of the land and in offering the remedial measures to those who are dissatisfied with their teaching profession. The policy makers and the implementors must try to bring job satisfaction among teachers.

Let us hope for the best services of teachers in deciding the destiny of our nation.

Dr. D. Ramakrishnaiah
Dr. D. Bhaskara Rao

CONTENTS

1

INTRODUCTION

1. The Process of Occupational Choice

One's occupation is the watershed down which the rest of his life flows. So if one has to be happy in his life he must be satisfied and happy in his occupation. To get satisfaction in his job, in turn, he must choose it wisely.

Choice of a job emerges as a result of the interplay of a multiplicity of factors. It is mainly the result of an interaction between factors pertaining to the job and those that characterise the chooser. Great vocational psychologists like Burnstein, Hollender, Super and many others consider occupational choice as a developmental process over a periods of years, that ends in a compromise between interests, capacities, values etc., of the individual on the one hand and opportunities on the other.

People work for different reasons. Some work just to earn money, some others work to utilise their talents and get satisfaction, recognition and social status. The first significant study on job satisfaction conducted by Hoppock (1935) reported that work rather than leisure brings more satisfaction. Morse, et al., (1954) made a survey on attitudes toward work and reported that work had a double function : (1) it enabled people to get money to support their families and themselves; and (2) it gave people a feeling of 'place' or 'role' in the society.

Prestige, power, salary, leisure and other features of a job are no doubt important, but these features become meaningful only to those who value them. The value of a particular feature of a job felt by the chooser is in turn determined by his personality, social and psychological background. This is implied in the proposition of Thompson (1947) that jobs differ in their attractiveness from person to person depending upon the need pattern of value system of the individual.

2. The Place of the Teacher in Ancient India

The significance of the teaching profession in any society can not be over emphasised. The luster with which our ancestors were interested in the 'teacher' may be gleaned from the hierarchy of their Gods: 'Matrudevo Bhava, Pitrudevo Bhava, Acharyadevo Bhava'. First mother is God, second father is God and third, 'Acharya' or 'Guru' or the 'Teacher' is God. Further, it is said 'Guru Brahma, Guru Vishnu, Gurudevo Maheswarah', which implies that the teacher is the Creator, the Sustainer and Ultimate Liberator.

Centuries ago in this land of Vedas, certain principles which had something noble and uplifting about them were held stead fastly. These principles were emphasized in those famous verses in Sanskrit, which the teacher and the taught recited together and considered the essence of their mūtual relationship; "Saha nau avatu/Saha nau bhunaktu/Saha Viryam Karavavahai/Tejasvi nau adhitamastu/Ma vidvisavahai/": 'May He protect us both: may He save us both; may we do together great deeds; may over learning be bright; may we not hate each other'. Though the same lines are recited today one does not always find the same zeal and the same enthusiasm issuing therefrom. The teacher's image has unquestionably changed from an 'inner-directed' to that of a 'stereotype'

3. Teaching Profession then and Now

Altekar (1961), while explaining the status enjoyed by the teachers in ancient times, said that the teacher was paid the highest reverence by all people including the rulers.

The teacher was looked upon as 'Guru' or 'Acharya' and was given the top most position in the professional hierarchy. Mukherji (1957) stated that the teacher had no need to worry his head over the mundane necessities of life in the olden days, and hence he was free to pursue his quest for knowledge. In those days he was a perfect model for the students in every aspect of life. He was totally responsible for the process of education. He was given full freedom in planning the curriculum, methods of instruction and evaluation. The student and the society used to 'look up' at the 'Acharya' for guidance and not 'look down' upon him as it is being done today.

There used to be a very close relationship between the teacher and the taught in the olden days. The relationship was founded more on love and affection rather than on authority. It was so intimate, that one was giving shelter to the other whenever there was a need.

Today, though along with other professions like medicine, law and engineering, teaching is also considered as a profession, nay, it is said to be the noblest of all professions; people do not think of the teacher as a professional worker in the same sense, status and reverence in which they consider the doctor, the lawyer, or the engineer. A teacher does not enjoy a social status as is enjoyed by lawyers, doctors or engineers. Why is this so ? Is it because teachers are poorly paid and their income is low ? Or is it because the majority of the teachers are from the poorer sections of the society ? If so, are there no lawyers and engineers whose income is less than that of the teachers ? Or, is it because teachers have failed to impress the society about the importance and the dignity of their work ?

Anjaneyulu (1971) pointed out that in addition to the loss of special recognition, the profession has been infested with a number of other evils. Enormous rise in the work load, lack of security of service-especially under private managements, growing indiscipline among the students and too much domination by the non-official politician bosses are only some of the evils. It is no exaggeration to say that there was a time when ministers had to seek appointment with Vice-Chancellors to meet them. Now Vice-Chancellors queue up to see ministers and officials (Subrahmanian, 1987).

Gone are the days when the teacher was glorified in the true sense of the word. The situation relating to the teacher's status and the teacher-pupil relationship seen today is quite contrary to what was obtained in those days.

4. Discontent in the Teaching Profession

True enough, it is said that a large number of teachers of the present day have no interest in their profession. They continue in the profession only as mechanical wage earners. The facilities and incentives offered in this profession are so meagre that many of the talented persons do not think of becoming teachers but seek positions elsewhere. Lack of recognition of the teachers in this country is a very sore point. They have not yet been given the same footing as a doctor, a lawyer or an I.A.S. officer in the society. The significance of the role of the teacher is hardly recognised, though it has become a fashion to observe the teachers' day. The teachers of today suffer from neglect, indifference and insecurity. We always expect of a lot from a teacher who has so little power and alarmingly meagre facilities.

The net result is there appears to be a widespread dissatisfaction at present in the teaching profession as a whole. Many seem to repent over their wrong choice and would be too willing to change their job in favour of some other lucrative one, if only opportunities are available.

In this connection it is befitting to quote the oftquoted quotation of Mr. Henry Van Dyke: 'He (the teacher) lives in obscurity and contents with hardship. For him no trumpets blare, no chariots, no golden decorations are decreed ..... patient in his duty, he quickens the indolence, encourages the eager and steadies the unstable.... He lights many candles which in later years will shine back to cheer him. This is his reward'.

Dissatisfaction of the individual, whatever may be the occupation in which he is engaged, results in professional stagnation. A dissatisfied teacher is lost not only to himself but also to the entire society. A dissatisfied teacher spells disaster to the country's future. Dissatisfaction among the workers is undesirable and dangerous in any profession; it is just suicidal if it occurs in the teaching profession (The Education Commission, 1966).

Pagel and Price (1980) listed different causes for the dissatisfaction of teachers. They were: (1) lack of planning time, (2) tedious paper and clerical work, (3) an out-of-touch and autocratic administration, (4) disruptive and unmotivated students, (5) non-teaching activities, such as faculty meetings and time wasting workshops, (6) uncooperative parents, (7) lack of autonomy to prescribe curriculum, (8) feelings of failure, and (9) low occupational prestige. Therefore, a better understanding of the causes for job satisfaction/dissatisfaction is desirable not because it will enable us to make them completely satisfied, but because it may help the administrators to relieve that intense and painful dissatisfaction which injures both the individual and the society in which he lives.

5. Role and Importance of the Teacher

The Education Commission (1966) has very aptly observed that, 'the future of the nation is shaped in her classrooms'. It is the teacher that moulds the most precious material of the land, viz., the boys and the girls in their most impressionable period of development in the required shapes.

The teacher has a powerful and abiding influence in the formation of the character of every future citizen. He acts as a pivot for the transmission of intellectual and technical skills and cultural traditions from one generation to the other. The responsibility of the teachers is, therefore, very great. There is no gain saying, therefore, the nation's, well being depends on the teacher's well being.

Saiyidain (1950) made the role of teacher quite illustrative when he said that the teacher had to patiently cut, out of a crude and unshaped stone, a thing of beauty. His role, today, more than ever, has become exceedingly crucial in the national attempt to bring about several positive changes in the society, national progress and national integration. It is increasingly realised by all those concerned with education of children that the standard of education in schools and colleges has considerably fallen. In any scheme of improvement of the teaching and standards in schools and colleges it is the teacher who has a key role to play. Unless and until he is a fully competent person, greatly interested and involved in his work and does his job satisfactorily, all other efforts that are taken to effect any improvement in the field of teaching are bound to fail.

The University Education Commission (1948) emphasised the importance of the teacher and his responsibility. The commission was categorical about the need for improving his status, salaries, service conditions, and about providing facilities for the pursuit of knowledge and performing his duties satisfactorily. In creative work like teaching, job satisfaction remains the 'sine-qua-non' and plays a very significant role in attracting and retaining the right type of persons in the profession.

6. Job Satisfaction

Job satisfaction involves liking for the work and acceptance of the pressures and aspirations connected with that work (Anjaneyulu, 1970). Scheneider and Snyder (1975) explained job satisfaction as follows . "It is most adequately conceptualized as a personalistic evaluation of conditions existing on the job (work, supervision) or outcomes that arise as a result of having a job (Pay, security). Job satisfaction is the perception of internal responses (i.e., feelings)".

All types of work are not inherently satisfying. People engaged in the work which is not satisfying in itself naturally look for satisfaction from sources external to it. But job satisfaction does promote happiness, success and efficiency in one's professional activity.

Every profession has got certain aspects conducive for job satisfaction. At the same time it has other aspects that lead to dissatisfaction. Teaching profession is no exception. If it is possible to isolate the factors of dissatisfaction, attempts can be made either to change the dissatisfying conditions or to reduce their intensity so as to increase the holding power of the profession. There is no gainsaying the fact that unless the teacher is satisfied with his occupation, he cannot deliver the goods.

7. Importance of the Study

As pointed out earlier, now-a-days there is a general feeling that the teachers do not have satisfaction in their jobs. There seems to be a growing discontentment on the part of the teachers towards their job as a result of which standards of education are falling. Is it a fact that the teachers are really dissatisfied inspite of the different plans and programmes which have been implemented to improve their lot ?

Studies on job satisfaction seem to have begun with the famous Hawthorne studies conducted by Elton Mayo at the Western Electric Company in the 1920's. Most of the studies conducted so far are in industrial setting in examining the effects of physical conditions, design of equipment etc., on job satisfaction and productivity. Elton Mayo and his co-workers started very much in this direction. During the course of their investigations, however, they became convinced that factors of a social nature also affect job satisfaction and productivity. The human relations school was thus born, which saw the function of the industrial psychologist as seeking to improve the happiness of the worker, and through this to imrove productivity. The implicit assumption, of course, was that the satisfied worker produced more.

The traditional model of job satisfaction is that it consists of the total body of feelings — about the nature of the job, promotion prospects, nature of supervision and so on — that an individual has about his job. If the sum total of influence of these factors give rise to feelings of satisfaction, the individual has job satisfaction. On the other hand if on the whole they give rise to feelings of dissatisfaction, the individual is dissatisfied. Changing any one of these influences will lead in the direction of job satisfaction or dissatisfaction depending upon the nature of the change.

Locke (1969), however, emphasises the concept of value fulfilment rather than expectation. Satisfaction occurs when the job fulfils what one values. Just as expectations, values vary from group to group and between individuals within the group.

In Andhra Pradesh and some other States under the 10+2+3 pattern, the +2 stage has been separated from the schools and regular colleges and a separate institution, called the junior college, has been evolved. Though the qualifications of teachers employed in Degree colleges and Junior colleges is same, there is a vast difference in their pay structure. Agitations by teachers were witnessed demanding equalisation of the pay structure and also other fringe benefits of both categories of teachers. What is the effect of the difference in the level of teaching and pay on the job satisfaction of the teachers employed in Junior Colleges ?

Further, the colleges in Andhra Pradesh are controlled by two types of managements — government and private. Has the type of management under which the teachers work, any effect on the job satisfaction of teachers ? Very often it is felt that teachers in government colleges will be more satisfied with their jobs than teachers working under private managements. But investigations by Venkata Rami Reddy and Krishna Reddy (1978); Venkata Rami Reddy and Babjan (1980) and Venkatarami Reddy and Ramakrishnaiah (1981) showed that teachers in private institutions were more satisfied with their job than those in government colleges.

Similarly, is there any significant difference between the job satisfaction of men and women teachers ? What are the other correlates of job satisfaction ? Is it related to attitude towards teaching ? Not much is known about these as very few empirical studies have been carried out especially on Indian samples. Investigation into these factors may throw light on many aspects of job satisfaction.

The progress and standard of any nation cannot be beyond the standard of her system of education and the standard of her educational institutions. The standard of any educational institutions in turn, cannot rise beyond the levels of its teachers. It is, therefore, emphasised by different Committees and Commissions that high quality personnel, who have the necessary aptitude for teaching and favourable attitude towards teaching should be selected for the teaching profession. Further, it is believed that certain personality traits are desirable for the teaching profession. It would be rewarding, therefore, to identify the type of attitude and personality characteristics that are conducive for driving satisfaction in the teaching profession. This knowledge may help in selecting the best suited to the teaching profession.

Thus, the present study 'Job Satisfaction of College Teachers' is designed to analyse the job satisfaction of the teachers relation to different variables like management, sex, level of teaching, attitude towards teaching, personality traits, etc.

2

REVIEW OF LITERATURE

1. The Teacher

Mukherji (1957) observed that four terms are used to refer to the teacher, viz. **'Acharya'**, **'Guru'** , **'Sikshaka'** and **'Upadhyaya'**. It may be noted that the term **'Acharya'** was reserved by Patanjali for application to the highest type of teacher, an original thinker and master like Panini, while the other terms were used with reference to the ordinary teachers.

To quote Gupta (1973), "As teachers, we tend to forget that out roles are determined to a large extent by the expectations of the pupils". One might ask what ideals or qualities a teacher should develop and posses so as to fit in with his changing roles. One can not but recall the dictum laid down in the 13th chapter of the **'BHAGAVADGITA'** about the characteristics of a real teacher : absence of pride, freedom from hypocrisy, non-violence, forgiving nature, straightforwardness, service of the preceptor, purity of mind and body, steadfastness and self control.

2. The Teacher — Then and Now

The teacher in India has always been held in high esteem. Tradition has attributed to him certain desirable personal qualities which he will do well to cultivate, in order to win and deserve that esteem. If the teacher is to secure and retain his rightful place, if he has to accomplish all that he might with his pupils, and if he has to find satisfaction in his work, he must know the qualities and qualifications required for the purpose and must strive to achieve them as far as possible.

Saiyidain (1950) made the role of the teacher quite illustrative when he said that the teacher has to patiently cut from a crude and unshaped stone, proportion and balance. Altekar (1951) while explaining the status enjoyed by teachers in ancient India, said that the teacher was paid the highest reverence by all people including the rulers. The teacher was called **'Guru'** and **'Acharya'** and was given the top most position in professional hierarchy.

Saiyidain further observed that we should take care to do nothing that will undermine the teachers's dignity and self respect. In this connection, there is a need not only for improving their material prospects but also according them proper social recognition which would cost the community nothing, except the cultivation of a better sense of values and greater social sensitiveness.

Mukerji (1947) found that in the ancient times the relationship between the teacher and the pupil was so intimate, that one was given shelter to the other whenever there was a need.

According to Apte (1961) the teacher in those days was not confronted with any financial problems. Mukherji (1957) states that the teacher then had no need to worry his head over the mundane necessities of life, and hence was free to pursue his quest for knowledge. But today the teacher finds himself handicapped not only by lower salary and lower status but also by longer hours of work and lack of facilities (Rao, 1966).

3. Opinions and Suggestions Given by Commissions and Committees About Teaching Staff

Many Commissions and Committees, appointed by the Government of India from time to time have examined various aspects of teachers and forwarded recommendations regarding their status, salaries, conditions of service, facilities, etc. The opinions of some of the committees and commissions are worth mentioning.

A. The University Education Commission (1948)

The University Education Commission, under the chairmanship of Dr. S. Radhakrishnan, examined various aspects of the teaching staff and emphasised the importance of the teacher and his responsibility. The commission was categorical about the need for improving his status, salaries, service conditions, and about providing facilities for the pursuit of knowledge and performing his duties satisfactorily.

The Commission further said that the success of educational process depends so much on the character and ability of the teacher that in any plan of university reform the main concern must be for securing adequate staff with qualifications necessary for the discharge of its many sided duties. It also opined that the success of a teacher will be measured not in terms of percentage of passes alone, nor even by the original contributions to knowledge, important though they are, but equally though the quality and character of men and women he has taught and developed.

It was felt that the main cause for deterioration of standards of teaching and of discipline may be due to the indifference with which teachers are treated today by the public. Hence due respect must be given to the teaching profession in order to improve the standards of teaching.

The Commission also emphasised the need for providing the necessary facilities such as books, journals and laboratories with out which the teacher cannot keep pace with the advancement of knowledge and carryout significant investigations. Further, it also stated that university teachers should be paid salaries on par with central services. Further, conditions regarding provident fund, leave and hours of work should be definitely laid down. It stressed on the need for refresher courses for the teachers to help them have up-to-date knowledge.

The Commission also pointed out that participation in political campaigns for electing members to the different bodies was one of the causes for the deterioration of the standards of education.

B. Secondary Education Commission (1954)

The Secondary Education Commission appointed by the Government of India, under the chairmanship of Dr. A. Lakshmana Swamy Mudaliar, also stressed on the need for improving the general conditions of teachers.

The Commission emphasised the reconstruction of the teacher in terms of his professional training and his economic status in particular and the status in the school and in the community in general. It laid great emphasis on paying adequate salary keeping in view the price index. It also suggested that other aspects, such as working conditions, service, job security, leave facilities, work load, retirement benefits, etc., should be given for the teacher so that he can do his job more successfully. It further recommended that amenities like education for children, housing schemes, rail travel concessions, in service programmes, medical facilities, etc., should be provided.

C. The Education Commission (1966)

"The future of India is now being shaped in her classroom" was the statement with which the Commission under the Chairmanship of Dr. Kothari opened its report. It emphasised that to make any process of education a success, the quality, competence and character of the teachers were the most important aspects.

In the opinion of the Commission, it is necessary that intensive and continued efforts be made to raise the economic, social and professional status of the teachers in order to attract young men and women of ability to the profession and to retain them in it as dedicated, enthusiastic and contended workers.

It also emphasised the principle of parity in remuneration to all the teachers with the same qualifications, doing similar work. There is a great deal of disparity in the remuneration of teachers of various ranks in higher education. The engineers and medical men are paid higher than those in the humanities. Moreover, there is a difference between the pay scales of the teachers in the affiliated schools and central schools. This should be reduced to a minimum. The teachers in the government schools, local bodies and private organisations have to be paid the same scale of pay. It also stressed the need to follow the principle of parity at all levels even among the different States.

It further opined that teachers should be free to exercise all civic rights and should be eligible for any public office. It also said that provision should be made for promotional chances within the profession. It recommended facilities for accommodation and such other benefits for the teachers to attract and retain men of talent the profession.

The Commission also states that awards should be given at the state level and national level to motivate the teachers to do their job most efficiently.

4. Job Satisfaction

According to Blum and Naylor (1968) job satisfaction is the result of various attitudes possessed by an employee. In a narrow sense, their attitudes are related to the job and are concerned with such specific factors as wages, supervision, steadiness of employment, conditions of work, opportunities for advancement, recognition of ability, fair evaluation of work, social relations on the job, prompt settlement of grievances, fair treatment by employer and other. similar factors.

However, other aspects such as employee's age, health, temperament, and level of aspiration should be considered. Again his family relationships, social status and activities in organisations, like labour, political or social, contribute ultimately to job satisfaction.

According to Gilmer (1966) job satisfaction or dissatisfaction is " the result of various attitudes, the person holds toward his job, toward related factors and toward life in general". Job satisfaction is a complex phenomenon, as described by Rao (1970), having multiple inter-correlated causal factors: personal, social, cultural and economic. Blum (1956) also stated that a more comprehensive approach to the problem of job satisfaction requires that many additional factors — physical, social, temperamental and personal factors — be included for correct assessment.

According to Katzel (1964) job satisfaction is the verbal expression of an incumbent's evaluation of his job. The verbal evaluation is made operational by some form of attitude questionnaire or scale by means of which the incumbent rates his job on a continuum of 'like — dislike', or approximate synonyms, such as 'satisfied — dissatisfied'.

Thus it is apparent from the foregoing definition that job satisfaction is a species of affect or hedonic tone, for which the stimuli are, events or conditions experienced in connection with the job or occupation. This circumstance is of considerable assistance to the understanding of job satisfaction since it permits examination of the subject in the context of the more general and fairly well documented conceptions of affect and motivation.

A theoretical view of job satisfaction as hedonic tone, according to Blum and Naylor (1968), may be summarised as containing the following elements :

1. The events or conditions experienced by a person in his job or occupation which arouse, among other responses,

feelings or affects which he can verbalise on a continuum of 'like — dislike', 'pleasant — unpleasant', 'satisfactory — unsatisfactory' or similar evaluative or hedonic dimensions.

2. People differ markedly in the degree of job satisfaction. In addition to errors of measurement, the variance in job satisfaction may be attributed to (a) differences in the stimuli i.e., features of the job and (b) differences in the job incumbents.
3. The intra-individual sources of job satisfaction may be accounted for largely in terms of the concept of adaptation levels of the related concept of personal values.

Thus there are numerous definitions and meanings for the concept of job satisfaction. To conclude, different operational definitions of job satisfaction given by Wanous and Lawler (1972) may be quoted.

1. "Overall job satisfaction is the sum of job facet satisfaction across all facets of a job".
2. "Job satisfaction has been conceptualized as a weighted sum of job facet satisfaction".
3. "Job satisfaction has been operationalised as the sum of goal attainment or need fulfilment when summed across job facets".
4. "Job satisfaction has been operationalised as a discrepancy between ' how much is there now' and 'how much should there be'.

5. Theories of Job Satisfaction.

Several theories have been propounded concerning the dynamics of job satisfaction and its general impact upon worker behaviours. A brief mention of some important theories seems appropriate.

A. Herzberg's Two-factors Theory

No theory of job satisfaction has received as much attention or has been subjected to as much criticism as the model proposed by Herzberg, Mausner, and Snyderman (1959). Because of its popularity among personnel managers and because of its somewhat uncertain status as an accurate model for job satisfaction it has been examined in detail by different authors.

Basic Study: The original study of Herzberg, Mausner, and Snyderman was concerned with an investigation into the causes of job satisfaction and job dissatisfaction among engineers and accountants. Their method was quite simple. They interviewed each person individually. Each worker was asked to describe, in detail, times when he felt exceptionally good or exceptionally bad about his job. The interviews were then 'content analysed' to see

1. What kind of things were mentioned when people described the times at which they were satisfied with their job,
2. What kind of things were mentioned when people were describing times at which they were dissatisfied with their job, and
3. Whether the kinds of things described in these two different circumstances were different.

The results of their study did indicate that things which were associated with high satisfaction (satisfiers) were somewhat different from the things which were associated with situations of low satisfaction (dissatisfiers). They found that the descriptions of good periods included such things as achievement, recognition, advancement, responsibility, etc. All of these things seemed to relate to the actual content of the job. They were therefore called 'content factors'. Descriptions of dissatisfying work periods seemed to be filled with items dealing with company policy, supervision, salary, and working conditions. These items were seemed to relate to the context in which a person performed his task and were therefore referred to as 'context factors'.

The Model: Thus, Herzberg, Mausner and Snyderman postulated two general classes of work variables — 'satisfiers' and 'dissatisfiers'. Satisfiers are those things which lead to job satisfaction. They are generally job 'content factors' or 'motivators'. Dissatisfiers are those things which result in job dissatisfaction. They are generally job 'context' or 'hygiene' factors.

To quote the authors, "Man tends to actualise himself in every area of his life, and his job is one of the most important areas. The conditions that surround the doing of the job cannot give him this basic satisfaction, they do not have this potentiality. It is only from the performance of a task that the individual can get the rewards that will reinforce his aspirations. It is clear that although the factors relating to the doing of the job and the factors defining the job context serve as goals for the employee, the nature of the motivating qualities of the two kinds of factors are essentially different. Factors in the job context meet the needs of the individual for avoiding unpleasant situations. In contrast to this motivation by meeting avoidance needs, the job factors reward the needs of the individual to reach his aspirations. These effects on the individual can be conceptualised as actuating approach rather than avoidance behaviour. Since it is in the approach sense that the term motivation is most commonly used, we designate the job factors as the 'motivators', as opposed to the extra job factors, which we have labelled as the factors of 'hygiene'. It should be understood that both kinds of factors meet the needs of the employee; but it is primarily the 'motivators' that serve to bring about the kind of job satisfaction...." (Herzberg, *et al.*, 1959).

Because the model postulates two general classes of variables — one class which can satisfy but not dissatisfy, and the other one which causes dissatisfaction but not satisfaction — the model has been designated as Herzberg's Two factor theory.

Major Criticism of the Model : Blum and Nylor (1968) say that in the process of the study the authors had to make the implicit assumption that the people being interviewed had both the ability and the desire to report accurately on the conditions which make them satisfied or dissatisfied with their jobs. If this is not so, then the results may be only an artifact of the 'set' people carried into the interview situation. For this reason, the study has been severely criticised. The major objection is that when a person is asked to tell about something good, he is apt to attribute the causes of it to his own accomplishments and achievements (content items); we all like to satisfy our need for esteem. Similarly, when someone is asked to tell about an unpleasant or dissatisfying work experience, he is more apt to blame others for this (context items), than he is to blame himself. Many attribute Herzberg's findings to this simple tendency on the part of the people.

Evidence bearing on the model: Since the original publications of the model, a number of studies have attempted to provide evidence or other wise concerning its validity. Unfortunately the results are contradictory in nature. Porter (1966) has provided a brief but comprehensive summary of all such research.

Evidence in favour of the theory: Myers (1964) found that, for a representative sample of employees in a manufacturing company, satisfaction was related to intrinsic work factors and dissatisfaction to extrinsic factors. Likewise, Schwartz, Jenusaitis and Stark (1963), in a study of lower level supervisors, found the appropriate relationship between satisfaction — dissatisfaction and intrinsic - extrinsic factors.

Evidence against the theory: Studies by Friedlander (1963), Ewen (1964), Wernimont (1964), and Kornhauser (1965) seem to support Dunnette's (1965) conclusion that ".... the two factor notion of job satisfaction is an over-simplified representation of the motivational milieu of the world of work". Reviewing the literature, Blum and Naylor (1968) pointed out that the factors involved in feelings of satisfaction and dissatisfaction of not appear to divide themselves as neatly as assumed by Herzberg's original studies.

Savage (1967) supported Herzberg's theory with a few minor exceptions, the most obvious of which was that good interpersonal relations of teachers, especially with students, were motivational rather than hygienic.

Soliman (1970) found that when the environment (organisation) provides adequately for the satisfaction of all kinds of needs, the motivators become more powerful sources of satisfaction than hygiene factors. If the environment deprives people of all kinds of needs, hygiene factors become more powerful sources of dissatisfaction than motivators.

Sarveswara Rao (1972) found that promotions and achievement which are prominent intrinsic factor, acted as bipolar variables. So also, company policies and practices acted as bipolar variables. This fact goes against the contention of the dual-factor theory. One of the significant findings which fundamentally violates the postulates of the theory is, that hygienes contributed significantly more to satisfaction than to dissatisfaction.

B. Maslow's Theory

Jobs which are able to satisfy most of the maslow's (1943) needs, would be jobs which would result in greater satisfaction on the part of the employee.

One way of defining motivation is to talk in terms of a particular state of the individual — a state of imbalance or disequilibrium — as defining a motivated person. The person is motivated to correct any such imbalance, that is, he seeks some way of obtaining relief. Thus one might talk of a motivational cycle as a process having three distinct parts:

1. Need or motive i.e., a state of psychological or physiological imbalance.

2. Response of motivated behaviour i.e., an action directed toward alleviating the imbalance.
3. Goal i.e., that which has to be obtained to reduce the imbalance, the object of the motivated behaviour.

Psychologists interested in motivation have spent considerable time discussing different types of needs. Maslow (1943) has proposed an interesting theory concerning human needs and their effect upon human behaviour. He suggests that human needs may be classified into five different groups or classes:

1. *Physiological needs:* These are the basic needs of the organism such as food, water, oxygen and sleep. They also include the somewhat less basic needs such as sex or activity.
2. *Safety needs*: Here Maslow is talking about the need of a person for a generally ordered existence in a stable environment which is relatively free of threats to the safety of the person's existence.
3. *Love needs*: These are the needs for affectionate relations with other individuals and the need for one to have a recognised place as a group member — the need to be accepted by one's peers.
4. *Esteem needs*: The need of a stable firmly based self-evaluation. The need for self-respect, self-esteem, and for the esteem of others.
5. *Self-actualisation needs*: The needs for self-fulfilment. The need to achieve one's full capacity for doing.

The important thing about Maslow's theory, however, is not so much his classification system as it is in the fact that he considers these five need classes to form a 'hierarchy of needs'. That is, it proceeds from very basic needs (physiological needs and safety needs) to a cluster of higher social needs (love needs, esteem needs and self-actualisation needs).

The hierarchy concept is critical to Maslow, since his basic premises are:

1. The behaviour of any person is dominated and determined by the most basic groups of needs which are unfulfiled.
2. The individual will systematically satisfy his needs, starting with the most basic and moving up the hierarchy.
3. More basic need groups are said to be pre-potent in that they will take precedence over all those higher in the hierarchy.

Blai (1982) hypothesised that, in the work environment, degrees of self assessed job satisfactions vary with the strength of the psychological needs satisfied. The degree of satisfaction of any person is dependent upon the extent of fulfilment of his needs. If the structure of the work situation is such that it is not possible for an employee to select goals or to obtain goals which are necessary to satisfy his needs, then frustration — instigated behaviour is likely to occur. It is therefore important that a system of goals or rewards be available to the employee that well satisfy whatever needs he brings into the work situation.

C. Vroom's Theory

Vroom (1964) has proposed a theory of human motivation which, although quite general in form, takes as its context the individual in the world of work. It is probably the first such attempt at formal motivation 'model building' in industrial psychology. Vroom has drawn very heavily on the work of the great social psychologist, Kurt Lewin. Like Lewin, Vroom uses the basic concept of valance as a key notion. He defines valance as 'the attractiveness of a goal or outcome', or 'the anticipated satisfaction from an outcome'. Vroom suggests that job satisfaction is a reflection of how desirable a person finds his job. Vroom outlines the town propositions as follows:

1. The valance of an outcome to a person is a monotonically increasing function of the algebraic sum of the products of the valances for all other outcomes and his conceptions of its instrumentality for the attainment of these other outcomes.
2. The force on a person to perform an act is monotonically increasing function of the algebraic sum of the products of the valances of all outcomes and the strength of his experiences that the act will be followed by the attainment of these outcomes.

Vroom suggests that job satisfaction is a reflection of how desirable a person finds his job. Thus, it was a measure of a persons's valance for his work situation. His model predicted the direct relationship between the valance of his job and turnover and absenteeism. Vroom equated job satisfaction with the valance of the job or work role. The overall valance of work role is useful in predicting behaviour in relation to the total work role.

D. Other Theories

Other theories of job satisfaction are not so popular as the above theories. But a few researches were undertaken applying these theories.

Activation theory: Scott (1966) suggested that 'activation theory' was a very appropriate model for understanding the behaviour in work environment. Briefly, activation theory states that the human organism needs stimulation and variety in its environment, with out which motivation will suffer and frustration may result. Smith, Kendall and Hulin (1969) defined job satisfaction as feeling of affective responses to the work situation. In addition, they posited that these responses are best explained by a discrepancy between the work motivation attitudes and the incentives offered by the organisations.

The inducement contributions theory (March and Simon, 1958), the Cognitive dissonance theory (Festinger, 1957) and the Inequity theory (Adams, 1963) have similar conceptualisations. The basic postulate of these theories is that job satisfaction levels are related to the perceived differences between what is expected or desired as a fair and reasonable return (individual motivation) and what is actually experienced in the job situation (organisatioal incentives).

6. Motivational Factors and Job Satisfaction

One of the earliest community wide surveys on job satisfaction was conducted by Hoppock (1935). Eighty eight per cent of 351 employed adults answered the lengthy questionnaire. The results obtained in the study indicated that 15 per cent of the sample had a negative attitude or dissatisfaction.

Hoppock (1935) conducted a survey on people in the teaching profession also. Five hundred teachers from 51 urban and rural communities in the north-eastern United States, estimated their job satisfaction on four attitude scales. Of this group, the 100 most satisfied and 100 least satisfied were asked about 200 questions. A comparison of their answers differentiated the satisfied from the dissatisfied teachers in the following areas:

(a) The satisfied showed fewer indications of emotional maladjustments.

(b) The satisfied were more religious.

(c) The satisfied enjoyed better human relationships with

their superiors and associates.

(d) The satisfied were teaching in the cities of over 10,000 population.

(e) The satisfied felt more successful.

(f) Family influence and social status were more among the satisfied.

(g) The satisfied 'selected' their vocations.

(h) Monotony and fatigue were reported more frequently by the dissatisfied.

(i) The satisfied averaged 7.5 years older.

Weitz and Nuckolos (1955) found that the decision to accept a new job would depend on expectations or anticipations of value fulfilments. To the extent that the expectations failed to materialise, job satisfaction would be relatively low and the likelyhood of quitting the job would be relatively great.

Herzberg, et al., (1957) pointed out that for people at higher occupational and/or educational levels, intrinsic aspects of the job go up in importance, while security drops off considerably. This is no doubt due to the greater 'marketability' possessed by the people in the higher occupational strata.

Crites (1961) analysed three relatively new measures of work motives and values and identified the following five orthogonal factors: material security Vs. job freedom; personal status Vs. Social service; social approach; system; and structure.

On 93 subjects matched for equal satisfaction on motivator and hygiene aspects of their jobs, it was found that the work itself and opportunity for advancement accounted for nearly all the variance in overall job satisfaction (Halpern, 1966).

Hackman and Lawler (1971) found that when jobs are high on the four core dimensions (variety, autonomy, task identity, feedback), employees who are desirous of higher order need satisfaction (obtaining feelings of accomplishment, personal growth) tend to be treated by supervisors as doing high quality work.

Schmidt (1976) pointed out the importance of motivational factors like achievement, recognition, advancement, responsibility and work itself for job satisfaction.

According to Hackman and Oldham (1976) a job high in motivating potential will not affect all individuals in the same way. In particular, people who strongly value and desire personal feelings of accomplishment and growth, would respond very positive to a job which is high on the core dimensions; individuals who do not value personal growth and accomplishment my find such a job anxiety-arousing and may be uncomfortably 'stretched' by it.

From a motivational point of view, Sergiovanni (1975) suggested that over the long haul external standards and impersonal control mechanisms, unduly programme teacher activity and behaviour and reduce the amount of discretion at the teaching level and also lower the mount of influence which teachers and students have over classroom activity.

According to Schmidt (1976) administrators are highly motivated by achievement, recognition and advancement in their profession.

Robert's (1977) study indicated that teachers ranked challenging work, good interpersonal relations, achievement of objectives, good wages, and fair and competent supervision as the most important of the thirteen job motivation factors.

Two important sources of job satisfaction have been suggested by faris (1977). The motivator factors commonly associated with meaningful work experiences appeared to provide an intrinsic source of job satisfaction. In addition to this, perceived success attained through achievement on the job and advancement through the organisational hierarchy, appeared to be major determinants of job satisfaction.

According to Blum (1961), a person might select a job where elements of security and other hygiene factors are high. Other persons, less concerned with security, choose jobs in which motivators or satisfiers are high. Williams' (1965) findings that low risk takers are more concerned with intrinsic characteristics, support Blum's (1961) conclusions.

According to Davis (1981), the primary sources of satisfaction of teachers were in aspects of working with students, intellectual stimulation, autonomy, holidays, and job security. Teacher satisfaction according to Daly (1981) is affected primarily by objective feedback or individual perception as to the prevailing performance level of the school.

Karugu's (1981) study indicated that the Kenyan educators in the sample groups identified job security, sense of building the nation, chance to continue learning, love of jobs itself (Noble), love for children, extracurricular activities, and communication with teachers, parents, and pupils as the most satisfying job factors in their current positions and also as the factors which cause them to retain their positions.

Teachers as a total group, indicated that they were most satisfied in the following areas: social service, creativity, moral values, and responsibility (Gordon, 1981).

Kuhn (1982) found that satisfied teachers centered around intrinsic aspects of work, predominantly, helping students. It was found that satisfaction was a result of a achievement on the job, interpersonal relational and recognition; and satisfaction was likely to result in feelings of increased job commitment (Hayeslip, 1983).

The most important job dimensions motivating employees were work itself, achievement, relationship with peers, working conditions and relationship with supervisors (Al-Khaldi, 1983).

Ahmed (1984) found that the most important predictors for teachers' feelings of job satisfaction were the amount of pay offered by the job, the degree of help received from superiors, and the amount of say teachers had in decision making. Least important predictors for job satisfaction were found to be opportunity for promotion and the degree of fairness of work load.

Satisfaction influences how individuals describe their jobs. Satisfied individuals may see their jobs as more 'complex' than dissatisfied individuals (Loher, et al., 1985).

Birmingham (1985) found that teachers were most satisfied with intrinsic reinforces such as social service, creativity, variety and ability utilization.

7. Dissatisfaction, Stress and Burnout

News paper headlines that emphasize teacher strikes, teacher burnout and stress, and assaults on school employees suggest that many teachers are not satisfied. A number of studies conducted through out the 1970s and into the 1980s indicate a gradual education in teacher satisfaction (Encyclopedia of Educational Research, 1982).

Fuller and Miskel (1972) found that about 89 per cent of the teachers participating in their study were satisfied or very satisfied with their jobs, but Bentzen, Williams and Heckman (1980), in an investigation conducted in the late 1970s, reported that slightly more than 75 per cent of the teachers were satisfied with their jobs. In the latter study, important differences in job satisfaction were discovered at the various levels of teaching, with elementary teachers expressing more satisfaction with their jobs than secondary teachers.

Causes of teacher dissatisfaction and low morale vary. They

include questioning and criticizing of school goals and policies, lack of enthusiasm for teaching, rejection or lack of follow-up on administrative directives (Cook, 1979), absenteeism (Educational Research Service, 1980), and fragmentation-a general feeling of being pulled in different directions (Klugman, Carter, & Israel, 1979). Stapleton, Croft, Frankiewicz (1979) found a positive relationship between teacher job dissatisfaction and teacher brinkmanship, which they defined as teacher behaviour that attempts to challenge the authority structure of the school while attempting to avoid its negative sanctions.

Employee stress and burnout are also frequently perceived to be symptoms of dissatisfaction and low morale. Psychological stress is believed to a manifested by feelings of frustration, great pressure, and a lack of control over one's emotions and environment (Werner, 1980). Maslach (1978) defines burnout as emotional exhaustion caused by job stress. Among the more important indicators of burnout are a loss of concern for and detachment from the people with whom one works; a cynical and dehumanized perception of students, accompanied by deterioration in the quality of teaching; depression; increased use of sick leave; and efforts to leave the profession (Walsh, 1979).

Although stress and burnout are typically viewed as symptoms of dissatisfaction, it should be emphasized that this relationship may not be as strong as assumed. For example, one study found that two-thirds of teachers reported that their jobs were stressful, but 86 per cent said that they usually or always liked their work (American Academy of Family Physicians, 1979). Too much stress, however, can be harmful (Cooper and Marshall, 1976; Girdano and Everly, 1979; Cichon and Koff, 1980).

With regard to teacher stress, Quick and Quick (1979) believe that four groups of factors create work stress: (1) role factors, (2) job factors, (3) physical factors, and (4) interpersonal factors. Based upon a survey of its members, the New York State United Teachers Organisation contends that the most important factor contributing to stress is the effect of disruptive children; incompetent administrators are identified as the second most important cause of stress (Urban Teachers Report more stress, 1980).

In their research on Chicago teachers, Cichon and Koff (1980) found that the more important causes of teacher stress are problems of disruption and threats to the teachers' physical, professional, and personal well-being. In this connection, an NEA Survey of its membership in 1980 ("Teacher Opinion Poll : Attacks on Teachers" 1980) estimated that 113,000 of the country's 2,184,000 public school teachers were physically attacked by students during a twelve-month period. Suggested causes of teacher burnout are usually believed to be similar to those associated with stress Bloch, 1978; Weiskopf, 1980).

A number of investigations into the causes of teachers' dissatisfaction have been conducted. An NEA survey ("Teacher opinion Poll : Job Satisfaction", 1980), found that a majority of teachers felt that the following factors, listed in order of frequency of identification, had a negative effect on their job satisfaction :

1. Public attitudes toward the schools,
2. Treatment of education by the media,
3. Student attitudes toward learning,
4. Salary, and
5. Status of teachers in the community.

In addition, 49 per cent of the teachers indicated that student behaviour had a negative effect upon their job satisfaction.

Glass, et al., (1979), Pagel and Price (1980) found that the factors contributing most to job dissatisfaction, in order of importance, were:

1. lack of planning time,
2. tedious paper and clerical work,
3. an out-of-touch and autocratic administration,
4. disruptive and unmotivated students,
5. non-teaching activities, such as faculty meetings and "time wasting workshops",
6. uncooperative parents,
7. lack of autonomy to prescribe curriculum,
8. feeling of failure, and
9. low occupational prestige.

In Adler's (1980) study, respondents saw external agents viz., co-workers, supervisors, the orgtanization in general, customers, as more responsible for occasions of dissatisfaction than for occasions of job satisfaction.

In Davis' (1981) study, the major source of dissatisfaction was in teacher-administration interaction through politics and policies at the local, state, and federal levels, 97 per cent of the teachers reported that teaching was not a profession because of the low salary, lack of prestige, and teachers' lack of control.

Karugu (1981) found that the following job factors as dissatisfying and as reasons for wanting to resign current jobs: poor pay, poor promotion methods by merit, lack of recognition, no chance for advancement, no house allowance for married women, no loan privileges, frequent supervision and administrative policies, and delay of school supplies and maintenance.

Teachers working in the schools managed by private firms indicated that company policies and practices, advancement, recognition and social status were areas in which they found the least job satisfaction or dissatisfaction (Gordon, 1981).

Hayeslip's (1983) findings also suggested that major sources of dissatisfaction were administrative policies and actions as well as interpersonal relations with fellow officers.

Minnesota teachers were dissatisfied with the extrinsic reinforcers, of advancement, compensation, company policies and practices and recognition (Birmingham, 1985).

8. Job Characteristics and Job Satisfaction

A questionnaire based upon the 14 need as specified by Maslow (1954) was completed by a sample of 470 persons in a wide range of occupations. It was found that the most important job characteristics that served as satisfiers were interesting duties (mentioned by 53% of the sample), job security (45%) and self actualisation (42%) (Blair, 1964).

Paliwal & Paliwal (1974) conducted a study on the need importance in relation to personal characteristics of 52 industrial employees. The results indicated that the skilled, semi-skilled and unskilled groups expressed equally strongly the need for dignified behaviour, giving this need the first place of importance. Need for wage increase was almost the same for all the three groups. Need for housing varied from group to group — the unskilled feeling it least and the skilled feeling it highly strongly.

Friedlander (1964) in a study on 80 evening course students of whom about half were full-time employees, administered two questionnaires consisting of 18 possible job characteristics. Job characteristics such as achievement, challenging assignments, recognition and the work itself were viewed as most important to both satisfaction and dissatisfaction. Other characteristics such as employee benefits, merit increases, working conditions, effect of job on home life, job security and technical competence of the supervisor were of relatively minor importance.

The Herzberg theory (Herzberg, et al., 1959) as applied by Ford (1969) emphasises job characteristics rather than individual differences. The theory suggests that jobs with opportunities for achievement, recognition, responsibility, advancement and growth in competence are those that enhance motivation and job satisfaction.

Robert (1977) stated that teachers ranked challenging work, good interpersonal relations, achievement of objectives, good wages and fair and competent supervision as the most important job motivation factors. In a study by Hooker (1977), it was found that authority and decision making were rated as being the most satisfying variables and compensation was rated as being the most dissatisfying variables of the study.

In Miskal's (1974) study, the business managers evidence attitudes with high-risk propensity and less concern for extrinsic factors. The two educational administration groups, appearing in the middle of the continuum were similar in their attitudes to teachers in having a high concern for extrinsic factors and security; but when risk was attached to intrinsic factors, they resembled the business managers.

Goble's (1977) job satisfaction survey showed that a majority of workers in broiler processing plant, were dissatisfied with their work. Those workers who were least satisfied with co-workers, seemed to have more family-illness-related-absences, than did those who were more acceptable to others.

According to Chen (1977), the strongest sources of satisfaction for Chinese school teachers were : moral value, social service, and co-workers. Prevalent sources of dissatisfaction were : advancement, company policies and practices, supervision-technical, compensation, and supervision-human relations. The subject taught by the teachers was a source of job satisfaction.

In the studies carried out by Rao (1971), Lahiri and Srivastava (1967), supervisory relations and relations with co-employees are included in hygienes, while in Marr and Mathur's (1973), they fail in the job content factor. In a study by Marr and Mathur (1973), it was observed that the largest number of teacher educators were satisfied with the fact that they found their work interesting.

In fact, Friedlander's (1966) study showed that job content factors are important for high status white-collar workers.

Glickon (1977) conducted a study on the job satisfaction of social workers. They ranked their job satisfaction in the following order. Satisfaction with co-workers highest, followed by satisfaction with supervision, the work itself, pay and lowest satisfaction with promotional opportunity.

Aspects of job satisfaction were found to be strongly related to perceived task characteristics (Caldwell and O'Reilly III, 1982). Further, they argued that satisfied job incumbents may describe their jobs favourably in terms of job characteristics, rather than in terms of variations in job dimensions, leading to differences in job satisfaction.

9. Nature of Work and Job Satisfaction

The nature of the work done is very important element of job satisfaction. In fact, it probably can be said that it is the major determiner of job satisfaction.

Herzberg et al. (1959) found that positive events are dominated by reference to intrinsic aspects of the job itself, while negative events are dominated by references to extrinsic aspects of the job situation.

Anjaneyulu's (1968) study on the job satisfaction of secondary school teachers indicated that the factors which contributed to dissatisfaction were lack of academic freedom and heavy load of work.

Perumal (1969) also expressed the view that the assignment of any extra work to a teacher should be determined in the light of the work load; extra work should be assigned preferably to those who have the least number of periods of work.

According to Gangappa (1969), the multiplicity of tasks and duties makes one loose interest in his job and subjects him to all kinds of worries and maladjustments.

Armstrong (1971) found that satisfaction with the content factor made the greatest contribution to overall job satisfaction, regardless of occupational level.

Hackman and Lawler (1971) suggested that intrinsically satisfying jobs should (a) allow the worker to feel personally responsible for his work (autonomy), (b) provide meaningful outcomes (variety and task identity), and (c) provide adequate knowledge of results (feedback).

- White collar employees were more Preoccupied with the content of the work to be done and with subordinates and were more likely to have taken job because they liked the type of work (Locke and Whiting, 1974).

Clarke (1977) found that internal factors were more satisfying than external factors for most satisfied and most dissatisfied teachers. External factors were more dissatisfying than internal factors for both groups. Internal and external factors appeared to be related to job satisfaction and external factors appeared to be related to job dissatisfaction. According to Chen (1977), however, there was no linear relationship between the two variables.

Vickroy,/et al. (1982) reported that employees tended to be less satisfied when working on boring tasks.

10. Work Environment and Job Satisfaction

It has been recognised that the work environment satisfied many of the needs possessed by the worker as an individual. The extent to which the various segments of the job environment contribute toward satisfaction of these needs, determines the job satisfaction of the worker.

Numerous studies conducted in Britain have shown how lighting, temperature, noise, etc., affect the efficiency and personal well-being of the worker (Smith, 1945).

American Vocational Association (AVA) Research Bulletin No. 3 (1948) reported that more equipment in the Home economics department brought more satisfaction to home economics teachers. Similarly National Educational Association (NEA) Research Bullitin (1957) pointed out that acquisition of teaching materials and suitable classroom situations were related to job satisfaction.

Rudd and Wiseman (1962) found that inadequate equipment and supplies as well as lack of other facilities have often been a source of low morale and dissatisfaction. Gilmer (1966) believed that working conditions were more important for female workers than for male workers, especially for married ones.

Rohila (1966) found that if the physical environment in which the work is done, is unhealthy, it may contribute to a sense of uneasiness and that work done in poor physical conditions over a long period of time may result in dissatisfaction with the job.

Anjaneyulu (1968) divided the factors of dissatisfaction into three categories : (1) strong dissatisfiers, (2) weak dissatisfiers, and (3) conditional dissatisfiers. The third group of dissatisfiers would cease to cause dissatisfaction if the situation was changed. Factors like frequent transfers, low standard of pupils, interference of politicians which was peculiar in certain managements have caused conditional dissatisfaction.

Pestonjee, Akhtar and Siddiqui (1971) found that there was tendency among the lower levels of employees to resist change like introduction of electronic data processing system in their work.

Englhardt (1973) observed that job satisfaction of teachers decreased as the size of the class increased. Satisfaction also had a direct relation to the principal's considerations to the teaching staff.

According to Neeraja Dwivedi and Pestonjee (1975), the work environment satisfies many of the needs of the worker as an individual.

Umstot, Bell (Jr) and Mitchell (1976) investigated the effects of job enrichment and goal setting on employee productivity and satisfaction in a well-controlled simulated job environment. The results indicate that job enrichment had a substantial impact on job satisfaction but little effect on productivity. Goal setting on the other hand, had a major impact on productivity and a less substantial impact on satisfaction. In the second phase (after two day's work) people with unenriched jobs worked under the enrichment conditions and people originally without goals, were assigned goals. Job enrichment, again had a positive effect on job satisfaction, while goal setting had a positive effect on performance.

11. Job Behaviour and Job Satisfaction

Vroom (1964) has done an excellent job of examining the relationship between job satisfaction and various aspects of job behaviour, and perhaps sumarising his findings is the best way of getting an over view. He categorised the studies in terms of which job behaviour was correlated with job satisfaction. Of the seven studies which related job satisfaction to turnover, that were examined by Vroom, all indicated a negative relationship. That is, the higher a worker's satisfaction the less apt he was to leave the job.

A moderate and consistent relationship has generally been found across various samples between greater job satisfaction and propensity to remain with the organisation (Brayfield and Crockett, 1955; Herzberg, et al., 1957; Vroom, 1964; Porter and Steers, 1973).

Porter, Steers and Mowday (1974) indicated that the attitudes held by an individual are predictive of subsequent turnover behaviour, with individuals who ultimately leave the organisation having less favourable attitudes than individuals who stay. Patterns of attitudes across time suggest that this inverse relationship between favourable attitudes and turnover is generally stronger as individuals approach the point at which they leave the organisation.

Job related factors linked to stress include role ambiguity, role conflict, role overload, unwanted overtime, high job concentration, low utilization of abilities, low participation, low complexity of work (Caplan, et al., 1975), management-supervision, organizational climate, and group conflict (Matteson and Ivancevich, 1979; Ivancevich and Matteson, 1980).

Although job satisfaction was found to be negatively related to absence behaviour when simple correlations were conducted, partial correlations of job satisfaction with absenteeism showed no consistent relationship (Cheloha and Farr, 1980).

For organizations, stress is important no only from the disease and physical health perspective but also from the psychological perspective. That is, stress has been implicated as a factor that leads to job dissatisfaction, absenteeism, and voluntary turnover (Ivancevich, Matteson and Preston, 1982). Intent to quit is a reasonable component of a stress model because it has been found to lead to voluntary turnover and absenteeism (Mobley, et al., 1979; Michaels and Spector, 1982).

Smith (1982) Indicated that elementary teachers were voluntarily absent more often than secondary teachers. Attitudes and behaviours of withdrawal were likely outcomes of dissatisfaction (Hayeslip, 1983).

Sharp (1984) found that principals who plan to retire from the system early are less satisfied with their jobs than principals who plan to stay in the system until at least normal retirement age.

12. Management and Job Satisfaction

The possible cause of employee dissatisfaction and low morale stems from the different frames of reference of administrators and teachers. This disparity is frequently conceptualized as conflict between the bureaucratic orientation of the administration and the professional orientation of the staff (Blau and Scott, 1962; Etzioni, 1964). A bureaucratic orientation emphasizes staff compliance with rules, regulations, and loyalty to the administration. A professional orientation, in contrast, emphasizes desire for autonomy and control over one's work environment and allegiance to one's subject matter and/or clients rather than to the organization itself. According to this conceptualization teachers are assumed to have professional orientation, whereas administrators are believed to have bureaucratic orientation (Corwin, 1965). It should be noted that some writers have questioned whether all teachers possess a professional orientation and all administrators have a bureaucratic orientation (Henson, 1978; De Young, 1980).

Stagner, Flabee and Wood (1952) found that job satisfaction was related to better employee - employer relationship. When the behaviour of administrators conformed with teachers' expectations of the formers role, satisfaction was high; non conformity produced high dissatisfaction (Bidwell, 1959).

California Institute of Technology (1953-54) conducted a series of surveys of employee opinion and concluded that the employees expressed a great desire for information from management. Sommers (1969) observed that most of the teachers felt that there was a lack of communication between teachers and administrators. Suehr (1962) also found that communication was one of the most vital areas in the whole morale process. It was most conspicuous by its absence, and consequently in tended to be a major source of dissatisfaction.

Anjaneyulu (1968) in his study on job satisfaction of secondary school teachers, educationists, inspecting officers, headmasters and retired teachers, found that in committee schools, the teachers were dissatisfied because of lack of job security, rigid and orthodox service conditions and too much of domination by the management. In mission schools, the factors were low standards of pupils, lack of parental co-operation and lack of right prospects in the job. In local board schools, the factors were too much interference by politicians lack of social status and non-availability of suitable accommodation, equipment and furniture. In government schools, rigid and orthodox service conditions, lack of parental co-operation and frequent transfers to distant places were the factors, producing dissatisfaction.

Merill-II (1969) noted that both the elementary teachers and principals were equally dissatisfied with company practices and polices as well as with authority. Butler (1961) observed that degree of satisfaction was related to feeling of freedom or lack of it, that was allowed by the management, in the classroom.

The company or organization was found to be causing the highest percentage of both satisfying and dissatisfying events with emphasis on money, working conditions, promotions, amount of work and recognition (Locke and Whiting, 1974).

Bernard and Kulandaivel (1976) studied job satisfaction of high school teachers working under different managements and found that the teachers of aided schools appeared to be better satisfied than the teachers from municipal and government schools. It was also found that teachers working under different managements had different problems.

Smith (1977) found the satisfying elements in the principalship to be directly controlled by the principals themselves while control of the dissatisfying elements rested with the upper level school district management.

Venkatarami Reddy and Krishna Reddy (1978) observed that the teachers employed under private managements were the most satisfied while thole in the government managements were the least satisfied. Similar results were obtained by Venkatarami Reddy and Babjan (1980); and Venkatarami Reddy and Ramakrishnaiah (1981). In a comparative study of job satisfaction, Tabatabai (1981) revealed that private sector employees were more satisfied with their job than public sector employees.

Results of Dodge's (1983) study revealed that proclamation factors accounted for 33 per cent of the variance in job satisfaction while the personal variables accounted for 2 per cent of the variance.

Chopra (1986) found that the teachers working in schools with open climate are likely to show higher over all job satisfaction than their counterparts in closed climate schools. Further, in open climate, school teachers exhibit higher job satisfaction in respect of two areas, namely 'Supervisor' and 'Identification with the Institution'.

13. Principal and Job Satisfaction

One of the most frequently cited reasons give by former teachers for having left the profession was dissatisfaction with their principals, according to Browning (1963) and Yuskiewicy and Donaldson (1972).

Sommers (1969) reported that the principal is the most important determinant of teacher morale. Englhardt (1973) found that satisfaction had a direct relation to principal's consideration to the teaching staff. According to Ahuja (1976) dissatisfaction increases when one has to work under an incapable, inefficient and indifferent head or boss.

According to Bloland and Selby (1980), an important factor

in teacher career change is dissatisfaction with the principals which may stem in part from the principal's role often unintentional, in reducing or eliminating teacher opportunity for creativity in the classroom. Lipham et al., (1982 found that the staff perceptions of principal's leadership was significantly and positively related to job satisfaction.

Teacher satisfaction may also be influenced by the perceived ability of the principal to provide rewards for high quality teaching performance (Daly, 1981). Teachers-principal relations and interfaculty relationships have a great effect on teacher's job satisfaction (Mokry, A-I, 1981).

A positive association was found to exist between the level of teacher job satisfaction and the principal's perceived level of aloofness (Holder, 1985).

14. Supervision and Job Satisfaction

Supervision has been found to have a significant relation to job satisfaction by several investigators. A number of investigators believe it to be one of the important, if not the most important, factors. One of the significant findings of the Hawthrone studies was that it was possible to change the attitudes of the employees by developing a co-operative spirit between workers and supervisors (Roethlisberger and Dickson, 1939).

According to Rohila (1966) a decentralised organization provides each individual with more freedom and opportunities for self — expression and hence persons in such an organization are likely to be better adjusted than those in a centralised organization.

In Locke and Whiting's (1974) study, blue collar workers saw their supervisors and co-workers as agents of dissatisfaction, while white collar attributed dissatisfying events to subordinates and the union.

It was found by Gowin (1975) that school's innovativeness increased with the principal's and teacher's education, teacher's experience, and the proportion of teachers who are male. Teacher's characteristics accounted for more of the variance than did principal's characteristics. Contextual variables were of primary importance in the low income schools whereas principal's characteristics were more salient in the middle income schools. Teacher's characteristics were salient in both the settings.

Arvey, Dewhirst and Boling (1976) found that supervisory

goal clarifying and planning activities and participation in goal setting are positively associated with satisfaction of subordinates.

Schmidt (1976) found that supervision was one of the highly dissatisfying factors to the administrator.

15. Co-Workers and Job Satisfaction

Many investigators reported the importance of good co-workers or interpersonal relations for job satisfaction. According to Neeraja Dwivedi (1977), friends, co-workers, members of the family and neighbours exercise their influence on the individual and affect his job satisfaction.

Vanjeist (1951) stated that persons who were rated high in interpersonal desirability by their fellow employees were the most satisfied with their jobs.

Schutz (1958) postulated that interpersonal relations involve three fundamental values or need orientations among the interactive persons: inclusion, affection and control. Depending on the pattern of the values among group members, they may be described as compatible or incompatible. However, it supported the notion that group members who are incompatible with respect to these interpersonal values are less satisfied with their groups and less attracted to them than are members of more compatible groups. His work supports the hypothesis that satisfaction depends on the degree to which one's values regarding interpersonal behaviour are realised in groups.

Savage (1967) replicated the Herzberg study with teachers in Georgia using the interview technique. The results of his study, generally supported Herzberg's theory with a few minor exceptions, the most obvious of which was that good interpersonal relations, especially with students, were motivational rather than hygienic. A study conducted on teachers by Wickstrom (1971) also supported savage's (1967) findings that among teachers good interpersonal relations is a motivator.

Robert (1977) found that teachers ranked good interpersonal relations as one of the most important job motivation factors among teachers. In Glicken's (1977) study on the job satisfaction of social workers, satisfaction with co-workers was given the highest place. Ramakrishnaiah (1980) also found that 93 per cent of the college teachers who were highly satisfied in their job, expressed that they have cordial relationship with their colleagues.

In Locke and Whiting's study (1974) blue collar workers more often saw their co-workers as agents of dissatisfaction. Affiliation was the need on the part of teachers to establish and maintain positive interpersonal relationships with colleagues. Teachers whole affiliation needs were frequently unmet tend to report dissatisfaction with teaching (Cruickshank, 1982).

Schmidt (1976) found that absence of good interpersonal relations, was highly dissatisfying to the administrators. Davis (1981) also found that 80 per cent of the teachers' problems were emanating only from teacher-colleague relationship.

16. Students and Job Satisfaction

In ancient times the relationship between the teacher and the pupil was so intimate that one was giving shelter to the other whenever there was need (Mukerji, 1947). But today the situation is entirely different. Controlling the students has become one of the major tasks of any teacher. But teachers who reported control problems did not as a group report dissatisfaction with teaching (Cruickshank, 1982).

Roger (1953) found that a large majority of male elementary teachers were very much satisfied with classroom teaching, especially in the area of teacher-pupil relationships. Lindgren and patton (1958) reported that attitudes of high school teachers were less favourable toward children and toward current education theory and practice than were the attitudes of teachers in the lower grades.

Anjaneyulu (1968) made an observation that satisfied teachers rated a large number of their students as excellent, good and average on pupils' qualities and behaviour, than dissatisfied teachers. Dissatisfied teachers noted a large number of their students as poor and below average. Hansen and Stanley (1969) found interpersonal relations with students as one of the principal motive powers for teachers.

Smith (1978) found that working with children was cited most often by teachers as a source of satisfaction with their jobs. Job satisfaction of teachers was positively related with "students' linking for teachers and teachers' liking for students" (Anand, 1971). Parelius (1982) studied 32 members of different faculties and found that the majority of respondents were displeased with a large number of poorly prepared and unmotivated students.

Secondary teachers reported that students' irresponsibility, apathy, and poor attendance made teaching difficult (Davis, 1981).

17. Needs and Job Satisfaction

Needs work as propellors to motivate an individual to attain need based goals. These goals change in view of the individuals' educational attainments, age, income, work experience, factory environment, family responsibilities and several other personal and social factors. This has been borne out by studies conducted by Ganguli (1954), Singh and Wherry (1963), Lahiri and Chowdhary (1966), Schwerz, et al., (1966), Kappor (1967), Desai (1968), Mukherjee (1968) and several other investigators in various industries.

Schaffer (1953) has proposed a hypothesis that overall satisfaction will vary directly with the extent to which those needs of an individual which can be satisfied in a job are actually satisfied, the stronger the need, the more closely will job satisfaction depend on its fulfilments.

Similarly, Pestonjee (1973) observed that job satisfaction is generated by the individual's perception of how well his job, on the whole, is satisfying his various needs.

King and Brass (1970) proposed a hierarchy for access to managerial positions on the basis of race. They observed that in the absence of higher level needs, the lowest level of needs become prepotent. As one level of needs become satisfied, it ceases to be a source of concern. They comment that little has been done by organizations to mobilise the needs of black employees for the satisfaction of their ego and self-actualisation needs.

Scherf (1974) found that the desire for existence needs increased as the satisfaction with them decreased. He concluded that real improvement of satisfaction could occur only if man's meeting of his relatedness needs is facilitated along with the improvement of his economic welfare.

As a result of his study, Morse (1953) advanced a hypothesis that satisfaction depends basically upon what an individual wants from the world and what he gets. He developed four indices of the job satisfaction. The first is related to 'content' of the job, the second is related to 'identification with the job', the third is related to 'financial and job status satisfaction' and the fourth is related to 'pride and group performance'.

According to Friedlander (1966) work can be a very important source of satisfaction for socially derived needs and, in consequence, a means towards the realisation of satisfaction in life in general.

In the theory of organizational behaviour (Korman, 1970) has emphasised the role of self-esteem in work outcomes. Within a balanced theoretical framework, the general thrust of the approach is that, all other things being equal, high self-esteem persons are motivated to perform well on a task in order to maintain their self-image of competence. Low self-esteem persons on the other hand, are not motivated to perform well since poor performance for them is consistent with their self image of relative importance.

Slocum and Strawser (1972) collected data from both black and non-black Certified Public Accountants (CPAs) in the United States to test the racial differences in job attitudes. Results indicated that the self-actualisation and compensation need categories were the most important and the most deficient areas for both groups of CPAs. The results also indicate that the black respondents reported more needs deficiency in the social needs category than the others in CPAs.

An attempt was made by Mayadeb (1972) to find out if the perceived importance of different job factors or needs vary with the types of jobs i.e., engineers, medical representatives and clerks. It was found that the perceived importance of job factors varies with the type of job and the variation depends on the divergence of the type of occupation.

Miller (1974) administered a questionnaire to 702 teachers and conducted interviews with a random sample of multiple job-holding and non-multiple job-holding teachers. The desire to achieve a higher standard of living and to satisfy social and psychological needs, not fulfilled through class room teaching were indicated as the main reasons for public school teachers to take up other jobs while continuing as teachers.

In the study of Arvey and Mussio (1974), the culturally disadvantaged clerical employees indicated that the following outcomes were more important to them than to the culturally advantages clerical employees: steady and secure employment, praise and getting along with co-workers. In contrast the advantages group showed that 'accomplishment' was more important to them than to disadvantaged group.

In a study by Chen (1977), both satisfied and dissatisfied teachers showed a need for respect. The most important vocational needs of teachers as identified by Gordon (1981) were achievement, utilization of ability, creativity, working conditions, responsibility and recognition.

18. Suitability and Job Satisfaction

Super (1939) found that lack of congruence between job requirements and the individual's abilities was the primary reason for dissatisfaction. In support of this finding Brayfield (1957) observed that suitability of work was very important for job satisfaction and general mental health of the individual.

Blum and Naylor (1968) observed that job dissatisfaction may be the result of a lack of vocational guidance. They further stated that a person who is 'too good' or 'not good enough' for a job in terms of his abilities and interests, is not likely to be satisfied with his job.

Siegal (1969) also found that employees who were either insufficiently challenged by their work or who were engaged in activities that were too demanding relative to their intellectual capabilities were often dissatisfied with their jobs.

19. Security and Job Satisfaction

Security is one of the most frequently studied factors. Blum (1952) reported that security was less important to the better educated person, perhaps because there was not so much fear of lay off in the kind of jobs that the highly educated obtained, or the highly educated were justifiably more confident of being able to find other jobs if necessary.

Blum and Naylor (1968) made an observation that security contributes to job satisfaction, but cautioned that 'secure' is social as well as economic. Hence it is believed that social security and economic security are essential to be happy in any job. Kalanidhi (1973) reported that the women workers, in industry treated security as the most important job factor. Similar results were obtained by the Fortune Survey (1947). It stated that security for old age was one of the five factors significantly related to job satisfaction. In a manufacturing organization both male and female groups described job security to be the source of highest satisfaction (Wills, 1982).

20. Rewards and Job Satisfaction

A worker is likely to be satisfied as long as the magnitude of the rewards he or she gets equals or exceeds the rewards of comparable others and will be dissatisfied upon discovering that the magnitude of his or her awards are lower than that of those of others (Stouffer, et al., 1949).

Lawler (1971) suggests that pay satisfaction is a function of two perceptions: (1) the amount of the pay he feels he should receive, and (2) the amount of pay he feels he does receive. The amount of pay a person feels he should receive, in turn, is hypothesised to be a function of (1) his perceived personal job inputs, (2) his perceived job characteristics, (3) his non-monetary outcomes from work, and (4) his pay history.

The type of pay system (individual incentive, group incentive and hourly incentive) was found to be significantly related to pay satisfaction, when the effects of pay level and worker demographic characteristics were controlled (Schwab and Wallace, 1974).

Locke and Whiting (1974) found that the company or organization was viewed as causing the highest percentage of both satisfying and dissatisfying events, with emphasis on promotions and recognition.

According to Bizman (1976) when the satisfaction of a given need can be evaluated according to some internal stimuli, its level will be determined more by the absolute than by the relative magnitude of the reward, and vice-versa, when internal stimuli do not exist.

In the areas of employee satisfaction, goal setting alone enhanced satisfaction as much as the formal feedback groups in the areas of people on the present job and supervision on the present assignment. The self-feedback group showed no increase in satisfaction on promotion potential, present pay, work on the present job, co-workers and supervision, while the other three groups (including the goal setting only group) showed improvement in their level of satisfaction. Again self-feedback alone may do little to enhance productivity or satisfaction (Kim and Hamner, 1976).

Spuck (1974) examined the relationship between the following eight categories of rewards available to teachers in high schools and teacher behaviours of absenteeism, recruitment and retention:

1. Material inducements (Monetary rewards) — extrinsic
2. Support and recognition of community — environmental
3. Physical conditions — environmental
4. Pride of workmanship — intrinsic
5. Social interaction with peers — intrinsic
6. Agreement with distinct goals and policy — intrinsic

7. Ability to influence school policy — extrinsic
8. Environmental working conditions — environmental.

Spuck concluded that the existing behavioural theory emphasises the role of environmental and extrinsic rewards in accounting for employee behaviours related to joining and remaining in the organization. Intrinsic rewards are thought to be related to employee behaviours one on the job but not specially related to recruitment and retention of functionaries. This exploration of reward structures in public high schools suggest, that intrinsic incentives are highly related, individually and in combination with other reward categories, to all three employee behaviours included in this study : recruitment, absenteeism and retention.

Latham and Yukl (1976) studied 45 women typists and found that satisfaction declined slightly in both goal-setting conditions, by some of the women typists to their supervisor and suggested that the dissatisfaction was duc primarily to the quality aspect of the goal-setting programme.

21. Recognition and Praise and Job Satisfaction

Johnson (1967) and Hansen and Stanley (1969) found that recognition enhanced satisfaction. Kay, et al., (1963) showed that most subordinates felt that they deserved more favourable appraisals than they received. On the contrary Vroom (1964) believed that if a worker expects to be praised or criticised for effective or ineffective performance he loses all motivation.

Merill-II (1969) found that meagre recognition led to dissatisfaction among teachers. Robinson (1960) concluded that teachers were more interested in public recognition than in recognition from other professionals. Thus recognition is one of the most significant factors that influences the satisfaction of the teacher.

22. Advancement and Job Satisfaction

Blum (1952) stated that opportunity for advancement was most important to sales, clerical and skilled personnel and least important to the unskilled. Spector (1956) assessed the impact of promotional opportunities on job satisfaction in a laboratory situation and concluded that meagre chances of promotion were causing dissatisfaction.

Herzberg, et al., (1959) suggested that job enrichment or vertical enlargement of the job are conducive to psychological growth of the worker. Regardless of advanced degrees and credentials acquired, in terms of prestige, a classroom teacher still appears to be one step above the student and one step below the lowest level administrator (Bloland and Selby, 1980). In a manufacturing organization, advancement was the source of least satisfaction for both male and female groups (Wills, 1982).

23. Qualification and Job Satisfaction

Rao (1970) found that there was significant relationship between job satisfaction and education level of individuals. Carrell and Elbert (1974), in a study on postal clerks found that the educational qualification of the employees was one of the significant determinants of job satisfaction.

Happock (1935), Sinha and Sarma (1962), Anand (1972), Weaver (1974), and Bernard and Kulandaivel (1976) concluded that there was no relationship between level of education and job satisfaction among employees of various occupations.

The teachers with Bachelor degrees were more satisfied with their work situation than those who had master degrees, particularly in the areas of supervision and co-workers (Weiner, 1981).

Teachers with master or higher degrees were more critical of the professional environment (Smith, 1982). Al-Khaldi (1983) found that employees with higher educational levels were less satisfied with their salary than those with lower education levels.

24. Marital Status and Job Satisfaction

Neeraja Dwivedi and Pestonjee (1975) conducted a study on a group of 240 blue-collar workers who were working under a financial incentive scheme in a leading locomotive works and found that as far as marital status was concerned married workers showed higher job satisfaction than unmarried workers.

It was concluded by Weinroth (1977) that age, teaching experience, and age of children in the home affect the motivational needs, job satisfaction, and career aspirations of married women teachers.

Smith (1977) found that husband's marital adjustment was correlated with women's job satisfaction. Those who were generally happy and satisfied, tended to reflect that feeling in both the major areas of their lives — work and family.

Generally, married adults are better adjusted than their unmarried counterparts (Srole, et al., 1962; Orden and Bradburn, 1968; Bradburn; 1969). As adjustment is positively related to job satisfaction (Kates, 1950; Herzberg et al., 1957; Anand, 1977; Balasubramanyam and Narayanan, 1977; Venkatarami Reddy and Krishna Reddy, 1978) one may expect that married teachers would be more satisfied with their jobs.

However, the few studies that were carried out in this area obtained contradictory results. AVA (1948), Redfer (1964), Venkatarami Reddy and Krishna Reddy (1978), and Ramakrishnaiah (1980) reported no relationship between the two variables, while Butler (1961) found that unmarried beginning teachers were more satisfied than their married counterparts. However, Inlow (1951), NEA (1957) and Venkatarami Reddy and Babjan (1980) found that married teachers were more satisfied. Sinha and Nair (1965) and Chen (1977) also obtained similar results on factory workers. Married teachers seem to be more satisfied with their teaching positions than unmarried teachers (Smith, 1982).

25. Salary and Job Satisfaction

Anjaneyulu (1968) found that inadequate salary was one of the most common causes for dissatisfaction among school teachers.

Those who were working under financial incentives had better job satisfaction than those who were under no such incentives (Pestonjee, 1971). These findings laid support to Ganguli's (1964) prediction that for the present and in the foreseeable future, money will remain as an important incentive for Indian workers.

In this age of materialism and run-away inflation, man's worth is judged by the size of his bank balance according to Mishra (1972). Thus economic factors tend to overshadow all others. A radical improvement in the economic status will do much to attract and retain good teachers.

Neeraja Dwivedi and Pestonjee (1975) conducted a study on 'Socio-personal correlates of job satisfaction' in which 240 blue-collar workers who were working under a financial incentive scheme were studied. The workers belonging to the high income group were found to be satisfied with their job. Income generally affected job satisfaction. However age and tenure of service were more effective correlates of job satisfaction than income and marital status.

In Robert's (1977) study, teachers ranked good wages as one of the most important job motivation factors. Similarly, Shaver (1977) observed that the biggest contribution among journalism graduates to job dissatisfaction was low salary.

In the same line, Schmidt (1976) concluded that salary was highly dissatisfying to the administrators when it was not effectively present.

Roger (1953) also found that the major dissatisfaction were inadequate salary, and factors related to the disproportionate number of women on the teaching staff.

It is very unfortunate that the scales of pay of teachers are lower than other categories of employees who possess similar or even lower qualifications, experience and responsibilities, observed Perumal (1969). He added that such a disparity promotes an unhealthy and undesirable competition and as a result, teachers become a disgusted and a dissatisfied lot.

According to Brown (1973) "An incentive is an objective goal which is capable of satisfying what we are aware of subjectively as a need, drive or desire". So monetary incentive or financial need or drive is one of the most and primary motives of work. Blum (1956) and Blum and Naylor (1968) states that in most of the studies financial incentives were found to be the most effective determinants of job satisfaction.

Counts (1978) conducted a study on public school teachers and found that inadequate salaries and the narrow salary range between beginning and retiring teachers were among the principal reasons for leaving the teaching profession.

Eckert, Stecklein and Sagan (1959) administered a questionnaire to 706 college faculty members and found that 'low salaries' was quoted as one of the three most common reasons for job dissatisfaction. Anand (1972) also found that salary was significantly related to job satisfaction.

From a study on a nationwide sample of 4000 fully employed males, Weaver (1974) found that there was a strong positive relationship between job satisfaction and satisfaction with income.

Greene (1973) found that merit pay caused satisfaction and increased the correlation between job satisfaction and pay. Orpen (1981) suggested, from an experimental study, that it was the absolute amount of pay received under the different schemes, viz., continuous reinforcement conditions (CR) and production-partial reinforcement conditions (PR) and production arbitrary reinforcement condition (AR), rather than their distinguishing characteristic (nature) which determined the employee satisfaction with it.

Surbida (1984) indicated that overall, principals responded that they were satisfied with their jobs and their salaries. In Kentle's (1985) study income was rated highly important by 54 per cent of the respondents; however, only 36 per cent were satisfied with their income.

But there are a few instances where it can be observed that the influence of pay on job satisfaction is insignificant. According to Mayadeb (1972) salary was not the main factor which men, working in different positions as engineers, medical representatives and clerks, wanted from their jobs. Butler (1961) and Ramakrishnaiah (1980) reported no difference in the level of satisfaction among different salaried groups.

26. Occupational Level and Job Satisfaction

Frier (1954) conducted an extensive study to determine the influence of job status on job satisfaction. It was observed that occupational status was the most influential factor in creating differences in job satisfaction.

Porter (1962) found that in general those in lower management positions were dissatisfied than managers in top level positions. He also stated that higher levels of employment offer more ego satisfaction, more status, pay and self-direction.

Teachers' prestige is the image of respect in the eyes of the people or the position of authority in the minds of their fellowmen (Chu, 1964).

The Education Commission (1966) emphasised that — "Intrinsic and continuous efforts are necessary to raise the economic; social and professional status of teachers and to attract talented young persons into the profession".

Shingwekar (1966) also opined that in the present times educational reconstruction can be brought about only when we raise the position and status of the teachers.

Nayyar (1967) said it is difficult to have a disciplined society as long as our teachers are frustrated. We have to put a full stop to the entry of frustrated persons in the teaching profession. Now-a-days, it is seen that those who are fit nowhere, do find a place in the teaching profession. Such persons neither have a happy life for themselves nor do they work to make successful citizens out of their pupils.

Anjaneyulu (1968) found that post-graduate teachers expressed dissatisfaction in the job on account of lack of social status.

A survey on highly skilled and skilled personnel indicated that occupational level was an important variable in determining employees satisfaction.

One of the important reasons for the slow progress of the professional growth of teachers is lack of interest and indifference on the part of teachers themselves towards their profession. In order to promote the growth of the teaching profession, therefore, it is essential that professional consciousness should be developed among teachers (Katti and Bennur, 1971).

Nixon and Gue (1975) studied woman administrators and women teachers and found that administrators were satisfied with their professional role than teachers.

Askar (1981) observed that society's perception of teaching is below the teachers' expectations.

Teachers who are active in the teacher associations were more satisfied with their jobs and their occupational status (Smith, 1982).

Ray (1982) concluded that the higher the level of the occupation, the higher the morale of the worker and the achievement need was an important mediator of the relationship between job level and job satisfaction. Therefore, the level of employment is one of the factors that contributes to job satisfaction.

Smith (1982) however, found that elementary teachers perceive that they have more job satisfaction and a better professional environment than secondary teachers. Birmingham (1985) also reported that elementary teachers were more satisfied than their secondary colleagues.

Ramakrishnaiah (1980) observed that socio-economic status of the teachers did not have any bearing on their job satisfaction.

27. Sex and Job Satisfaction

That certain personal characteristics like sex, age, intelligence, and mental health or adjustment should be related to job satisfaction, is not surprising. Work is an aspect of the total life experience. Hence, to some extent our attitude towards work reflects our personal history.

Bange (1944) and stockford and Kunze (1950) found that women workers were more satisfied than men. Morse (1953) observed that a higher overall level of job satisfaction has been reported in various studies for women than for men. According to his work is generally a less consuming element in the lives of women and hence of somewhat lesser importance to their status in the community.

Studies on elementary and secondary school teachers (Chase, 1951; and Belesco and Alutto, 1972) have reported that women teachers tended to be more satisfied with their job than men teachers. Bernard and Kulandivel (1976) also found that women teachers expressed greater job satisfaction compared to their men counterparts.

In a study on 240 secondary school teachers, Venkatarami Reddy and Krishna Reddy (1978) found that women teachers were more satisfied than men teachers. Venkatarami Reddy and Babjan (1980); and Venkatarami Reddy and Ramakrishnaiah (1981) also obtained similar results.

Female teachers tend to be more satisfied with their current teaching profession and they perceive a more favourable professional environment than male teachers (Smith, 1982). Lewis (1982) and Birmingham (1985) also found that women teachers were more satisfied with their job than men teachers.

In some studies women were found to be less satisfied than men. For example, Hulin and Smith (1964) found that women workers in 3 of the 4 plants surveyed were less satisfied than their men counterparts. Hollen and Gemmill (1976) reported that women teaching professionals experienced less perceived participation in decision making, less overall job satisfaction, and more job related tension than their men counterparts.

Gobel (1977) also found that women workers evidenced more dissatisfaction with work than did their men counterparts but they expressed more satisfaction with pay. Similarly, Chen (1977) observed that men teachers were more satisfied with their jobs than were women teachers.

Englhardt (1973) and Weaver (1977) however, did not find any significant difference between men and women workers with regard to their job satisfaction. Cohen's (1977) study also showed that men and women teachers are remarkably similar, sex was found to be unrelated to organizational affiliation, job consciousness, degree of participation in the local association and degree of participation in the job actions. Similarly, Atteberry (1977) reported no significant relationship between sex and job satisfaction of elementary school principals.

Among the university professors it was found that either no significant sex differences in job satisfaction exist or that, if found, the differences are not psychologically meaningful (Smith and plant, 1982). Surbida (1984) found that there was no significant relationship between principals' sex and their ratings of their overall job satisfaction.

28. Age and Job Satisfaction

Age is also one of the most important variables in exercising its influence on job satisfaction. But the relationship between them is again complex as pointed by Hulin (1977) since it is confounded with job level, income, personal and family needs and expectations.

Neeraja Dwivedi and Pestonjee (1975) also reported that age was the important factor which played a significant role in the determination of job satisfaction. Holdaway (1978) reported that both facet and overall satisfaction were related to age of the teacher. Kentle (1985) also found that age was significantly related to job satisfaction.

Richard and Dewhirst (1979) disclosed that age demonstrated a significant positive relationship with extrinsic satisfaction and there was no such relationship between age and intrinsic satisfaction. Godkin (1982) also found a positive correlation between the age of respondents and the level of expected satisfaction on their job.

Hull and Kolstad (1942) observed the results of several investigations and concluded that job satisfaction was relatively high at the start, dropped slowly to the fifth or eighth year, then raised again with more time on the job. The highest morale was reached after the twentieth year. Herzberg et al., (1957) in their review of research and opinion also reported that, in general job satisfaction was high among young workers, low among middle aged employees and it would increase again after the middle age.

Sinha and Sarma (1962) and Anand (1972) observed a significant relationship between age and job satisfaction. Altimus and Tersine (1973) found that younger workers were significantly lower in satisfaction with work itself, esteem, self-actualisation and total work satisfaction.

Mokry, A-I (1981) in a study, found that the young female teachers begin their job with enthusiasm, hope and satisfaction and older female teachers end up with feeling of frustration, disappointment and dissatisfaction, where as young male teachers begin their job with low or average feelings of satisfaction and end up with a somewhat better level of satisfaction.

Salch and Otis (1964) reported that job satisfaction increased upto 60 years of age and then declined in the terminal period of 60-65 years among the managers in different companies. Belasco and Alutto's (1972) study indicated that the most satisfied teachers tended to be older an teaching in the elementary school. Similar results were obtained by Smith (1982) and Al-Khaldi (1983). Birmingham (1985) also observed that teachers over 55 years of age and under 25 were the most satisfied.

But three studies conducted by Rao (1970), Pestonjee and Singh (1973), Anand (1977) reported that there was no significant relationship between age and job satisfaction of workers. Surbida (1984) also observed that there was no significant relationship between principal's ages and their ratings of their overall job satisfaction.

29. Experience and Job Satisfaction

According to Siegel (1969), job experience is related to satisfaction in a rather interesting fashion. As one might expect, new employees tend to be relatively well satisfied with their jobs. This 'honeymoon', however, terminates after a period of time unless the worker feels that he is making a rather steady progress towards the satisfaction of his occupational and social needs.

Almost every company employees a large number of persons who after several years with the company feel that advancement or salary increases have not been forthcoming with sufficient regularity and that they are working at a dead-end job. The effect of this is to cause a perceptible decline in the prevailing level of job satisfaction during the several years following the start of employment. The level of job satisfaction appears to increase again after six or seven years and reaches a maximum for workers who have remained with a company for about 20 years (Hull and Kolstad, 1942). This is undoubtedly due to the fact that the most dissatisfied employees have sought other employment either voluntarily or involuntarily. In addition, employees who have been encouraged to remain with the company for as long a period as 20 years have probably been provided with the kind of incentives that lead to feelings of job satisfaction.

Neeraja Dwivedi and Pestonjee (1975) found that job satisfaction increased with increasing experience for a period of 10 years and after that it starts going down. Hodge (1977) observed that the level of job satisfaction increased for both Negro and White professors as years of employment at the institutions increase in number.

Weinroth (1977) indicated that experienced teachers, over 55 years of age, with older children, had lower motivation and higher job satisfaction in the intrinsic area compared to (1) the young, childless inexperienced teachers, and (2) older, experienced teachers with school aged children. Young inexperienced teachers with pre-school children wanted less work pressure and were less satisfied with the amount of pressure on the job than older, experienced teachers with school aged children. Lewis (1982) also found that teachers who had continuous experience in the current school were more satisfied that others.

But Rao (1970) found that there was no association between job satisfaction and experience. Anand (1977) and Ramakrishnaiah (1980) in their studies pointed out that the years of experience possessed by teachers had no role to play in the determination of job satisfaction. No significant relationship existed between the number of years served as a principal and ratings of subjects and their overall job satisfaction (Surbida, 1984).

30. Family Background and Job Satisfaction

Family background has been found to be a significant determinant of vocational adjustment. The U.S. Department of Labour (1949) in a follow up study of school leavers noted that a well integrated family life seemed to increase the likelihood of satisfactory vocational adjustment. Sucher (1962) working with teachers found the childhood background to be highly related to their vocational adjustment. Teachers with high morale as compared to those with low morale indicated that both their parents were happy in their respective occupations, that their childhood family was very close, and that they had their parents' expectations.

Cohen (1977) found that work ideology plays a great part in employee's motivation to engage in militant job actions. Such ideology is learned in the home and is a product of background variables.

31. Size of the Family and Job Satisfaction

Morse (1953) studied white-collar workers and indicated that the more the dependents one had the less the satisfaction he had with the job. Pestonjee and Singh (1973) also found in a study on supervisors that morale was significantly related to number of dependents. Family size was found to decrease satisfaction with time available for domestic activities, job and avocations (Bryson, Bryson and Johnson, 1978).

However, in a study of college teachers, it was found that the size of the family did not have any bearing on their job satisfaction (Ramakrishnaiah, 1980).

32. Personality and Job Satisfaction

The study of personality seeks to discover the reasons for a wide range of human behaviours, to account for their occurrence, and to assess their roles in the total person (Gordon, 1963). When the demographic and situational factors are capable of influencing the individual's satisfaction in either way, one's personality will certainly play a vital role in determining the job satisfaction/ dissatisfaction. As rightly pointed out by Vroom (1964) any study of job satisfaction should include both sets of variables viz., work role and personality variables.

Blum and Naylor (1968) observed that security must be considered as an important dimension of personality as it affects job satisfaction. An insecure person will remain insecure even though his job is secure. Family background and many similar factors contribute to the individual's security.

McConaughy and Palmer (1969) found that personality traits of federal field executives in South California were significantly related to their job satisfaction.

Gupta (1977) made an attempt to see the personality structure of the primary school teachers. It was found that on factors E, F and Q3 of 16 personality factors of Cattell, the subjects were slightly deviant and on factor 'N' they were strongly deviant and on the rest of the factors, they took average positions.

Heckert (1977) found that personal ideology influences behaviour and job satisfaction more than do the perceived press of peer group or organization. Hence, it was conjectured that external influences upon behaviour are mediated by the isolation of the classroom. Within the classroom teachers behave more consistently with personal beliefs than they do in areas of high visibility. Anand (1977) observed that it is the personality of a person which determines job satisfaction in the profession of school teaching.

It was found by Rim (1977) that men with high protestant ethic values preferred most self-realisation and intrinsic work satisfaction while men with low protestant ethic values preferred most self realisation and social contact; their least important functions were security and power. Women high on protestant ethical values preferred social contact and self-realisation and security. All women subjects ranked patterning of time and power as the least preferred functions of work.

Studies conducted by Hoppock (1935), Gellmon (1939), Kates (1950), Inlow (1951), and Blum (1956) showed that there was a positive relationship between personality factors and job satisfaction. On the other hand, according to Hulin (1977) the relationships among personality measures and job satisfaction had shown no trends which were of sufficient generality to be summarized. Similarly Hughes (1972) reported that employed subjects did not possess consistently the personality orientation appropriate to their jobs; and when the subjects were classified into groups as 'consistent' and 'inconsistent', it was found that there was no significant difference between the two mean job satisfaction scores.

Lusk (1980) studied the relationship between personality factors and teacher effectiveness on a group of prospective teachers. The four personality factors which predicted the effectiveness in student teachers were : (1) (The personality factor of group — dependent/self sufficient may be used to predict effectiveness in student teaching). Student teachers who exhibit higher levels of group dependence are perceived as being more effective in student teaching by public school supervisors that are student teachers who exhibit lower levels of group dependence. (2) (The personality factor of expedient/conscientious may be used to predict effectiveness in student teaching). Student teachers who exited higher levels of conscientiousness are perceived as being more effective in student teaching by public school supervisors than are student teachers who exhibit lower levels of conscientiousness. (3) (The personality factor of practical/imaginative may be used to predict effectiveness in student teaching). Student teachers who are more imaginative as perceived as being more effective in student teaching by university supervisors than are student teachers who are more practical. (4) (The personality factor of shy/venturesome may be used to predict effectiveness in student teaching). Student teachers who are characterized as venture some are perceived as being more effective in student teaching by university supervisors than are student teachers who are characterized as shy.

Houge (1980) observed that special education teachers were more sensitive to others, pragmatic, imaginative, shrewder, and experimental/ open minded. The major difference was in the high group dependency needs of the regular class teachers as compared to special education teachers.

High school principals possessed low levels of psychological conditions thought to be tied to job stress — Anxiety, Depression, Irritation and Somatic complaints — and own amounts of stresses such as role ambiguity and Role conflict. Some organizational factors of job stresses were found to have an impact upon the job satisfaction of the principals (Domian, 1981).

Kuhn's (1982) Study on teacher personality type and job satisfaction, indicated that extroverts tended to be more satisfied with their careers than introvert teachers. There tended to be higher mean satisfaction indicated by teachers having extrovert, sensing and judging characteristics.

(a) Adjustment

Peck (1936), in a study of teachers found that women were more critical of their jobs and were less adjusted with work than were men. Smith observed that many researchers assumed that job satisfaction was primarily affected by personal maladjustment.

Satisfied teachers showed fewer indications of emotional maladjustment than the dissatisfied teachers (Hoppock, 1935). Kates (1950) studied the relationship between job dissatisfaction and the Rorschach's maladjustment. The results showed that there was significant relationship between the two measured variables.

One important factor about the individual which must be taken into consideration if there is to be a complete understanding of job satisfaction, is his adjustment to his life. If he is not well adjusted in life, in school, with friends, with family etc., if he has a long list of 'gripes' about being 'done wrong', it is probable that sooner or later — probably sooner — he will find gripes and accompanying dissatisfaction in the job (Blun and Naylor, 1968).

Orpen (1974) studied 91 white employees to test the hypothesis that 'the correlation between job satisfaction and personality adjustment would be reduced when the influence of social desirability was statistically removed. It was interesting to note that the mean correlation between the indicators of job satisfaction and social desirability indicated 7 per cent of the variance in job satisfaction scores could be accounted for by differences in social-desirability.

Women who were poorly adjusted with their jobs had less job satisfaction than well adjusted workers (Kalanidhi, 1973). Fisher and Hanna (1931) showed that vocational maladjustment was the reflection of emotional maladjustment breaded with in the worker dissatisfaction and thwarts him in his search for happiness and success. Krishna Reddy (1976) found that better adjusted teachers exhibited greater satisfaction in their jobs than less adjusted teachers.

(b) Anxiety

Another important dimension of personality is anxiety. Sarala (1971) investigated into the relationship between job satisfaction and anxiety and found that there was an inverse relationship between anxiety and job satisfaction. It was shown that the high anxious group was less satisfied with the job than the low and moderate anxious groups.

The characteristic of the emotionally unstable is the degree to which they allow one situation to affect a totally different situation. Thus a slight exchange of words with co-worker can have the individual 'tied up in Knots' not only on the job but even at home after the day's work is done. Similarly, such a person will bring a home situation to the job, much more often than a stable individual will (Blum and Naylor, 1968).

Teachers reporting higher levels of satisfaction reported lower job tension. They also showed less militant attitudes. Thus it was concluded that high satisfaction levels are associated with the desirable organizational outcomes of reduced job tension and less militant attitudes, (Belasco and Alutto, 1972).

Srivastava and Sinha (1972) also found that there was an inverse relationship between job satisfaction and job anxiety. In addition, high, moderate and low job anxiety groups differed significantly from each other with regard to level of job satisfaction.

Ivancevich (1974) studied the effects of shorter week on employees and found that there was a significant education in anxiety and stress of the workers. Thus the anxiety of an individual certainly influences his job satisfaction.

Arora (1986) found that the dissatisfied teachers possess a higher level of anxiety than the satisfied teachers. Similarly the 'satisfied more experienced' teachers possess a significantly lower level of anxiety than that of the 'dissatisfied more experienced' teachers, but the anxiety level of the less experienced teachers of both satisfied and dissatisfied groups is quite similar.

(c) Authoritarianism

Foa (1957) studied the workers' expectation in relation to satisfaction with supervisor among sailors and found that those with authoritarian expectations were more likely to be satisfied with whatever behaviour was adopted by their officers than were sailors with less authoritarian expectations.

Pestonjee and Singh (1972) found that there was an inverse relationship between job satisfaction of supervisors and authoritarianism.

McGowan (1981) reported that authoritarianism of the management did not correlate significantly with job satisfaction of public school teachers.

(d) Neuroticism

One of the dimensions of personality is emotional stability or 'neurotic tendency'. An individual's emotional stability is likely to manifest itself in satisfaction or dissatisfaction in a specific job. Kornhauser and Sharp (1932) conducted an investigation on female employees of the Kimberly — Clark Corporation and found that of the 25 most neurotic, 16 were more dissatisfied than the average and of the 25 most stable, only 3 were dissatisfied. McMurry (1932) also reported in a study on bank employees that neurotic tendency accounted for a slight degree of the variability in work attitudes among women employees. In both these studies the evidence is that neurotic tendency leads to job dissatisfaction only when the job itself is one of greater strain.

Hoppock (1935) found that satisfied teachers showed fewer indications of emotional maladjustment which was due to neuroticism. If a teacher was neurotic, he was emotionally maladjusted and dissatisfied with the job. Mehdi and Sinha (1971) found a negative correlation between job satisfaction and neuroticism in their study on teachers. Balasubramanyam and Narayanan (1977) attempted to explore the relationship between the personality dimensions of extorversion - introversion and neuroticism and job satisfaction.

The findings showed that there was no relationship between extroversion and job satisfaction. However, neuroticism was found to affect job satisfaction. In general an individual's emotional stability seems to contribute to job satisfaction and extroversion seems to be unrelated to job satisfaction.

In his study on 591 teachers working in government and aided higher secondary schools of Delhi, Anand (1977) found that there was a significant positive correlation between job satisfaction and extroversion, and a negative correlation between job satisfaction and neuroticism. Similarly Fisher and Hanna (1931) found that job satisfaction and neuroticism were negatively related. Mehdi and Sinha (1971) also found that job satisfaction was more in low neurotic group of teachers than in high neurotic group. So, it is evident that neuroticism is an important contributor to job satisfaction.

33. Attitude Towards Teaching

Investigations carried on by Cook, Leeds and Callis (1956), the pioneers in the area of attitude towards teaching, led them to conclude that attitude of teachers towards children and school work can be measured with high reliability and that they are significantly correlated.

Variables like security, chance for advancement, good working conditions, pleasing environment, chance to serve society, work with young people, prestige, personal satisfaction, social contacts and other factors were seen as advantages by prospective teachers (Fox and Richey, 1948). But there were disadvantages, including low pay, restricted private life, poor working conditions, monotony, parental disapproval, responsibility, 'nerve strain', too many bosses, low social standing, lack of prestige, lack of academic freedom, little tenure, politics and other factors mentioned by those not intending to teach.

According to Best (1948) persons who choose teaching as a profession believed teaching profession to be more secure, less over crowded, involved less physical strain; there was more opportunity for proper home life, more adequate life time income; that it was easier to gain the needed education and that there was less opposition from parents and relatives compared to certain other profession.

Kearney and Rocchio (1955) found significant difference between the attitudes of elementary school teachers of self-contained classrooms and teachers of special subjects. They remarked that teachers who have the same pupils throughout the day are concerned not only with the subject matter but also with pupils' interests and physical and mental health, while teachers of special subjects are interested only in subject matter coverage.

Teachers who get along well with pupils tend to be co-operative, friendly, objective and emotionally stable, and to a lesser degree manifest sociability, social ascendancy, and masculinity in emotions and interests. Those who do not have high rapport with pupils tend to be critical and intolerant, hostile and belligerent, hypersensitive, depressed, and emotionally unstable, and to a lesser degree tend toward submissiveness, shyness, seclusiveness, and femininety (Leeds, 1956).

Beamer and Ledbetter (1957) investigated the relationship between the MTAI and social service preferences as measured by the Kuder (1953), feeling that this is the one interest area that might be related to teacher attitudes. The MTAI and the Kuder were administered to 164 experienced teachers attending North Texas State College. The mean MTAI score was 70 with a standard deviation of 29. The mean Kuder social service score was 57 with a standard deviation of 10. The correlation between the two measures was 0.35. However, there were variations for male and female and for elementary and secondary school teachers. Although male teachers scored lower than female teachers on the MTAI, they scored higher on the Kuder; although secondary school teachers scored somewhat lower than elementary school teachers on the MATAI, they scored somewhat higher on the Kuder. No interaction effects between sex and teaching level were given, and no over all rationale for the findings offered, but the investigators concluded, 'if these tests are valid, then this study strongly indicates that many persons are now engaged in teaching who do not exhibit the two essential characteristics of teachers (interest in social service and permissive attitude towards children)'.

Cook et al., (1956) reported the results of a study in which pupils in the tenth and twelfth grades of four high schools were asked to name the subjects taken during the years with the two teachers they liked most and those whom they liked least. There was no difference in the sex or age of the teachers most often liked and disliked but the difference in the MTAI scores was pronounced, the mean of the liked group (n = 50) being 39 and the mean of the disliked group (n = 50) being 18.

The high school teacher with undesirable teacher-pupil relations, who creates an atmosphere of fear and tension, and thinks in terms of the subject matter to be covered rather than in terms of what the pupils need, feel, know, and can do, is more likely to fail pupils than a teacher who is able to maintain harmonious relations with his pupils and who is interested in pupils as pupils (Rocchio and Kearney, 1956).

Several studies suggest that pupils value warmth and friendliness in their teachers. Ryans (1960) found this to be one of three factors characterising teachers' behaviours, attitudes, and beliefs. Jenkins and Lippitt (1951) also reported this as a dominant theme in teacher interview and questionnaire responses but found that power and control were also persistent aspects of teacher — pupil relationships, as reported by both teachers and pupils.

The conflict felt by teachers between the problem of discipline and the desire to be liked by their pupils appears to be a major source of anxiety for them (Alexander, 1951; Travers, Robinowitz, and Nemovicher, 1953). It comes as no surprise then to find that teachers have regarded stealing, cheating and other forms of extroversive pupil behaviour threatening to class room protocol, as the most serious kind of behaviour problems in children (Wickman, 1928; Thompson, 1940; Mitchell, 1943; Slobertz, 1950; Stouffer, 1956; and Hunter, 1957). Teachers indicate, clearly that more withdrawn forms of behaviour, including hypersensitivity, suspiciousness, and fearfulness, are among the least serious. Teachers evidently codify desirable and problem behaviours in terms of classroom decorum rather than student mental health.

This attitude toward classroom behaviour problem is seemingly widespread, being found even in a french study (Xydias, 1956) cited by Coladarci (1958). Some observers has, none the less, reported evidence of increasing teacher sophistication. Johnson (1955) and Slobertz (1950, 1951) both felt that elementary school teachers were employing constructive remedial procedures in dealing with the withdrawn child. Teachers and students appear to share similar conceptions of educational values (Jervis and Congdon, 1958) and of the ideal student (Schuhle, 1957; Fager, 1958; Brown, 1960). They even prefer students who are also most liked by other students (Gronlund, 1953). Teachers are moderately successful, however, in judging how the students themselves feel about one another.

Harvey, et al., (1966) classified pre-school teachers as either abstract or concrete after rating on factors such as flexibility, attitude towards rules, encouragement of childrens' independence and activity, need for structure and punitiveness. They found that the more abstract teachers differed from the more concrete teachers in an educationally favourable direction on all dimensions.

Faculty members who completed their graduate work in highly competitive schools and those currently employed in prestigious academic institutions hold more positive attitudes toward competition than their colleagues from less prestigious schools. A level of involvement in faculty governance and tenure, were strongest single predictors of one's attitude toward competition (Lopuch, 1985).

34. Attitude Change

The modification of teacher attitudes in a desirable direction has been the objective of many training programmes. The studies report modifications of teacher judgments about pupils towards greater accord with those of child specialists in both cases as a result of closer interaction between teacher and professional in conjunction with specific class room problems (Stern, Stern and Bloom, 1956; Harring, Stern and Cruickshank, 1958).

The Harring study reports the use of several specially devised tests for measuring the changes in the attitudes of teachers toward exceptional children. The limitations of conventional training programme in modifying teacher attitudes were observed in studies by Travers and Robinowitz (1953) and Robinowitz and Travers (1955) which showed evidence of improvement only in the areas of pupil control, pupil-teacher tension, and mutual pupil-teacher participation after training in a progressive programme but not in a conventional or conservative one. No differences between students in the two programmes were found before of during the training period.

35. Sex and Attitude Towards Teaching

Women teachers obtained a higher mean score of 76 compared to their men counterparts whose mean score was 61 on the MTAI

(Beamer and Ledbetter, 1957). Similarly, in their investigation with a 50 item questionnaire, Lindgreen and Pattan (1958) reported that men teachers were less favourably disposed to children and current educational theory and practice than women teachers.

In a very exacting study Ryans (1960) observed that at the elementary school level, men and women teachers differed in only four of the personal-social characteristics studied; men were less responsible and business like in classroom behaviour and more favourable towards democratic classroom practices, more inclined towards permissive, child-centered educational view points, and more emotionally stable than women. At the secondary school level, differences between the sexes were fairly general and pronounced with women tending to attain significantly higher scores on the scales measuring friendly, responsible, stimulating classroom behaviour, favourable attitude toward pupils, democratic classroom practices, permissive educational view points, and verbal understanding. However, men teachers scored significantly higher on emotional stability. Thus men teachers at both elementary and secondary levels were more emotionally stable than their women counterparts.

Women teachers had a significantly more favourable attitude towards teaching than their men counterparts (Ramakrishnaiah, 1980). Similarly, Anand's (1986) study revealed that a greater percentage of women teachers cherish favourable attitude towards students as compared to men teachers.

36. Level of Teaching and Attitude Towards Teaching

Lindgreen and Pattan (1958) hypothesised that the attitudes of high school teachers are less favourable toward children and toward current educational theory and practice than are the attitudes of teachers in the lower grades. When the questionnaire was scored with a key based on favourable attitudes toward children and acceptance of current educational theory and practice, the hypothesis was supported at the 0.05 level of significance, i.e., non high school teachers scored higher than high school teachers.

In a study conducted by Beamer and Ledbetter (1957) with MTAI, elementary teachers (N=87) obtained a slightly higher mean score of 74 compared to secondary teachers (N=54) who obtained a mean of 70. Wandt (1954) also reported that elementary school teachers held more positive attitude towards students compared to secondary school teachers.

In the teacher characteristics study directed by Ryans (1960) certain dimensions of teacher attitudes, verbal understandings, educational view points and emotional stability were investigated. Among the trends in the data with regard to level of teaching were:

1. The attitudes of elementary school teachers towards pupils, administrators, fellow teachers, and non-administrative personnel were markedly more favourable than were similar attitudes of secondary school teachers.
2. The educational view points expressed by secondary school teachers were more traditional while those of elementary teachers were more permissive.
3. It was also found that the actual pupil behaviour in the classroom (based on the observers' assessments) did not appear to be related to the attitudes held by teachers.

Ramakrishnaiah (1980) found that there was no significant difference between junior lecturers and senior lecturers in their attitude towards teaching.

Austin (1985) found significant differences between the attitudes of teachers and principals concerning various aspects of main-streaming practices: Teachers showed a great deal of concern about classroom behaviour and academic progress of students, whereas principals tended to show a greater concern about philosophy of students. Teachers tended to be more influenced by involvement in special education programmes.

Anand's (1986) study showed that the attitude of teachers towards students bears a significant and positive correlation with their job satisfaction.

37. Experience/Age and Attitude Toward Teaching

Beamer and Ledbetter (1957) examined the MTAI scores of various types of educational personnel. The subjects were 212 students enrolled in graduate courses at North Texas State College, sub-divided into male and female, elementary and secondary school teachers, guidance workers, administrators, and inexperienced education majors. The experienced personnel guidance workers (N=27) had the highest mean score of 84, and the administrators the lowest (M=56). The inexperienced education majors (N=48) had a higher mean score (M=90) compared to the mean score of 70 of experienced teachers (N=164).

Ryans (1960) observed that generally the older teachers (55

years and above) were at a disadvantage' compared to the younger teachers except from the standpoint of responsible, business like, systematic vs. evading, unplanned, slipshod classroom behaviour; and learning centered (traditional) Vs. child-centered (Permissive) educational view points. He also observed that trends with regard to extent of teaching experience are not substantially different from those noted when teachers were classified according to age.

A study conducted on college teachers by Ramakrishnaiah (1980) showed that differences in teaching experience did not have any significant effect on attitude towards teaching.

38. Marital Status and Attitude Towards Teaching

According to Ryans (1960), there are systematic differences between married and unmarried teachers with respect to various classroom behaviour and attitudes, but these differences often vary according to school level, grade and subject taught. For example, at the elementary school level, the married group attained more favourable scores in business like classroom behaviour and child-centered educational view points; at the secondary school level, the single group attained more favourable scores on the same variables. Ryans suggested that, despite general trends, it is probably more important to recognise the interaction of marital status with grade or subject taught when considering the teacher characteristics under study.

Ramakrishnaiah (1980) concluded that the unmarried teachers had a significantly more favourable attitude towards teaching than their married counterparts.

3

STATEMENT OF THE PROBLEM AND HYPOTHESES

No good life is conceivable without education. Education is a purposeful and organised activity between the educator and the educand which helps the later to lead a gracious and harmonious life. Hence, from time immemorial the teacher occupied an important position and enjoyed very great respect in the society and the world at large. But at present the teaching profession is being looked down as inferior to many other professions in the society.

If one has to be happy in his life, he must be satisfied and happy in his occupation. Dissatisfaction in the job is like a contagious disease and, if a teacher is not satisfies with his job he may produce dissatisfaction and maladjustment among the students with whom he comes across. Therefore, it is essential to see that the teachers are satisfied in their occupation, so that they can shape the best citizens for the future society.

But, are the present day college teachers satisfied with their occupation ? When we compare the teacher (the 'Guru') of the olden days, with the present day teacher, there seems to be a lot of differences. The teacher of the Gurukula' was completely satisfied with his job and used to be proud of his occupation. But today those who take up teaching profession seem to take it up just because they could not get entry into other occupations; and they will be watching for the slightest opportunity to leave it and take up some other lucrative profession. That is why every Education Commission without exception categorically pointed out the need for improving the teacher's status, salaries, service conditions and for providing adequate facilities for the pursuit of knowledge and for performing his duties satisfactorily.

Though the teachers occupy an important place in the development of the nation, not much attention has been paid by researchers to the study of job satisfaction of teachers unlike that shown in the case of industrial or clerical workers. Are the teachers satisfied or dissatisfied with their job ? If dissatisfied what are the causes for the dissatisfaction ? Do men and women college teachers differ in the level of their job satisfaction ? Has management anything to do with the job satisfaction of college teachers ? In other words do the college teachers working under different managements differ in the level of their job satisfaction ? Is there any significant difference between teachers working in junior colleges and degree colleges in the level of their job satisfaction.

What is the relationship between personal and demographic variables and the job satisfaction of teachers ? What personality factors affect one's job satisfaction.

Very few empirical studies have been carried out, especially on Indian samples, to investigate into these aspects.

1. Statement of the Problem

Hence, the present study was designed to make an in-depth study of job satisfaction of college teachers in relation to variables like attitude towards teaching, management, sex, level of teaching, marital status, experience, personality factors, etc.

2. Objectives of the Study

The major objective of the study are :

1. to estimate the general level of job satisfaction among the college teachers;
2. to identify the different factors in the teaching profession with which the teachers are satisfied/dissatisfied;
3. to find out the relationship between personal and demographic variables and job satisfaction of teachers;

4. to find out the relationship between attitude towards teaching and job satisfaction;
5. to identify the personality factors which influence the level of job satisfaction;
6. to make a comparative study of the personality profiles of satisfied and dissatisfied teachers.

Apart from these, the relationship different variables bear with the attitude of the teachers towards teaching was also sought to be analysed and the following additional objectives were set up for study.

7. to find out whether the college teachers have a favourable or unfavourable attitude towards teaching;
8. to find out the influence of personal and demographic variables on attitude towards teaching;
9. to identify the personality characteristics that affect attitude towards teaching;
10. to make a comparative analysis of the personality profiles of teachers who have a favourable attitude and those who have a negative attitude towards teaching; and
11. to develop multiple regression equations to predict job satisfaction and attitude towards teaching.

3. Specific Questions to be Answered

The study is designed to answer the following specific questions:

1. Are the college teachers satisfied with their job ?
2. What are the job factors on which the teachers are satisfied/dissatisfied ?
3. What is the relationship between personal and demographic variables and the level of satisfaction of teachers on the various job factors and total job satisfaction ?
4. Is there any relationship between job satisfaction and attitude towards teaching ?
5. Which personality characteristics of the teachers play a significant role in influencing the level of their job satisfaction ?
6. Is there any significant difference between the personality profiles of satisfied and dissatisfied teachers ?
7. Have the college teachers a favourable attitude towards teaching ?

8. Do personal and demographic variables influence the attitude of the teachers towards teaching ?
9. What personality factors affect the teachers' attitude towards teaching ?
10. Is there any significant difference between the personality profiles of the teachers who have a favourable attitude and those who have an unfavourable attitude towards teaching ?
11. Which of the independent variables turn out to be significant predictors of job satisfaction ?
12. Which of the independent variables turn out to be significant predictors of attitude towards ?

4. Hypotheses

Based upon the above, the following hypotheses were set up for investigation :

1. In general college teachers are satisfied with their job.
2. The different job factors would contribute to the satisfaction of the teachers.
3. Teachers working in government and private colleges do not differ significantly in the level of their job satisfaction.
4. There would not be any significant difference in the level of job satisfaction of men and women teacher.
5. Teachers working in junior colleges would be less satisfied with their jobs than those working in degree colleges.
6. Differences in attitude towards teaching contribute to differences in job satisfaction.
7. There would be a significant difference between the level of job satisfaction of the teachers who have the minimum required qualification and those who have more than the required qualification.
8. The level of job satisfaction of married teachers would not be significantly different from that of unmarried teachers.
9. Teachers with different levels of experience differ in the level of their job satisfaction.
10. Teachers belonging to different age groups differ in the level of their job satisfaction.
11. The size of the family of the teachers would have a significant bearing on their job satisfaction.
12. Differences in the personality characteristics of the teachers

would contribute to differences in the level of their job satisfaction.

13. There would be a significant difference between the personality profiles of satisfied an dissatisfied teachers.
14. College teachers in general have a favourable attitude towards teaching.
15. There would not be any significant difference in the attitude of teachers working in government and private colleges.
16. Men and Women teachers would not differ significantly in their attitude towards teaching.
17. Degree college teachers and junior college teachers would not differ in their attitude towards teaching.
18. Teachers who have the minimum required qualification and those who have more than the required qualification differ in their attitude towards teaching.
19. Married and unmarried college teachers would not differ significantly with regard to their attitude towards teaching.
20. Experience would not have any significant bearing on the attitude of the college teachers towards teaching.
21. Teachers of different age groups differ in their attitude towards teaching.
22. Size of the family of the teachers would not have any significant influence on their attitude towards teaching.
23. Teachers differing in their personality characteristics differ in their attitude towards teaching.
24. There would be a significant difference in the personality profiles of teachers who have a favourable attitude and those who have an unfavourable attitude towards teaching.

would contribute to differences in the level of their job satisfaction.

13. There would be a significant difference between the personality profiles of satisfied and dissatisfied teachers.
14. College teachers in general have a favourable attitude towards teaching.
15. There would not be any significant difference in the attitude of teachers working in government and private colleges.
16. Men and women teachers would not differ significantly in their attitude towards teaching.
17. Degree college teachers and junior college teachers would not differ in their attitude towards teaching.
18. Teachers who have the minimum required qualification and those who have more than the required qualification [illegible] of their attitude towards teaching.
19. Married and unmarried college teachers would not differ significantly with regard to their attitude towards teaching.
20. Experience would not have any significant bearing on the attitude of the college teachers towards teaching.
21. Teachers of different age groups differ in their attitude towards teaching.
22. Size of the family of the teachers would not have any significant influence on their attitude towards teaching.
23. Teachers differing in their personality characteristics [illegible] attitude towards teaching.
24. There would be a significant difference in the personality profiles of teachers who have a favourable attitude and those who have an unfavourable attitude towards teaching.

4

VARIABLES STUDIED

The two dependent variables in the study are job satisfaction and attitude towards teaching. Attitude towards teaching is also treated as independent variable while analysing job satisfaction in relation with other variables like management, sex, experience, marital status, etc. A brief description of the variables included in the study is presented below:

1. Job Satisfaction

According to Blum and Naylor (1968), job satisfaction is the result of various attitudes possessed by an employee. In a narrow sense, their attitudes are related to the job and are concerned with such specific factors as wages, supervision, steadiness of employment, conditions of work, opportunities for advancement, recognition of ability, fair evaluation, social relations between workers, prompt settlement of grievances, fair treatment by employer and other similar factors.

Other aspects such as employee's age, health, temperament, level of aspiration, his family relationships social status, etc., also contribute to job satisfaction.

According to Katzel (1964), job satisfaction is the verbal expression of an incumbent's evaluation of his job. The verbal evaluation is made operational by some form of attitude questionnaire or scale by means of which the incumbent rates his job on a continuum of 'like-dislike'. Job satisfaction of the college teachers was measured by an inventory developed by the investigator.

2. Attitude Towards Teaching

One's attitude towards any occupation is defined by Miller (1934) as a measure of the positive or negative affect he has towards that occupation. According to the Advanced Learner's Dictionary of current English, attitude means 'way of feeling, thinking or behaving' (Hornby, 1985). The attitude of the teachers towards teaching was measured by an attitude scale developed by the investigator.

3. Management

Under the present set up of educational administration in Andhra Pradesh, the degree colleges as well as junior colleges are either under the direct control of the State government or are managed by private bodies. Thy type of management of the college in which an individual is working may have a significant influence on the level of his job satisfaction. Therefore, teachers working under the two types of managements were included in the study.

(a) Government Colleges: Government colleges are those managed and controlled directly by the state government. The appointment of teaching staff in these colleges is made by the state government. They can be transferred to any college in the state. All service conditions like pension, provident fund, retirement benefits etc., enjoyed by the state government employees hold good for the college teachers also. Their promotions are made on the basis of a seniority list prepared for the entire state. They have a greater scope for promotion to higher posts compared to teachers working under private management.

(b) Private Colleges: These colleges are controlled by private bodies. Appointment of teachers to these colleges are naturally made by the Board of management of the colleges. Usually, there would not be more than one or two colleges run by the same management. Therefore, the question of transfer of teachers from college to college arises very rarely. The work and conduct of the teachers in these colleges will be closely watched by the management. Possibilities for promotion, needless to point out, will be very limited.

4. Sex

Teacher of both the sexes were included in the study to find out whether there is any significant difference between men and women teachers with regard to the level of their job satisfaction.

5. Level of the Teacher

There are two grades or levels of colleges, viz., degree colleges and junior colleges, under the present set up of collegiate education in Andhra Pradesh. Junior colleges are those that prepare the students for intermediate (higher secondary or +2, as it is called in some states) examination. The duration of the intermediate course, is 2 years after the 10th class.

Degree colleges are those which prepare the students for the B.A./B.Sc./B.com., degree examinations. The duration of B.A./B.Sc./B.Com., course (+3 stage) is 3 years after the intermediate.

Persons with the same minimum educational qualification, M.A./M.Sc./M.Com., are recruited as lecturers to both the types of colleges. Naturally, therefore, some persons with M.A./M.Sc./ M.Com., are working in junior colleges, designated as Junior lecturers teaching intermediate students while some others with the same qualifications are working in degree colleges with higher salary and higher occupational status, designated as senior lecturers teaching degree students. This 'level of the teacher' may therefore have a significant influence on the extent of satisfaction in his job. Therefore, for the purpose of this investigation, the college teachers were, divided into 2 groups as junior lecturers (JLs) and senior lecturers (SLs) depending upon the college (junior/degree) in which they were working.

In some cases, the junior colleges and degree colleges are in the same campus under the same principal. In such cases, there will be JLs who are required to teach degree classes and also there will be SLs who teach intermediate classes depending upon the circumstances. Such teachers were not included in the study. Hence, juniors and seniors may be defined as follows:

(a) *Juniors*: Juniors are those lecturers, who were selected as junior lecturers and were teaching intermediate classes.

(b) *Seniors:* Seniors are those lecturers, who were selected as senior lecturers and were teaching degree classes.

6. Marital Status

Teachers who participated in the study were divided into two categories on the basis of their marital status, i.e., whether they were married or unmarried. Their job satisfaction and attitude scores were analysed to see whether marital status has any effect on job satisfaction and attitude towards teaching.

7. Age

Because of existence of contradictory research results about the relationship between age and job satisfaction; and age and attitude towards teaching, it was decided to include age as one of the variables in the present investigation. Information regarding the chronological age (in completed years) of the teachers was obtained through the personal data sheet and its relationship with job satisfaction was analysed.

8. Experience

The number of years the individual has worked as a teacher may have an influence on his job satisfaction. Hence, the teachers were divided into three sub-groups depending on their college teaching experience and the significance of the difference between the level of job satisfaction of the different sub-groups was tested.

9. Qualifications

While postgraduation in the concerned subject is the minimum required qualification for the college teachers, some have other qualifications as well. While the first group who have the minimum required qualification may be designated as suitably qualified, the other group may be called over qualified. Will variations in the level of qualification (suitable/over) bring about variations in the level of job satisfaction ? To probe into this, qualification was included as a variable in the study.

10. Size of the Family

Size of the family of teachers has been taken as another variable to see if it has any influence on the job satisfaction of the teachers. For the purpose of determining the size of the family, two children, aged less than fifteen years were considered as equivalent to one adult member. On the basis of this variable, the teachers were divided into 3 categories and the significance of the difference between the level of job satisfaction of the three groups was tested.

The 16 PF questionnaire (Cattell et al., 1970) was used to assess the personality of the teachers, and the effect of the 16 personality factors on their job satisfaction was analysed. A brief description of the meaning of low/high score on each of the 16 personality factors is given below:

11. Factor-A
(Low score) Reserved, detached, critical, aloof and stiff Vs. (High score) Warm hearted, outgoing, easy going and participating.

The person who scores low on Factor-A, is in no sense abnormal, but has a temperamental inclination to be cautious in emotional expression, uncompromising and critical in outlook, and awkwardly aloof in manner. He likes things or wards (e.g., machinery, logic), working alone, hard headed intellectual approaches, and rejection of compromise.

The person who scores high on Factor-A, will have characteristics of easy goingness, accessible emotions, interest in people, attentive to people, soft-hearted, kindly, adoptable etc. He likes occupations dealing with people and socially impressive situation. He is generally willing to "go along" with expediency. He readily forms active groups. He is generous in personal relations, less afraid of criticism, and better able to remember the names of the people.

12. Factor-B
(Low score) Low intelligence, concrete thinking Vs. (High score) More intelligence, abstract thinking.

The person scoring low on Factor-B tends to be slow to learn and grasp, dull, sluggish. His dullness may be simply a reflection of low intelligence.

The person who scores high on Factor-B tends to be quick to grasp ideas, a fast learner, intelligent. There is some correlation with level of culture and some with alertness.

13. Factor-C

(Low score) Affected by feelings, emotionally less stable, easily upset, changeable Vs. (High score) Emotionally stable, mature, faces reality, calm.

The person scoring low on Factor-C, is easily annoyed by things and people, is dissatisfied with the world situation, his family, the restriction of life, and his own health, and he feels unable to cope with life. He shows generalized neurotic responses in the form of phobias, psychosomatic disturbances, sleep disturbances, and hysterical and obsessional behaviour.

The person who scores high on Factor-C tends to be emotionally mature, stable, calm, realistic about life, unruffled, better able to maintain high group morale. He does not let emotional needs. Some times he may be a person making a resigned adjustment to unsolved emotional problems.

14. Factor-E

(Low score) Obedient, mild, easily led, docile, accommodating, i.e., submissiveness, Vs. (High score) Assertive, aggressive, competitive stubborn, i.e., dominance or ascendance.

The person who scores low on Factor-E tends to be submissive, dependent, considerate, diplomatic, expressive, conventional, conforming, easily upset by authority and humble. This passivity is part of many neurotic syndromes.

An individual scoring high on Factor-E tends to be assertive, independent minded, stern, hostile, unconventional, rebellious, tough-minded and authoritarian (managing others).

15. Factor-F

(Low score) Sober, taciturn, serious Vs. (High score) Enthusiastic, heedless, happy-go-lucky.

The person who scores low on Factor-F tends to be silent, introspective, full of cares, concerned, reflective, incommunicative, slow and cautious. He sticks to inner values.

The person who scores high on Factor-F tends to be quick, alert, cheerful, talkative, frank and expressive. He reflects the group.

16. Factor-G

(Low score) Disregards rules, expedient, Vs. (High Score) Conscientious, persistent, moralistic.

The person who scores low on Factor-G tends to be self-indulgent, slack, indolent and undependable. He dis-regards obligations to people. He lacks acceptance of group moral standards.

The person scoring high on Factor-G, tends to be responsible, emotionally disciplined, consistently ordered, determined, perservering, and dominated by sense of duty. He is concerned about moral standards and rules.

17. Factor-H

(Low score) Shy, timid, restrained, threat-sensitive Vs. (High score) Adventurous, "thick-skinned", Socially bold.

The individual, who scores low on Factor-H, reports himself to be intensely shy, tormented by an unreasonable sense of inferiority, slow and impeded in expressing himself, disliking occupations with personal contacts, preferring one or two close friends to large groups, and not able to keep in contact with all that is going on around him.

The person who scores high on Factor-H, tends to be friendly, adventurous and impulsive. He shows little inhibition by environmental threat, feels free to participate, and makes more socio-emotional than task-oriented remarks. He has a history of being more frequently involved in organizing clubs or teams. The individual will have interest in opposite sex and is associated with more heart attacks.

18. Factor-I

(Low score) Tough-minded, reject illusions Vs. (High score Tenderminded, sensitive, dependent.

The person who scores low on Factor-I, tends to be unsentimental, self-reliant and hard. He will have some sort of tough, masculine, practical, mature, group-solidarity generating and realistic temperamental dimensions. He holds responsibility, is unaffected by "Fancies", acts on logical evidence and does not dwell on physical disabilities.

The person who scores high on Factor-I, tends to be kindly,

gentle, and imaginative in inner life and in conversation. He seeks sympathy and help from others. He expects affection and attention from others. He acts on sensitive intuition. High score on Factor-I is associated primarily with an overprotected or , at least, sheltering from urgent demands of life upbringing.

19. Factor-L

(Low score) Trusting, conciliatory, accepting conditions. Vs. (High score) Suspecting, jealous, irritable.

The person who scores low on Factor-L, is one of the easy going. He lacks of ambition and striving, readily forgets difficulties and accepts personal unimportance. He tends to be adaptable, cheerful, uncompetitive, concerned about other people and a good team-worker.

The person who scores high on Factor-L, tends to be jealous, dogmatic, tyrannical, and easily irritable. He is often involved in his own ego, is self-opinionated, is uninfluenced by the views of prominent people and declines to be generous.

20. Factor-M

(Low score) Practical, conventional, careful, Vs. (High score), Imaginative, absent-minded, unconventional.

The person who scores low on Factor-M tends to do the right things, alert to practical needs and conventional. He is dependable in practical judgment, and earnest in thinking. He is concerned with immediate interests and issues. But sometimes, he is unimaginative.

The person who scores high on Factor-M, inclines to be disregardful of practical matters. He has higher internal, spasmodic anxiety and conflict tensions. He walks and talks in his sleep. He tends to feel in Group, unaccepted, but unconcerned. He participates and makes original leadership suggestions which are not immediately ignored, though in the long run his (partly impractical) suggestions turnout to be rejected. He expresses significantly more dissatisfaction with the group unity and the group's regard for rules of procedure.

21. Factor-N
(Low score) Forthright, natural, unpretentious Vs. (High score) polished, wordly, shrewed.

The person who scores low on Factor-N tends to be unsophisticated, sentimental and simple. He lacks self-insight. He contents with what comes. He has blind trust in human nature and has simple tastes. He gets warmly, emotionally involved. He has vague and injudicious mind.

The person who gets high score on Factor-N tend to be polished, experienced wordly and shrewd. He has exact and calculating mind. He is emotionally detached and disciplined, ambitious and possibly insecure. He is insightful regarding self and others.

22. Factor-O
(Low sore) Self-assured, pacid, secure, complacent Vs. (High score) Apprehensive, self-reproaching, insecure, worrying, troubled.

The person who scores low on Factor-O, tends to be self-confident, cheerful, placid and impenitent. He is expedient and insensitive to people's approval or disapproval. He is rudely vigorous and has no fears.

The person who scores high on Factor-O, tends to be depressed, worried, troubled, insecure, anxious and lonely. He is easily touched and overcome by moods. He has strong sense of obligation. He is sensitive to people's approval and disapproaval.

23. Factor- Q_1
(Low score) Conservative, respecting, established ideas, tolerant of traditional difficulties Vs. (High score) Experimenting, liberal, analytical, free-thinking.

The person who scores low on Factor-Q_1 tends to be conservative. He is reluctant to any change, inclined to go along with traditions, and tends to be interested in analytical "intellectual" thought. He respects established ideas.

The person who scores high on Factor-Q_1 is more well informed, more inclined to experiment with problem solutions, less inclined to moralize, less unquestioning about views generally, etc. In group dynamics he contributes significantly more remarks to discussion, a high percentage being of a critical nature.

24. Factor-Q_2

(Low score) Sociably group dependent, a "joiner" and sound follower Vs. (High score) Self-sufficient, resourceful, prefers own decisions.

The person who scores low on Factor-Q_2 goes with the group, definitely depends on social approval more, and is conventional and fashionable. He is a sound follower of the group.

The person who scores high on Factor-Q_2 is significantly more dissatisfied with the group integration, makes remarks which are more frequently independent solutions than questions, and tends to be rejected.

25. Factor-Q_3

(Low score) Uncontrolled, lax, follows own urges, careless of social rules. Vs. (High score) controlled, exacting will power, socially precise, compulsive, following self-image.

The person who scores low on Factor-Q_3 does not bother about social rules. He follows his own urges. He is negligent. He may feel maladjusted and may show maladjustment.

The person who scores high on Factor-Q_3 shows socially approved character responses, self-control, persistent, fore-right, considerateness of others, conscientiousness. He makes more remarks in committee than others, especially problem raising and solution-offering comments, receive fewer votes as hinderers, and fewer rejections at the end of the sessions.

26. Factor-Q_4

(Low score) Relaxed, tranquil, torpid, unfrustrated Vs. (High score) Tense, frustrated, driven, overwrought, fretful.

The person who scores low on Factor-Q_4 tends to be relaxed, calm and satisfied (not frustrated. In some situations, his over satisfaction can lead to laziness and low performance.

The person who scores high on Factor-Q_4 rarely achieves leadership. Also, he takes a poor view of the degree of group unity, its orderliness, and the quality of the existing leadership. High Q_4 is best interpreted as an "id" energy excited in excess of the ego strength capacity to discharge it, and which is therefore misdirected, converted into psychosomatic disturbances, anxiety, etc. and is generally disruptive of steady application and emotional balance.

27. Neuroticism

Scheier and Cattell (1961) defined neuroticism as those personality characteristics which actually differed significantly between clinically judged neurotics and normal. (1) over protection, (2) depressiveness, (3) submissiveness, and (4) anxiety were the four dimension of the personality characteristics which measure neuroticism. The neuroticism scale questionnaire developed by Scheier and Cattell was used to assess the neurotic level of the teachers to see its effect on job satisfaction and also on attitude of the teachers towards teaching.

[illegible] less satisfied [illegible] among men and women [illegible]

[illegible] teachers working in private colleges were more satisfied than teachers working in government colleges.

In the case of level, juniors were significantly less satisfied than seniors [illegible] college [illegible]

(2) [illegible] were more satisfied with academic [illegible] teachers [illegible] were less satisfied [illegible] academic [illegible] colleges.

[illegible] teachers did not [illegible] satisfaction with their co-teachers' attitude and their activities.

(i) *Girl students' personal activities and place of work:* Women teachers were more dissatisfied with the attitude of girl students' personal activities and place of work, than their men counterparts.

7. Teachers who had less favourable attitude towards teaching exhibited least satisfaction with their job, while teachers with more favourable attitude towards teaching exhibited the highest satisfaction in their job.

Therefore, the hypothesis 'Teachers differing in their attitude towards teaching, differ in their job satisfaction' was accepted.

Considering factorwise, it was found that teachers differing in their attitude towards teaching, did not differ significantly in their satisfaction with factors: physical facilities, fringe benefits, academic policies, and co-teachers. So, the above hypothesis was rejected in the case of the above factors and accepted in the case of the factors: Principal, parents and students, self esteem, entertainment, prestige and courses, and girl students, personal activities and place of work.

8. Teachers who had more than the required qualifications did not differ from those who had only the minimum required qualifications in their overall job satisfaction.

Hence, the hypothesis 'There would be a significant difference in the level of job satisfaction of teachers who have the minimum required qualifications and those who have more than the required qualifications' was rejected.

However, with regard to one job factor, i.e., academic policies, teachers who had extra qualifications were less satisfied than those

5

METHOD OF INVESTIGATION

This chapter describes the methods employed in the measurement of the variables, selection of the sample, collection of data, scoring the responses and analysis of the data.

1. Measurement of Variables

Out of the 27 variables (both dependent and independent) investigated in the present study, 8 are personal and demographic variables for which information was gathered through a personal data sheet and the remaining 19 variables were measured with suitable instruments. A brief description of the instruments employed is given in the following pages.

A. Job Satisfaction Inventory

i) Different Methods of Measuring Job Satisfaction

Among the various procedures used to measure job satisfaction, the most often use are: interviews, projective techniques, and attitude questionnaires (Hoppock, 1960; Kirkpatick, 1962; Katzel, 1964; Johnson, 1967; Blum and Naylor, 1968). Among the three again, the best specimens of job satisfactions measures are questionnaires constructed on the basis of attitude scaling methodology with evaluative type of items (Katzel, 1964; Blum and Naylor, 1968). That is, job satisfaction is operationally measured by obtaining the subjects's verbal rating of his job or of its various features on a scale of hedonic tone ('like — dislike' or 'satisfactory — unsatisfactory', etc.). This means that the existence of one or more distinct dimensions of evaluation may be shown to be reflected in the items and a scoring method must be devised which weighs each response in terms of the degree of affect expressed on a given dimension (Blum and Naylor, 1968). Job satisfaction questionnaires meeting these specifications can be constructed on any of the standard attitude scale rationales, such as those of Likert (1932), Thurstone (1946) or Gutman (1947).

ii) Meaning of Job Satisfaction

Job satisfaction is the result of various attitudes possessed by an employee (Blum and Naylor, 1968). In a narrow sense, their attitudes are related to the job and are concerned with such specific factors as : (1) wages, (2) supervision, (3) steadiness of employment, (4) conditions of work, (5) opportunities for advancement, (6) recognition of ability, (7) fair evaluation of work, (8) social relations on the job, (9) prompt settlement of grievances, (10) fair treatment by employer, and (11) other similar factors. Other aspects such as employee's age, health, temperament and level of aspirations should also be considered. Again his family relationships, social status activities in other organizations - labour, political or social contribute ultimately, to his job satisfaction.

In his study on job satisfaction, Hoppock (1935) proposed the following six major components of job satisfaction:

(a) The way the individual reacts to unpleasant situations,
(b) The facility with which he adjusts himself to others persons,
(c) His relative status in the social and economic group with which he identifies himself,
(d) The nature of the work in relation to his abilities, interests and preparation for the job,
(e) Security, and
(f) Loyalty.

According to Blum and Naylor (1968), ' these six items are not of the minute or specific characters measured in many studies on job satisfaction; possibly that is what is wrong with these studies. Hoppock's approach is to be commended for this reason that he is aware of the real factors which contribute to job satisfaction and does not get lost in the petty details'.

Vroom (1964) listed the following seven dimensions which go into job satisfaction:

(a) Attitude towards the company and company management,
(b) Attitude towards promotional opportunities,
(c) Attitude towards job content,
(d) Attitude towards supervision,
(e) Attitude towards financial rewards,
(f) Attitude towards working conditions, and,
(g) Attitude towards co-workers.

According to Katzel (1964) job satisfaction is the verbal expression of an incumbent's evaluation of his job. In short, job satisfaction is an attitude which is the result of many specific attitudes in three areas, viz., specific job factors, individual characteristics and group relationships outside the job.

iii) Construction of the Preliminary Form

Bearing the above important dimensions of job satisfaction in mind, a number of items (opinions) that are related to job satisfaction of college teachers were collected from a number of sources. Forty men and forty women college teachers were requested to write the factors in the form of statements which cause satisfaction or dissatisfaction to the teachers. These statements were sorted out and listed. This list of statements was supplemented by a careful study of related literature and informal interviews with college teachers, and a pool of 130 items was prepared. The pool of items, or universe of items as Gutman (1947) calls it, thus collected was refined by observing the following criteria laid down by different authors like Likert (1932), Edwards and Kilpatrick (1948), Guilford (1954) and others :

(a) The statements must be clear, precise and straight forward.
(b) They should be short and to the point.
(c) 'Double barelled' statements should be removed.
(d) They must be constructed as expressions of desired. behaviour, not as statements of fact.
(e) They must be in such a form that the ideas can be accepted or rejected.
(f) Both favourable and unfavourable statements must be included.
(g) Statements that could be endorsed by everyone or no one, must be avoided.
(h) Negative and positive statements must be arranged

randomly throughout the attitude scale so that any space error may be avoided.

The item pool thus refined, was presented to 10 experienced men and women college teachers who were requested to :

(a) add other statements that might be relevant to the subject
(b) point out redundant statements,
(c) mark ambiguous and 'double barreled' items, if any
(d) give suggestions for refining the items.

Their suggestions were incorporated and 91 item were selected to be included in the preliminary form. The items were randomised. Each of the items was arranged on a five point scale with the following alternatives — strongly Agree/Agree Doubtful, Disagree and Strongly Disagree. To avoid faking of the responses, the attitude scale was made anonyous.

(iv) Pilot Study: Item Analysis

The pilot study was conducted on 160 men and 160 women college teachers, selected by a multistage stratified random sampling procedure from 12 colleges belonging to S.V. University area which is a part of Andhra Pradesh State. The sample was distributed equally among the two kinds of managements (government and private) and the two levels of teachers (junior and senior). The pilot form of the job satisfaction inventory which is self-administering was administered to the sample of teachers individually in their respective colleges during leisure hours.

Even though the scale is self administering, as a matter of motivating the teaches, they were explained the purpose of the research, and the way they had to answer the items. They were also assured that the data would be used only for research work and would be kept confidential.

For the purpose of scoring, numerical weights were assigned as shown in Table 1, to each of the 5 categories of responses, viz., Strongly Agree, Agree, Doubtful, Disagree and Strongly Disagree as suggested by Likert (1932).

Table 1
Numerical Weights Given to the Five Alternative Responses

Type of statement	*Strongly Agree*	*Agree*	*Doubtful*	*Disagree*	*Strongly Disagree*
Positive	5	4	3	2	1
Negative	1	2	3	4	5

This method of assigning numerical weights to the responses is simple and highly satisfactory. Likert (1932) found that scores based upon this relatively simple assignment of integral weights correlated 0.99 with the complicated and time consuming normal deviate system of weighting.

After scoring the responses of the teachers as described above, item analysis was carried out by the method of criterion of internal consistency suggested by Likert (1932). The results obtained by this method of criterion of internal consistency agree very well with the results of the traditional method of item analysis, at the same time this method is far less laborious than the latter, and is advocated by many investigators like Likert (1932), Murphy and Likert (1937), Edwards (1969), to mention a few.

This method consists of rank ordering the respondents with respect to their total scores and taking a high group and a low group on the basis of the total score and calculating the internal consistency of each statement using the formula:

Internal consistency of any statement = The difference between the mean scores of the high and low groups on the statement.

In the present analysis the highest scoring 27 per cent and lowest scoring 27 per cent were taken to represent the criterion groups because with this tail proportions, the coefficient is most sensitive (Kelly, 1939). The difference between the mean scores of high and low groups on each of the items was tested for significance by applying 't' test and 70 items for which the 't' value was significant at or above 0.01 level ('t' = 2.61; df = 170) were selected to be included in the job satisfaction inventory using which the investigator conducted a study for his M. Phil thesis.

(v) Factor Analysis

In the present study, the above job satisfaction inventory with 70 items was administered to 320 college teachers, selected by a multistage random sampling procedure from three districts, viz., Chittoor, Guntur and Warangal which were selected at random from among the 21 districts of Andhra Pradesh. The sample was distributed equally among the two kinds of managements (Government and Private) and the two levels of teachers (Junior and Senior lecturers).

Table - 2
Distribution of the Sample of Teachers for Pilot Study

Government				Private				Total
Men		Women		Men		Women		
Seniors	Juniors	Seniors	Juniors	Seniors	Juniors	Seniors	Juniors	
40	40	40	40	40	40	40	40	320

The job satisfaction scale was administered to the sample of teachers individually during leisure hours after creating necessary motivation towards the work as explained earlier.

For the purpose of scoring, numerical weights were assigned to each of the 5 categories of responses form 5 to 1 in the case of positive statements and 1 to 5 in the case of negative statements as explained earlier.

The scores of the 320 teachers on the 70 statements of job satisfaction scale were factor analysed by applying varymax rotation (Overall and Klett, 1972) with a maximum of 19 factors.

(vi) Selection of Items for Final Form

The procedure of extracting factors until a residual factor emerged as suggested by Cattell (1956) and Rummel (1970) was followed in the selection of items. A residual factor was defined for this study as one for which fewer than three loadings could meet the joint condition of being equal or more than 0.35 as the highest loading for an item. Overall and Klett (1972) also suggested that those factors defined by 3 or 4 items (variables) having factor loadings of 0.35 and above alone were considered to be included in the final form. The number of items thus selected for the final form was 44. These items formed into 9 factors, each factor containing 3 or more items. The factors and the items grouped under each of them through factor analysis are described hereunder.

(a) Factor (F_1) : Principal

There were 11 items in this factor which describes the characteristics of the Principal or the treatment experienced by the college teachers from the principal. The qualities of the need of the institution and the way he deals with his subordinates, will no doubt have a profound effect on the job satisfaction of the teachers. The eleven items included in the factor are :

6. The principal does not give reasons for any change in my work.
7. The Principal gives contradictory orders from time to time.
11. There is a democratic spirit in the administration of the college.
13. Our Principal is sympathetic to my personal problems and grievances.
16. The Principal is interested in understanding the teachers' difficulties.
22. The Principal is impartial to all of us.
23. My ability and performance are recognised by the principal.
25. I have cordial relationships with my principal.
30. Our Principal is not efficient.
32. Our Principal trusts me.
34. We are allowed to give suggestions to the Principal for improving the quality of the work.

Since there are 11 items in the factor the highest possible score on this factor is 55 and the least possible score is 11.

(b) Factor (F_2) : Parents and Students

Four items, which are concerned with parents and students, are included in this factor. It is reasonable to assume that parental interest in the education of the children, and the quality of students and their interest in education do have a strong bearing in the level of job satisfaction of the teachers. The 4 items that were included in this factor are :

8. Parents are not interested in their children's education
9. I am dissatisfied with the poor quality of the students that come to colleges.
21. Students have interest in studies.
23. Parents do not feel the responsibility for their children's future.

As there are four items, the score on this factor variables between 4 and 20.

(c) Factor (F_3) : Physical Facilities

This factor is concerned with the physical facilities conducive for teaching, like lab, library, etc., and other facilities like staff room, etc., which make the place of work more comfortable. 5 items were included in this factor:

2. There are adequate washing and toilet facilities in the college.
5. There is an adequate laboratory for the college.
10. We have all the equipment and material necessary for teaching.
17. We have a well furnished staff room.
35. We do not have an adequate library for the college.

The score on this factor ranges between 5 and 25.

(d) Factor (F_4) : Self Esteem

This factor contains 7 items which explain the suitability of different abilities, interests, likings, etc., of teachers to the job and their feelings about their positions in the job. The following are the items included in the fourth factor.

3. I am a successful teacher
12. I like my job
14. There is a good relationship between myself and my students.
15. I feel important in my job
24. I am satisfied with this job because the future of the country is in the hands of teachers like me
27. I am getting fatigue rather quickly in this job.
41. My work is suitable to my abilities.

As there are 7 items in this factor, the sore varies between 7 and 35.

(e) Factor (F_5) : Fringe Benefits

This factor describes the attitude of teachers towards the fringe benefits like pension, casual leave, earned leave, medical leave, etc., they have in their profession. The items included in this factor are :

39. We get an adequate pension when we retire from the job.
42. My salary is less than what I deserve for the work.
44. We have adequate casual leave, earned leave and medical leave facilities.

The least and highest score on this factor are 3 and 15 respectively.

(f) Factor (F_6) : Entertainment, Prestige and Courses

As the name indicates, this factor describes about the availability of facilities for entertainment, the type of courses offered in the college, and prestige of the teaching profession, though these things not materially important to teachers, they are important to keep up the mental health of the teachers. The three items included in this factor are :

1. I am not satisfied because we do not have adequate play grounds, recreational and entertainment facilities in the college.
4. I am dissatisfied with the low social prestige value of teaching profession.
19. I am not satisfied because the courses offered are not job oriented.

The scores on this factor varies between 3 and 15.

(g) Factor (F_7) : Academic Policies

This factor deals with aspects related to the scope for academic advancement of the teachers, academic freedom the teachers have, etc., which do have an intrinsic effect on the job satisfaction of the teachers.

29. There are sufficient in service training programmes to keep us up-to-date about the new trends in knowledge.
33. Faculty Improvement Programme (FIP) facilities are readily available to us.
36. I have the freedom to take initiative in organizing projects, etc.
37. Advance information about the changes that are going to take place is given to the teachers.
40. I receive encouragement from my colleagues to try new methods.

As there are 5 items, the score on this factor varies between 5 and 25.

(h) Factor (F_8) : Co-teachers

This factor with three items is concerned with the conduct of the co-workers of the individual. Job satisfaction of the teachers is indeed affected by the behaviour of the co-workers. The items included in this factor are :

18. I am unhappy with the political affiliation of the teachers.
26. I am dissatisfied because we do not have a code of conduct.
38. I am dissatisfied because teachers who are highly disciplined are teased (made fun of) by their colleagues.

The score on the factor varies between 3 and 15.

(i) Factor (F_9) : Girl Students, Personal Activities and Place of Work

This factor deals with the feelings of teachers towards nature of students, interference of other activities with teaching and the distance of the place of work from one's native place. If students are not education oriented, if other activities interfere with the teaching work, teachers tend to be dissatisfied. Similarly, if they are posted to far away places, it becomes source of dissatisfaction especially for those who have immovable property like land, house, etc.

The three items included in this factor are :

20. Girl students are marriage oriented rather than education oriented.
28. I am not able to devote sufficient time to my profession due to interference of their activities.
31. I feel troubled because I am far away from my native place.

The score on this factor varies between 3 and 15.

The items were again randomised to avoid occurrence of items of the same factor continuously and the final form of the job satisfaction scale was prepared.

(vii) Validity

There are various methods of estimating the validity of a measuring instrument. The following types of validity were established for the job satisfaction scale that was developed.

(a) *Content validity* : This form of validity is established by evaluating the relevance of the test items individually and as a whole. Each item should be a sampling of that aspect which the test purports to measure and taken collectively, the items should constitute a representative sample of the variable that is measured.

In the construction of the present instrument, items were collected from a large number of college teachers. They were also supplemented by a review of related literature and by interviewing selected teachers to make sure that all possible items were included. Thus it can be reasonably assumed that the scale has content validity.

(b) *Item validity* : The discrimination power of each of the items was established. Thus each item of the job satisfaction inventory is valid, establishing the validity of the instrument in discriminating high and low groups on the aspect that is measured, viz., job satisfaction.

(c) *Factorial validity* : As explained above, all the items included in the final form of the job satisfaction scale had factor loadings of 0.35 or more. Each of the 9 factors consisted of 3 or more items. Overall and Klett (1972) stated that 50 per cent to 75 per cent of the total variance was enough to consider for prediction of any psychological and psychiatric domain. In the job satisfaction inventory, all the 9 factors put together were capable of predicting 67 per cent of the total variance in the domain of job satisfaction that was measured. So, it could be concluded that the inventory is factorially valid.

(d) *Intrinsic validity* : Guilford (1954) defined intrinsic validity as 'the degree to which a test measures what it measures'. This can also be stated in terms of how well the obtained scores measure the test's true score component. This validity is given by the square root of the proportion of true variance, i.e., square root of its reliability. The intrinsic validity of the job satisfaction inventory was, therefore 0.77 = 0.88

(e) *Criterion validity* : At the end of the job satisfaction inventory, two general items, viz.,

1. I am satisfied with my job (a) Strongly Agree
(b) Agree
(c) Disagree
(d) Strongly Disagree
2. I am satisfied with my job (a) Less than others
(b) As much as others
(c) More than others

were included to elicit a direct answer from the respondents about their satisfaction/dissatisfaction on their job.

On the basis of their answers to the first item, the 320 college teachers who participated in the pilot study were classified into four groups, as those who strongly agreed, agreed, disagreed and strongly disagreed with the item.

Those who gave 'strongly disagree' and 'disagree' responses were merged into one (dissatisfied group) and those who marked 'agree' and 'strongly agree' responses were combined into another satisfied group). The mean scores of the satisfied and dissatisfied groups as measured by the job satisfaction inventory were 149.09 and 127.95 respectively. To test whether these two mean scores were significantly different, 't' test was employed. The result of the 't' test is presented in the Table 3.

Table 3
Mean Scores and 't' Value of Satisfied and Dissatisfied Teachers

Group	*N*	*Mean*	*SD*	*t*
Satisfied	298	149.09	15.80	
				6.45***
Dissatisfied	22	127.95	14.77	

*** 't' significant at 0.001 level for 318 df.

The mean score (149.09, of those who were satisfied was greater than the mean score (127.95) of those who were dissatisfied. The obtained 't' value (t = 6.45) was highly significant even at 0.001 level for 318 df. (Fig. 1)

The 320 teachers were further classified on the basis of their responses to the second item, as those who were satisfied : (1) less than others, (2) as much as others, and (3) more than others. The mean scores of the three groups were :

Group 1 (less than others) : 132.71
Group 2 (as much as others): 146.19
Group 3 (more than others) : 151.09

showing that the mean scores were in the expected direction.

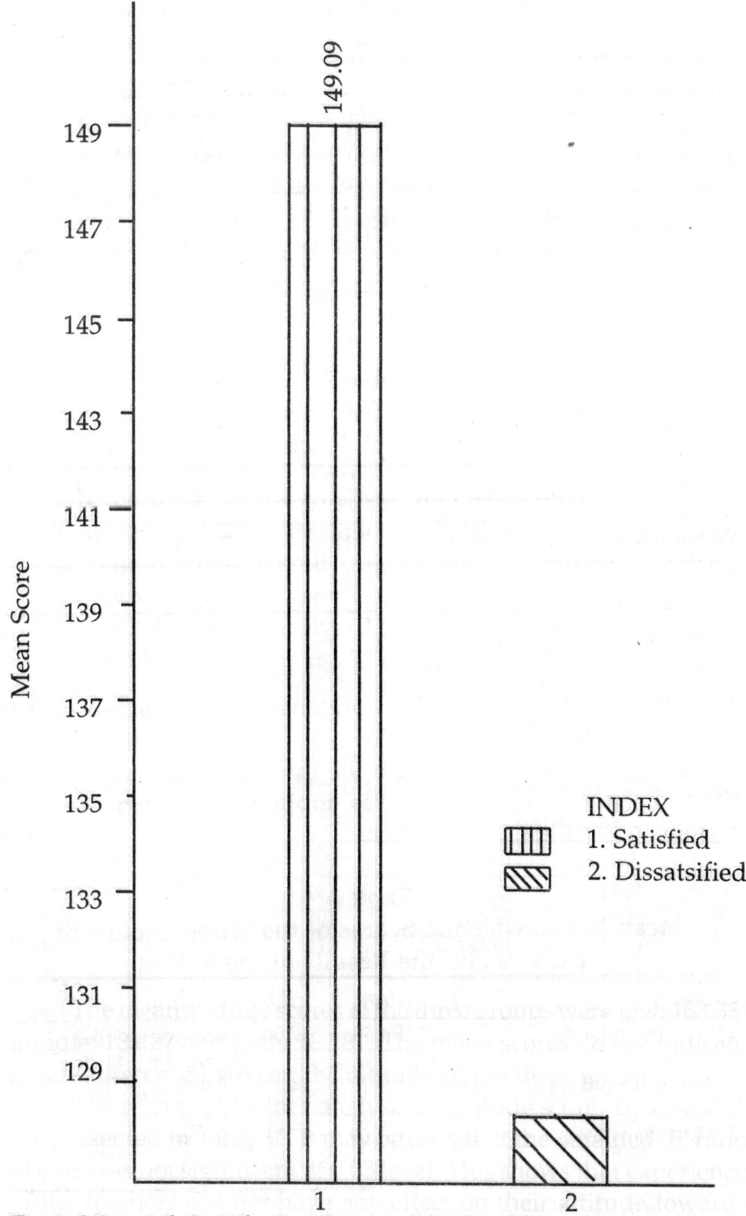

Fig. 1. Mean job Satisfaction Scores of the Teachers who have Rated Themselves as Satisfied and Dissatisfied in their Profession

Table 4
Mean Scores and SDs of Teachers who were Satisfied Less than Others, as much as Others and More than Others

Group	N	Mean	SD
1. Less than others	21	132.71	17.00
2. As much as others	150	146.19	14.30
3. More than others	149	151.09	17.31

The job satisfaction scores of the three groups of subjects were further analysed by one way ANOVA to find out whether there was any significant difference between the level of job satisfaction of the three groups.

Table 5
Result of ANOVA of the Job Satisfaction Scores of the Three Groups of Teachers

Source	SS	DF	MS	F
Between groups	6441.95	2	3220.98	12.55***
Within groups	81368.60	317	256.68	
Total	87810.55	319		

*** 'F' significant at 0.001 level.

The results of this analysis presented in Table 5.5 show that the 'F' ratio was significant at 0.001 level for 2 and 317 df, indicating a significant difference between the three groups with regard to their job satisfaction. 't' test was applied to find which group significantly differed from others.

Table 6
Mean Job Satisfaction Scores of the Three Groups of Teachers and the Results of the 't' Test

Group	N	Mean	SD	't' Values
1. Less then others	21	132.71	17.00	Between groups 1 and 2 = 3.47***
2. As much as others	150	146.19	14.30	Between groups 1 and 3 = 4.67***
3. More than others	149	151.09	17.31	Between groups 2 and 3 = 2.66

*** 't' significant at 0.001 level

From the 't' values presented in Table 6 it may be seen that each group differed significantly from the others.

(viii) Reliability

Split-half method was applied to calculate the reliability of the job satisfaction inventory. The scores on the odd and even numbered items were correlated using Pearson's formula for product moment correlation. This gave the reliability of the half test. The reliability of the half-test thus obtained was 0.63. This was corrected for full length of the test by Spearmen-Brown Prophecy formula. The reliability thus obtained was 0.77 (N = 60).

B. Attitude Scale to Measure Attitude Towards Teaching

Attitudes are a function of the individual's belief-value-matrix (Woodruff, 1942; Rhine, 1958). Favourable attitudes are said to result from perceptions that the attitude-object facilitates need satisfaction, while unfavourable attitudes result from perceptions that the attitude-objects block or hinder need satisfaction. Under this formulation the strength of an attitude will be dependent not only upon the individual's perceptions about the attitude-object but also on the dominant need(s) engaged by the attitude-object.

(i) Meaning of Attitude

In the dictionary of philosophy and psychology, Baldwin (1905) defined as 'readiness for attention or action of a definite sort'.

Allport (1929), prefers to treat attitude as 'a mental and neural state of readiness, organised through experience, exerting a directive or dynamic influence upon the individual's response to all objects and situations with which it is related'. This definition stresses that attitude is a generalised pattern in perception or action which is a result of integration of various experiences.

In the words of Kohler (1929), from the point of view of Gestalt Psychology, a change of attitude involves a definite psychological stress exerted upon a sensory field by a process originating in other parts of the nervous system.

Attitude is a tendency to act toward or against something in the environment which becomes, thereby, a positive or negative value (Bogardus, 1941).

'Attitudes are literally mental postures, guides for conduct to which each new experience is referred before a response is made' (Morgan, 1934).

In Warren's (1934) dictionary of psychology, attitude is defined as 'the specific mental disposition toward an incoming (or arising) experience whereby that experience is modified, or, a condition of readiness for a certain type or activity'.

Guilford (1954), defined attitude as 'personal disposition common to individuals, but possessed to different degrees, which impels them to react to objects, situations or propositions in ways that can be called favourable or unfavourable'.

An attitude is a dispositional readiness to respond for certain situations, persons, or objects in a constant manner which has been learned and has become one's typical mode of response' (Freeman, 1967). According to the Advanced Learners' Dictionary of Current English, attitude means 'way of feeling, thinking or believing' (Hornby, et al., 1968).

All the definitions cited above give importance to the degree of 'liking' or 'disliking' towards a psychological object and in line with the above, Thurstone (1946) defined attitude as 'the degree of positive or negative affect associated with some psychological object.

(ii) Different Methods of Measuring Attitude

Attitude can be measured in several ways. One's attitude is revealed in his behaviour. So it can be measured by direct observation of the overt behaviour of the individual. This has all the defects of observation, in addition to the difficulty of experimentally creating real situations, wherein the behaviour can be observed.

Projective techniques can also be used to assess an individual's attitude. The basis for the use of projective techniques to measure attitude is that attitude can be inferred by one's unconscious responses to certain stimuli like photographs, cartoons, etc. This method has all the disadvantages of projective techniques like difficulty in administration, scoring, low inter scorer reliability, etc.

The most common and popular method of estimating a person's attitude is through an attitude scale, where the individual is asked to express his opinion on several controversial statements about the psychological object. The logic behind the use of opinion to measure attitude is that there is a positive correlation between what people say about a subject and what they will do about it. To the extent people's actions correlate with their expressed opinion we can predict the former from the latter. Any single action, however, will be extremely unreliable from the point of view of measurement. A persons's particular actions cannot be predicted with a high degree of accuracy. This method of assessing attitude from expressed opinion is also subject to some limitations like faking of responses by the individual, where he tends to give socially acceptable responses, thereby, concealing his real attitude. But, this could be overcome in several ways like making the questionnaire anonymous, etc.

iii) Construction of the Preliminary Form

Bearing in mind the important dimensions of teaching like curriculum, students, teaching methods, teachers' status, merits and demerits of the teaching profession, etc., a number of items (opinions, related to attitude of teachers towards teaching were collected from a number of sources as in the case of the job satisfaction inventory. The item pool thus prepared was placed before 5 selected experienced college teachers who were asked to suggest changes, if any, to avoid ambiguity, repitition, etc., among the items. The suggestions made by them were incorporated and 90 items were selected to be included in the preliminary form. The items were randomised. Each of the items was arranged on a five point scale. The scale was made anonymous to avoid faking of the responses.

(iv) Item Analysis

As part of another investigation, the preliminary scale was administered to 274 B.Ed. trainees. The responses of the teachers trainees were scored by assigning integral weights of 5, 4, 3, 2, and 1 for positive statements and 1, 2, 3, 4, and 5 for negative statements as suggested by Likert, respectively for the five reasons Strongly Agree, Agree, Doubtful, Disagree and Strongly Disagree and item analysis was carried out by the procedure of criterion of internal consistency advocated by Likert (1932). 73 items that could significantly differentiate between high attitude and low attitude groups at or above 0.05 level were selected.

(v) Factor Analysis

This scale with 73 items was administered to the same sample which was used for the purpose of finalising job satisfaction inventory. The sample consisted of 160 men and 160 women college teachers selected by a multistage stratified random sampling procedures described earlier. The sample was distributed equally among the two kinds of managements (government and private) and the two levels of teachers (junior and senior teachers). The instrument was administered to the teachers along with the job satisfaction inventory after creating necessary rapport.

The responses were scored and the data obtained on the 320 subjects on the 73 statements of the attitude scale, was computerised to carryout factor analysis with a maximum of 15 factors by applying varymax rotation procedure (Overall and Klett, 1972).

(vi) Selection of the Statements for the Final Form

In selecting statements for the final study, the researcher followed the same procedure as that which was followed in that case of the job satisfaction inventory. The final form thus obtained consisted of 50 statements, which formed into 6 factors.

(vii) Validity

The validity of a measuring instrument can be estimated by various methods. The following types of validity were established for the present tool :

(a) *Content validity* : This means that each of the items should be relevant to the psychological concept being measured and all items put together should cover the entire range of the concept. As mentioned earlier, in the present investigation the item for the scale were collected from many sources like books journals, etc. The item pool was also supplemented by opinions collected from a sample of college teachers. Further, the item pool was gone through by judges to check up whether each of the items was relevant and also to see whether the items covered the entire range of items that can be thought of as appropriate to assess the concept under consideration. It may reasonably be assumed, therefore, that the instrument has content validity.

b) *Item validity* : As mentioned earlier only those items that could discriminate substantially between the high and low groups were included in the attitude scale.

c) *Factor validity* : Following the criterion, explained earlier, 6 factors covering 50 items were included in the final form of the attitude scale. All these factors put together were capable of predicting 63% of the total variance of the attitude of the teachers towards teaching. Hence the attitude scale can reasonably be well assumed to have factorial validity.

d) *Intrinsic Validity* : This can be stated in terms of how well the obtained scores measure the tests true score components. This validity is given by the square root of the proportion of true variance i.e., square root of its reliability as mentioned earlier. The intrinsic validity of the attitude scale thus obtained was 0.84 = 0.92.

e) *Criterion Validity* : At the end of the scale were added two general question :

(1) 'Do you like teaching ?' Yes/No

On the basis of their answers to this question, the teachers were classified into two groups as those who like teaching and those who do not like teaching. The mean scores of those who like teaching and those who do not like teaching were 182.78 and 163.38 respectively. To see whether the difference between the two groups was significant, 't' test was applied. (See Fig. 2)

Table 7
Mean Attitude Scores and SDs of the Teachers who Liked the Teaching and those who did not Like Teaching and the Results of 't' Test

Group	*N*	*Mean*	*SD*	*'t'value*
Like teaching	299	182.78	16.32	4.95***
Do not like teaching	21	163.38	17.44	

*** 't' significant at 0.001 level for 318 df.

The 't' value thus obtained was 4.95 highly significant even at 0.001 level for 318 df.

Another question that was included at the end was

2. If any other job where you get the same amount of salary and other benefits as in the teaching profession is offered, do you accept it in preference to teaching ? YES/NO

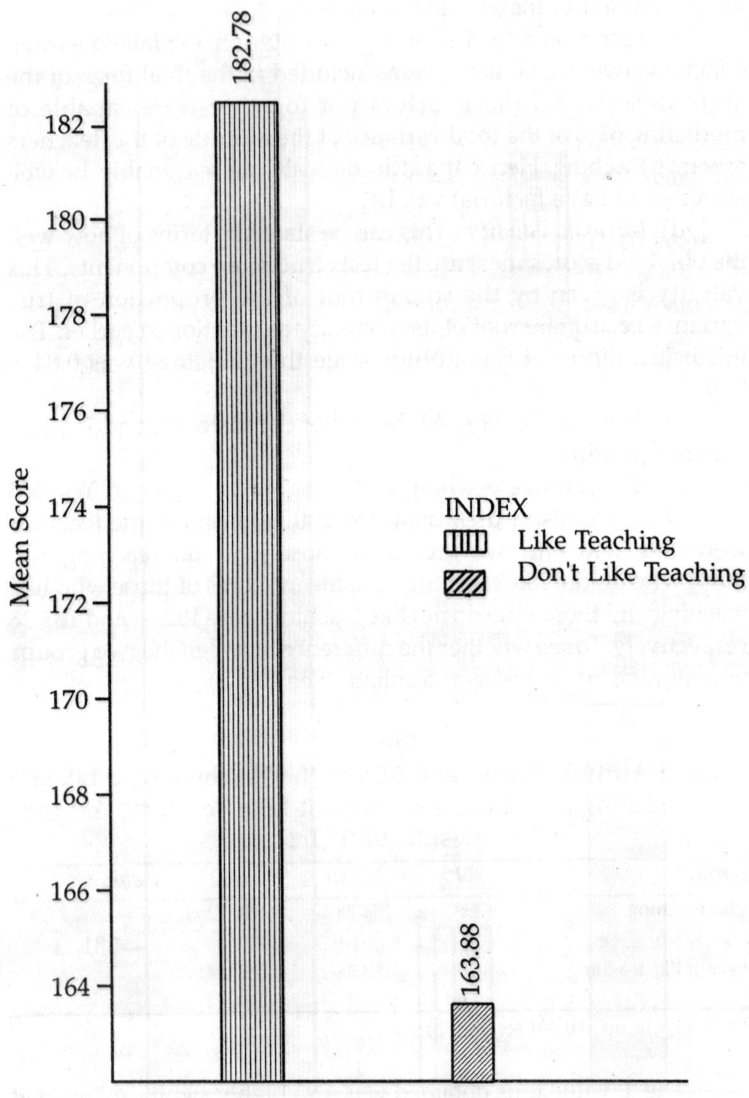

Fig. 2 : Mean Attitude of Teachers who have Stated that they (i) like teaching, and (ii)do not like teaching

The teacher were classified on the basis of their responses to this question as those who would like to continue in teaching and those who would like to take up other jobs. The mean attitude scores of those who would like to continue in teaching and those who would like to take up other jobs were 184.20 and 170.32 respectively showing that the mean scores are in the expected direction. To see the significance of the difference between the mean scores of the two groups, 't' test was applied. The results obtained are shown in Table 8.

Table 8
Mean Attitude Scores and SDs of the Teachers who would Like to Continue in Teaching and those who would Like to Take up Other Jobs and the Result of the 't' Test

Group	*N*	*Mean*	*SD*	*'t' value*
Teaching	261	184.20	16.63	6.31***
Other jobs	59	170.32	14.98	

*** 't' significant at 0.001 level

Here also the 't' value was significant at 0.001 level showing that the scale is able to differentiate between who would like to continue in the teaching profession and those who would like to leave it.

(viii) Reliability

Split-half method was used to find the reliability of the scale. The scores on the odd and even numbered items were correlated using Pearson's formula for product moment correlation. This gave the reliability of the half test. The reliability of the half test was 0.73. This was corrected for full length of the test by Spearmen-Brown Prophecy formula. The reliability thus obtained was 0.84 (N = 60).

C. 16 Personality Factor Questionnaire (16PF)

According to Cattel (1950) "Personality is that which permits a prediction of what a person will do in a given situation". His theory is based on personality sphere concept (Cattell, 1946, 1957, 1964) — a design to ensure initial item coverage for all the behaviour that commonly enters rating — and the dictionary description of personality. It focuses heavily on "source traits". Cattell defines source trait as the spring of the human behaviour. Much is becoming known about the nature of these dimensions through studies with ratings, with laboratory measures, and with real life situations. According to him, a trait of any variety is a mental structure which is a relatively fixed characteristic of the individual functioning from time to time in behaviour.

(i) Selection of the Tool and its Uses

Selection of a tool for measuring personality poses serious problems. One may cut a sorry figure in explaining for his/her choice. The selection of Cattell's *16 PF* test in the present research was also not arbitrary and has been made after a lot of deliberations and study of theory which has been supported amply by Stern (1921) and Allport (1937) in the following works.

Stern observes as under : "We have the right and obligation to develop a concept of trait as a definite doctrine, for in all activities of the person, there is, besides a variable portion, likewise a constant purposive portion, and this later we isolate as the concept of trait".

Allport's contention is equally forceful. He asserts that : "Traits are discovered not by deductive reasoning, not by faith, not by naming, and are themselves never directly observed. They are discovered only through an inference made necessary by the demonstrable consistency of the separate observable acts of behaviour".

Vernon (1963) says that a person's behaviour in any situation depends, of course, on specific features of that situation and on his temporary feelings or state of mind, but it depends also on his more enduring characteristics —abilities, habits and more general dispositions which may be called traits.

Cattell (1961) says that the source traits, as measured by the *16PF* test, are the spring of human behaviour. His definition of personality as given earlier is consistent with the contention of Marxi and Hillix (1973) that "the theory of personality is really identical with the general theory of behaviour, for Cattell's definition would fit the theories of behaviour".

In view of the above the theoretical as well as practical considerations Cattell's *16PF* questionnaire was selected. The *16PF* questionnaire is an objectively acceptable test devised by basic research in psychology to give the most complete coverage of personality possible in a brief time. Coverage of personality is ensured by the sixteen functionally, independent and psychologically meaningful dimensions isolated by over twenty years of factor analytical research on normal and clinical groups. Therefore, having a certain position on one factor does not prevent the person having some other position, whatever, on any other.

Experience with the *16PF* in clinical, educational, and industrial psychology shows that the use of the 16 traits gives actual prediction. In view of the above theoritical as well as practical considerations, Cattell's *16PF* questionnaire was selected to be used in the study.

(ii) Adaptation of the Instrument

Form — C of the *16PF* questionnaire was adapted for the present investigation. The English version of the instrument was translated into Telugu language. The copies of both English and Telugu versions were given to language experts and staff members of psychology department of the university for their comments on the translation. Their suggestions were carried out and the final form of the Telugu version was prepared. The *16PF* questionnaire, as its name implies, provides a multidimensional measurement of personality through normative scores on 16 bi-polar factors.

(iii) Validity

The twenty years of factor analytic work sponsoring this instrument lends empirical credence to its construct validity as a personality measure and predictor.

(iv) Reliability

The test-retest (four weeks interval between the two administrations) measures of reliability coefficients for the 16 factors were as follows :

Factor				
	A : 0.42	B : 0.40	C : 0.36	E : 0.34
	F : 0.41	G : 0.32	H : 0.49	I : 0.42
	L : 0.37	M : 0.31	N : 0.32	O : 0.29
	Q_1 : 0.52	Q_2 : 0.34	Q_3 : 0.37	Q_4 : 0.40

D. Neuroticism Scale Questionnaire (NSQ)

According to Freud's classical dictum "Anxiety is the central problem in neurosis". Most modern observers add — "Neurosis is the central problem in the society". The Neuroticism Scale Questionnaire (NSQ) developed by Scheier and Cattell (1961) is a very appropriate tool for measuring neurotic tendency, as it is brief, standard, and easily administered and scored. It is suitable for normal as well as abnormal adults and also adolescents.

(i) Description of the NSQ

Clinical studies with major personality dimensions showed that neurotics differed from normal not only on one dimension but on many dimensions. Thus, neurotic trend was a complex form, which was influenced by six personality dimensions viz., (1) over protection (Factor-I), (2) Depressiveness (Factor-F), (3) Submissiveness (Factor-E), (4) Worry (Factor-O), (5) Tension (Factor-Q_4), and (6) Ego weakness (Factor-C). Among the above six dimensions the last three dimensions measure a single factor, anxiety, which is the central problem in neurosis. The test provides only one separate sub-score for the last three dimensions — an anxiety score which may be stated as the fourth component of the test. The individual component scores describe the corresponding dimensions and the total score on all the four components measures neuroticism (Scheier and Cattell, 1961).

(ii) Adaptation of the NSQ

The NSQ was translated into Telugu language following the procedures described in the case of the *16PF* questionnaire.

(iii Reliability of the NSQ

The test-retest (with four weeks interval) reliability coefficient of the questionnaire was 0.78.

E. Personal Data

The data regarding the type of management of the college (Government/Private), sex of the teacher, level of teaching, qualifications, marital status, age, experience and size of the family was obtained through a carefully designed personal data sheet. The personal data sheet is given at the end of job satisfaction Inventory final form.

2. Design and Sample

The study was essentially of a 2^3 factorial design (2 managements X 2 sexes X 2 levels). The sample for the study was 480 college teachers equally distributed between the two managements (Government and Private), the two sexes (Men and Women and the two levels (Seniors and Juniors, of teaching. The sample was selected by a multistage stratified random sampling procedure.

The entire state of Andhra Pradesh was considered under three strata as Rayalaseema, Coastal Andhra and Telangana. From each of the strata one district was selected at random, viz., Chittoor in Rayalaseema, Guntur in Coastal Andhra and Warangal in Telangana. Thus, district was the sampling unit and region was the basis for stratification in the first stage.

In the second stage, stratification was made on the basis of the type of management of the college (Government and Private colleges), and level of the college (degree and junior colleges) and the sampling unit was the college. Thus all the colleges in each of the above three districts were divided into four sub-groups. From each of the four sub-groups 3 colleges were selected from each district, thus giving 12 X 3 = 36 colleges.

In the third stage, the sampling unit was the teacher and the stratification was made on the basis of the sex of the teacher and 60 male and 60 female teachers were selected at random from each of the 4 different sub-groups mentioned above, giving 480 teachers for this study. The distribution of the sample of teachers selected for the final study under different categories is shown in Table 9.

Table 9
Distribution of the Sample of Teachers Selected for the Final Study

Government				*Private*				*Total*
Seniors		*Juniors*		*Seniors*		*Juniors*		
Men	*Women*	*Men*	*Women*	*Men*	*Women*	*Men*	*Women*	
60	60	60	60	60	60	60	60	480

3. Administration and Scoring of the Instruments

The instruments viz., job satisfaction inventory, scale for measuring attitude towards teaching, *16PF* questionnaire, neuroticism questionnaire and personal data sheet which were self administering, were administered to the college teachers individually after establishing proper rapport with them as explained earlier. They were explained the purpose and importance of the study and the way in which they had to answer the different items. Sufficient time was given to the teachers to respond to the items.

The job satisfaction and attitude towards teaching inventories (which were five point scales) were scored by assigning numerical weights to each of the responses, as explained earlier.

The *16PF* questionnaire was scored as per the weights provided by the authors. Except the items in Factor-B, all other items were placed on a 3-point scale with weights from 0 to 2. The items in factor-B were given wights of '0' for wrong answers and '1' for right answers. The factor totals were obtained by adding the scores obtained on the items in each factor.

The neuroticism scale was also scored according to the weights given by the authors for the three alternative responses to each item. The total score was obtained by adding the weights for all the items in the instrument.

4. Analysis of the Data

The data thus collected was analysed using relevant statistical techniques like analysis of variance, 't' test etc., to find out whether differences in the independent variables accounted for significant differences in the dependent variables.

The profile similarity coefficient 'r^p' (Cattell, Eber and Tatsuoka, 1970) was computed to test whether there was any significant dissimilarity between the profiles of satisfied and dissatisfied teachers, and between the teachers having less favourable attitude and more favourable attitude towards teaching.

Multiple correlation coefficient 'R' was calculated by carrying out step-wise regression analysis to find out whether it was possible to predict the two dependent variables viz., job satisfaction and attitude towards teaching, with the help of the independent variables.

The usual levels of significance, viz., 0.05, 0.01, and 0.001 were employed to test the significance of the obtained values. The obtained numerical results were also adumbrated by graphical representation wherever necessary.

6

RESULTS AND DISCUSSION

SECTION : A
JOB SATISFACTION

1. Job Satisfaction of the College Teachers

The job satisfaction inventory was developed to measure the level of satisfaction/dissatisfaction of the teachers in their job as a whole and also to identify the most significant job factors causing satisfaction/dissatisfaction to the teachers.

Since the study aims at measuring the level of job satisfaction of the teachers and also to identify the factors with which the teachers were satisfied and those with which they were dissatisfied, the mean over all job satisfaction score of the sample of teacher and also the mean scores on the different factors were computed.

The mean over all job satisfaction scores of the subjects (Ss) and the mean scores obtained on different job factors are shown in Table 10.

It could be seen from Table 6.10 that the mean over all job satisfaction score of the Ss was 146.91. Since the job satisfaction inventory contains 44 items, with the score on any item ranging between 1 and 5, the total score on the instrument could range between 44 and 220 with a neutral point of 132 (44 x 3 = 132).

It may not be out of place to mention a few points about neutral point in this context.

Table 10
Mean Scores and SDs of the whole Group of Teachers on Different Job Factors and on Overall Job Satisfaction and the Results of 't' Test

Mean	*SD*	't'	*(df 958)*
Overall	146.91	16.06	20.34***
F_1	39.92	6.79	22.33***
F_2	10.02	3.33	12.99***
Mean	*SD*	't'	*(df 958)*
F_3	15.77	4.36	3.87***
F_4	28.06	3.46	44.70***
F_5	10.72	2.26	16.66***
F_6	9.24	2.53	2.11*
F_7	14.43	3.52	3.53***
F_8	8.47	2.35	4.96***
F_9	10.32	2.28	12.65***

Note: *** Significant at 0.001 level
** Not significant at 0.05 level

According to Krech, et al., (1962), McGrath (1964) and Newcomb, Turner and Coverse (1965) attitudes may be construed as varying in quality and intensity (or strength on a continuum from positive through neutral to negative. The strength or intensity of an attitude, positive or negative, is represented by the extremity of the position occupied by it on the continuum, becoming stronger as it goes outward from a neutral position. But the neutral point of the attitude continuum poses a problem with regard to its meaning and interpretation, to which several alternative solutions have been proposed.

First, one may consider the statement, that an attitude is neutral to be self-contradictory, indicating the presence of a response predisposition on the hand and the lack of a predisposition on the other. From this point of view, the neutral position on the attitude continuum represents no attitude towards the object in question (Shaw and Wright, 1967). This interpretation supports the idea of Krech and Crutchfield (1948) that "attitudes always have either a positive or negative sign; if they have no sign (i.e., are neutral or at the zero point), they can not be called attitudes at all."

The second alternative interpretation suggested by Shaw and Wright (1967) is that it represents the point of balance in the positive — negative evaluative conflict, thereby reflecting an ambivalent attitude, where ambivalence is used to indicate the existence of two or more attitudes toward the same referent or several referents possessing some degree of similarity of stimulus value and being grouped as a referent class.

The second interpretation suggested by Shaw and Wright seems to be more reasonable and has been adapted by investigators like Venkatarami Reddy (1978a, 1978b, 1979, 1980) Venkatarami Reddy and Ramakrishnaiah (1981) and Venkatarami Reddy (1984).

A mean score above the neutral point indicates satisfaction on the job, while a mean score below the neutral point shows dissatisfaction on the job. It is needless to point out, however, that a mean score of, say 133, just one point above the neutral point does not indicate definite satisfaction, as the little difference between the mean and the neutral point, may be due to error variance that is bound to occur in any investigation, more so in educational and psychological research. Hence, the difference between the mean score and the neutral point was tested for significance by applying t-test.

The obtained mean over all job satisfaction score of 146.91 is above the neutral point of 132. The 't' value for the difference between the mean score and the neutral point was 20.34, significant at 0.001 level. This indicates that the teachers were satisfied with their job in general.

Considering the different job factors, it may be seen that for factors 1, 3, 4, 5, 6, and 9, the mean scores were above the neutral points for the respective factors, while for factors: 2, 7 and 8, the mean scores were below the neutral points. The 't' values presented in the last column of Table 6.10 show that all the 't' values were significant at or above 0.05 level.

Hence it may be concluded that the teachers were satisfied with the six factors, viz., principal; physical facilities; self esteem; fringe benefits; entertainment, prestige and courses; and girl students, personal activities and place of work. They were dissatisfied with the three factors : parents and students; academic policies; and co-teachers.

An examination of the factors which caused dissatisfaction to the teachers revealed that the teachers were concerned about student unrest, frequent changes in the academic policies, lack of interest on the part of the parents on their children's education, political affiliation of their co-teachers, and non-implementation of a strict code of conduct for teachers. Locke and Whiting (1974) reported that blue collar workers more often saw their co-workers as agents of dissatisfaction. Davis (1981) also found that 80 per cent of the teachers' problems were emanating only from teacher-colleague relationships.

Dissatisfied teachers noted a large number of their students as poor, irresponsible, apathetic, poorly prepared and unmotivated (Anjaneyulu, 1968; Davis, 1981; and Parelius, 1982).

2. Type of Management, Sex and Level of the Teachers

The study was of a 2^3 factorial design with 2 types of management (government and private), 2 sexes (men and women) and 2 levels (seniors and juniors). The job satisfaction scores of the different subgroups of teachers were analysed to find the effect of type of management, sex and level of teaching, on their job satisfaction. The means and SDs of the over all job satisfaction scores of the different subgroups of teachers are presented in Table 11.

Table 11

Means and Sds of the Overall Job Satisfaction Scores of the Teachers Classified According to Type of Management, Sex and Level and the Results of the 't' Test.

Group	*Mean*	*SD*	*'t'*
Government	145.55	15.76	13.32***
Private	148.26	16.26	15.49***
Men	147.38	16.68	14.28***
Women	146.44	15.42	14.50***
Seniors	148.90	15.97	16.39***
Juniors	144.92	15.92	12.57***

Note: *** Significant at 0.001 level

It may be seen from the table that the mean scores of all the sub-groups were above the neutral point. 't' test was applied to see whether the difference between the mean scores and the neutral point was significant for the different subgroups of teacher. All the 't' values were significant at 0.001 level, indicating that all the categories of teachers were satisfied with their job (See Fig. 4).

The job satisfaction scores of the teachers were further analysed using analysis of variance of 2^3 factorial design to find whether there was any significant difference between the level of job satisfaction of teacher working under government and private managements, between men and woman teachers, and between senior and junior teachers. The results of this analysis are presented in Table 12.

Table 12
Results of ANOVA of the Overall Job Satisfaction Scores of the Teachers Classified According to Type of Management, Sex and Level

Source	*SS*	*df*	*MS*	*"F"*
Management (M)	880.21	1	880.21	3.38@
Sex (S)	106.41	1	106.41	0.41@
Level (L)	1904.03	1	1904.03	7.31**
M X S	83.33	1	83.33	0.32@
M X L	725.21	1	725.21	2.79@
S X L	826.88	1	826.88	3.18@
M X S X L	36.30	1	36.30	0.14@
Error	107534.00	472	260.37	—
Total	123491.00	479	—	—

Note: ** Significant at 0.01 level
@ Not significant at 0.05 level

It could be seen from the Table that the obtained 'F' ration for management was 3.38, not significant at 0.05 level for 1 and 472 df. From Table 11 it may be seen that mean overall job satisfaction score of teachers working in government colleges was 145.55. The mean score (148.26) of those working in the private colleges was slightly higher than that of the government college teachers. However, the difference between the two means was not significant as indicated by the 'F' value of 3.38 which is not significant at 0.05 level.

Similar results were obtained by Chen (1977) and Padmanabhaiah (1984) in their studies on school teachers.

Venkatarami Reddy and Krishna Reddy (1978); Venkatarami Reddy and Babjan (1980); and Venkatarami Reddy and Ramakrishnaiah (1981) reported that teachers working under private managements were more satisfied than those working in government institutions. The results of the present study were not in line with those of the above studies.

So, the hypothesis that 'Teachers working in government and private colleges do not differ significantly in in the level of their job satisfaction' was accepted.

The 'F' ratio (0.41) for sex was also not significant at 0.05 level for 1 and 472 df. The obtained mean scores of men and women teachers were 147.38 and 146.44 respectively. The insignificant 'F' ratio sex show that men and women teachers did not differ in the level of their job satisfaction.

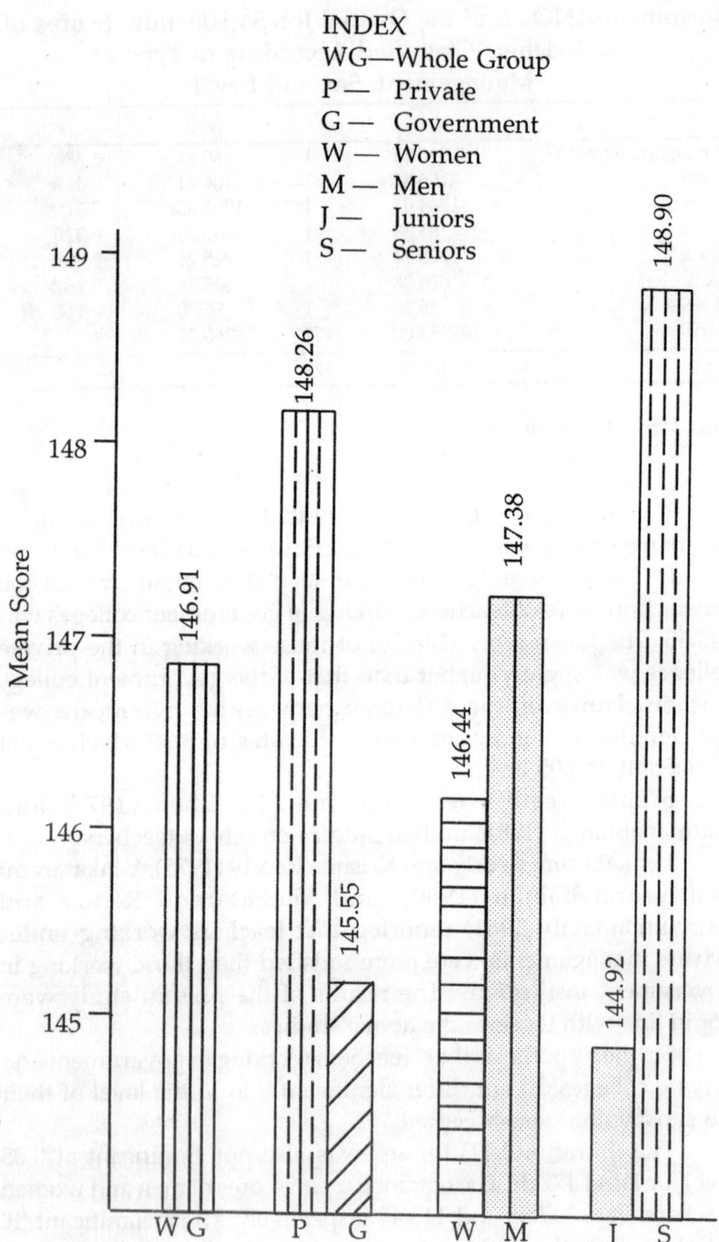

Fig. 4 : Mean Job Satisfaction Scores of Different Sub Groups of Teachers

Englehardt (1973), Atteberry (1977) Cohen (1977), Weaver (1977) and Padmanabhaiah (1984), also reported no significant difference between men and women with regard to their job satisfaction. The results of the present study are in line with the results of those studies.

However, women teachers were found to be more satisfied than men teachers in the studies of Chase (1951), Belasco and Allutto (1972), Bernard and Kulandivel (1976), Anand (1977), Venkatarami Reddy and Krishna Reddy (1978), Venkatarami Reddy and Babjan (1980) and Venkatarami Reddy and Ramakrishnaiah (1981).

Contradicting the above results, Hollen and Gemmil (1976), Chen (1977) and Gobel (1977) observed that women teachers exhibited less job satisfaction than their men counterparts.

From the results obtained in this study the hypothesis that 'There would not be any significant difference between the level of job satisfaction of men and women teachers' was accepted.

The 'F' ratio for level of teachers was 7.31, significant at 0.001 level for 1 and 472 df. This shows that there was a significant difference between the level of job satisfaction of teachers working in degree colleges and those working in junior colleges. From Table 11 it may be seen that the mean job satisfaction score of seniors (teachers working in the degree colleges) was 148.90 while that of the juniors (those working in junior colleges) was 144.92, indicating thereby, that the seniors were significantly more satisfied than the juniors.

The results are in the expected direction because under the present set up in Andhra Pradesh, where this investigation was conducted, the qualification for entering as lecturer either in the junior or degree college is the same. At times, the juniors claim that they do more work than the seniors since the strength of the classes they handle is usually more than the strength of the classes in degree colleges. But, yet they are paid less. The difference between the pay (1550-70-2250-80-3050) of a beginning junior lecturer and the pay (2200-75-2800-100-4000) of a senior lecturer is considerable. There have been agitations by the junior lecturers demanding that they should be paid on par with the lecturers in degree colleges. This explains the significant difference between the job satisfaction of senior and junior lecturers.

So the hypothesis that 'Teachers working in junior colleges would be less satisfied with their jobs than those working in degree colleges', was accepted.

The 'F' ratio (0.32) for the interaction effect between management and sex was not significant at 0.05 level, indicating that the difference between the job satisfaction of teachers working under the two managements is independent of the sex of the teachers. Since A x B interaction is identical with B x A interaction, it can be further stated that the difference between the level of job satisfaction of men and women teachers is independent of the type of management to which their colleges belonged (Edwards, 1968). The 'F' ratio for the other two factor interaction effects and that for the three factor interaction effect were also not significant at 0.05 level.

The factorwise job satisfaction scores of the Ss were analysed in the same way as was done with the overall job satisfaction scores, by applying analysis of variance of a 2^3 factorial design. The results of this analysis is presented in the following few pages.

(a) Factor-1 : Principal

The means and SDs of the job satisfaction scores of the different sub-groups of teaches on this factor are presented in Table 13.

Table 13
Means and SDs of the Job Satisfaction Scores of Different Subgroups of Teachers on Factor 1 (Principal)

Group	*Mean*	*SD*
Government	40.50	6.45
Private	39.33	7.07
Men	40.24	7.12
Women	39.60	6.44
Seniors	39.60	6.67
Juniors	40.23	6.90

It could be seen from the table that the mean scores of all the subgroups of teachers were above the neutral point (33). The satisfaction scores of the teachers were further analysed using analysis of variance of a 2^3 factorial design to find whether there was any significant difference between the level of satisfaction of different subgroups of teachers as measured by this factor.

None of the 'F' ratios for main effects was significant. This shows that teachers working in government and private colleges, did not differ in their level of satisfaction on this factor. Similarly, men and women teachers, and seniors and juniors also did not differ significantly in the level of their satisfaction with the principal.

However, these results based upon the 'F' ratios for main effects should be interpreted cautiously in view of the significant 'F' ratio for the interaction between management and level.

Table 14
Results of ANOVA of the Job Satisfaction Scores of Teachers Classified According to Type of Management, Sex and Level, on Factor 1 (Principal)

Source	*SS*	*df*	*MS*	*'F'*
Management (M)	164.50	1	164.50	3.61@
Sex (S)	50.00	1	50.00	1.10@
Level (L)	47.50	1	47.50	1.04@
M x S	57.88	1	57.88	1.27@
M x L	188.63	1	188.63	4.14*
S x L	16.50	1	16.50	0.36@
M x S x L	47.88	1	47.88	1.05@
Error	21502.95	472	45.56	—
Total	22075.84	479	—	—

Note: * Significant at 0.05 level
@ Not significant at 0.05 level

The interaction effect between management and sex was not significant ('F' = 1.27) at 0.05 level, indicating that the difference between the teachers working under the two managements with regard to their satisfaction with the principal is independent of the sex of the teachers and vice-versa. Similarly, the 'F' ratio of 0.36 for the S x L interaction was not significant at 0.05 level.

However, the 'F' ratio (4.14) for management x level was significant at 0.05 level. This indicates that the difference between the satisfaction of teachers working under the two managements, was not independent of the level of the teachers involved. To probe deep into this, the mean scores of the Ss classified according to management and level were analysed further.

The mean scores of the 4 subgroups of teachers presented in Table 15 show that so far as government colleges were concerned, seniors were significantly less satisfied that the juniors. But in private colleges there was no significant difference between the two categories of teachers. Further, there was no significant difference between the teachers working in government and private colleges in the case of juniors. But in the case of seniors, those in private colleges were significantly more satisfied than those in government colleges.

Table 15
Means and SDs of the Job Satisfaction Scores of Teachers Classified According to their Management and Level and the Results of the 't' test, on Factor 1 (Principal)

	Government	Private	
Juniors	N = 120 mean = 40.28 SD 7.01	120 40.19 6.75	t = 0.10@
Seniors	N = 120 Mean = 38.39 SD = 6.94	120 40.82 6.05	t = 2.89**
	t = 2.10*	t = 0.76@	

Note:** Significant at 0.01 level
*Significant at 0.05 level
@ Not significant at 0.05 level

That the juniors in government colleges were more satisfied with their principal than the seniors, may be because of the fact that almost all government junior colleges are located in the Mandal headquarters which are small towns and the staff strength of these junior colleges may not exceed 10. With such a small faculty, it is not difficult for the principals of these colleges to maintain close relationship with their colleagues and to satisfy their needs.

On the other hand most of the government degree colleges are quite big interms of staff and student strength. The faculty strength of these colleges ranges between 30 to 100 depending upon the strength of the students. Added to the large faculty strength, the staff of the government colleges are transferred frequently. Hence it may not be possible for the principals to maintain close relationship with all the faculty so as to satisfy their needs. Life in such colleges is mechanical and artificial. Under these circumstances, seniors working in government colleges were less satisfied with their principals than the juniors.

In the private colleges, juniors and seniors did not differ significantly ('t' = 0.76) from each other in the level of their satisfaction with their principals. Most of the private colleges (junior or degree) are established in the urban areas only. Teachers working in these institutions do not have transfers. More often than not most of the staff members of these colleges including the principals are either relatives of the management and/or highly obedient to the management. From entering into service until they retire, private college teachers work under one roof. Under such circumstances, the principals of these colleges have a closer rapport with the teachers and thereby cater to their needs more efficiently than those in the case of government colleges.

There was no significant ('t' =0.10) difference between the mean scores of juniors working in government and private colleges in the level of their satisfaction with their principal.

However, the mean scores of the seniors working in private colleges (40.82) was significantly higher than that (38.39) of those working in government colleges, indicating that seniors working in government colleges were less satisfied with their principals than those in private colleges. Principals in government degree colleges, as explained earlier, have limited scope to maintain cordial relationships with the faculty, unlike in the case of private colleges. This explains the significant interaction between management and level.

The three factor interaction (M x S x L) was not significant ('F' + 1.05). This shows that the M x S interaction was independent of the level of the teachers involved. Similarly, the M x L interaction was independent of the sex of the teachers and the S x L interaction was independent of the management under which the teachers were working.

Table 16
Means and SDs of the Job Satisfaction Scores of Different Subgroups of Teachers on Factor-2 (Parents and Students)

Group	*Mean*	*SD*
Government	9.90	3.41
Private	10.14	3.26
Men	9.63	3.41
Women	10.42	3.22
Seniors	10.15	3.40
Juniors	9.90	3.27

(b) Factor-2 : Parents and Students

To find the effect of type of management, sex and level on satisfaction of teachers on F_2 (parents and students), the scores of the different subgroups of teachers were analysed by applying ANOVA as in the earlier case. The means and SDs of the different subgroups of Ss are presented in Table 16 and the results of ANOVA are shown in Table 17.

As mentioned earlier, the mean scores of all the subgroups of Ss were below the neutral point (12) on this factor.

Table 17
Results of ANOVA of the Job Satisfaction Scores of Teachers Classified According to Type of Managements, Sex and Level, of Factor-2 (Parents and Students)

Source	*SS*	*df*	*MS*	*F*
Management (M)	6.79	1	6.79	0.62@
Sex (S)	74.44	1	74.44	6.79**
Level (L)	7.27	1	7.27	0.66@
M x S	40.23	1	40.23	3.67@
M x L	12.99	1	12.99	1.19@
S x L	5.40	1	5.40	0.49@
M x S x L	5.43	1	5.43	0.50@
Error	5172.22	472	10.96	
Total	5324.77	479		

Note:**Significant at 0.01 level.
@Not significant at 0.05 level.

Table 17 shows that the 'F' ration (0.62) for management was not significant at 0.05 level, indicating that teachers working in government and private colleges did not differ significantly from each other on this factor. The 'F' ratio for level was also not significant.

For sex, the 'F' ratio was 6.79; significant at 0.001 level. This shows that there was a significant difference between men and women teachers in the level of their satisfaction with F_2. Men teachers obtained a significantly lesser mean (9.63) score than the women teachers (10.42). In other words, men teacher were less satisfied with the attitude of students and their parents towards education than women teachers. It may be because that in the Indian culture, men rather than women hold responsibility for the raise or fall in their families. If the students and their parents do not show interest in education, men teachers with imbibed cultural background, naturally get dissatisfied.

None of the 'F; ratios for the two factor or three factor interactions were significant at 0.05 level.

(c) Factor-3 : Physical Facilities

The means and Sds of the different subgroups of teachers on factor-3 (physical facilities) are presented in Table 18.

The mean scores of some of the subgroups of teacher were above the neutral point (15, while those of other subgroups were slightly below or very nearly equal to the neutral point. Further analysis was carried out to test the significance of the difference among mean scores of different subgroups of teachers.

Table 18
Means and SDs of the Job Satisfaction Scores of Different Subgroups of Teachers on Factor-3 (Physical Facilities)

Group	*Mean*	*SD*
Government	14.20	4.13
Private	17.35	4.01
Group	Mean	SD
Men	16.28	4.05
Women	15.26	4.61
Seniors	16.71	4.03
Juniors	14.83	4.49

Table 19
Results of ANOVA of the Job Satisfaction Scores of Teachers Classified According to Type of Management, Sex and Level, on Factor-3 (Physical Facilities)

Source	*SS*	*df*	*MS*	*F*
Management (M)	1190.69	1	1190.69	78.65***
Sex (S)	124.06	1	124.06	8.19**
Level (L)	425.63	1	425.63	28.11***
M x S	0.13	1	0.13	0.01 @
M x L	118.07	1	118.07	7.80**
S x L	88.38	1	88.38	5.84*
M x S x L	31.94	1	31.94	2.11@
Error	7146.08	472	15.14	
Total	9124.98	479		

Note: *** Significant at 0.001 level
** Significant at 0.01 level
* Significant at 0.05 level
@ Not significant at 0.05 level

It could be seen from Table 19 that the 'F' ratios for management, sex and level were significant at or above 0.01 level.

The mean scores of the teachers working under government and private managements were 14.20 and 17.35 respectively. Teachers working in government collages were significantly less satisfied with physical facilities than those working in private colleges.

This result is not surprising. According to rules, if any college is to be started, the college must have its own building, furniture, good library, play ground, toilet and laboratory. In practice though the government insists on these facilities while giving permission to private managements to start a college, it does not bother about these rules if it wants to start a college because of political or other considerations. Under such circumstances lack of physical facilities is a real problem in many government colleges. This explains the above result.

The 'F' ratio (8.19) for sex was also significant at 0.01 level. The mean scores of men and women teachers were 16.28 and 15.26 respectively, indicating that men teachers were more satisfied than the women with physical facilities. Women in India are not as social as the women of developed countries. They need more privacy and do not mix freely with men. Thus, they are more bothered by inadequate facilities and expect better facilities. For example, toilet facilities, laboratory conditions, staff rooms, furniture, play ground, etc., were the items where improvement is needed as mentioned by the women teachers.

Similarly, senior and junior teachers also significantly differed ('F' = 28.11) in the level of their satisfaction with physical facilities. The mean scores of the seniors and juniors were 16.71 and 14.83 respectively, indicating that junior teachers were less satisfied than the seniors.

The junior colleges are established since 1969, to impart education at +2 level. Very few junior colleges have their own buildings. Many of them are maintained in high schools adopting shift system. That may be the reason for the junior teachers' less satisfaction with the physical facilities.

However, as mentioned earlier, these results obtained on the basis of the main effects, should be interpreted cautiously in view of the significant 'F' ratios for the interaction effects between management and level, and sex and level of the teachers.

The 'F' ratio for management X level was 7.80, significant at 0.01 level, indicating that the difference between the satisfaction of teachers working under the two managements was not independent of the level of the teachers. To probe into this aspect, the mean scores of the Ss, classified according to management and level were further analysed.

The mean scores of the 4 subgroups of teachers classified according to their management and level are presented in Table 20. It may be seen that in so far as government colleges were concerned, seniors obtained a significantly higher mean (15.63) score than the juniors (12.76).

As explained earlier, most of the government junior colleges have meagre facilities. Many of these colleges are maintained in high schools adopting shift system. That may be the reason for the lesser satisfaction of government junior college teachers with the physical facilities.

Table 20

Means and SDs of the Job Satisfaction Scores of Teachers Classified According to their Management and Level and the Results of the 't' Test of Factor - 3 (Physical facilities)

	Government	Private	
Juniors	N = 120 M = 12.76 SD = 3.85	N = 120 M = 16.90 SD = 4.07	t = 8.12***
Seniors	N = 120 M = 15.63 Sd = 3.70	N = 120 M = 17.79 SD = 3.81	t = 4.50***
	t = 5.98***	t = 1.75@	

Note: ***Significant at 0.001 level.
@Not significant at 0.05 level

There was no significant difference between the juniors and seniors working under private managements on this factor.

Comparing the mean scores of the Ss working in government and private managements, it may be seen that in the case of both juniors and seniors those working in private colleges were more satisfied with physical facilities than their counterparts in government colleges.

As already explained, the private managements are granted permission to start colleges only when facilities like building, furniture, playground, toilet, laboratory, etc., are available, where as the government does not follow its own guidelines when it wans to establish a college. Under these circumstances it is but natural that teachers working in government colleges, either juniors or seniors, are dissatisfied with the poor physical facilities.

It could be seen from Table 19 that the 'F' ratio (5.84) for sex X level interaction was also significant at 0.05 level. This shows that the difference between the satisfaction of men and women teachers was not independent of the level of the teachers and vice versa. To probe into this, the mean scores of the Ss classified according to their sex and level were further analysed using 't' test.

The results presented in Table 21 show that among seniors, men obtained a significantly higher mean score than women. Among men, seniors exhibited a greater satisfaction than the juniors. Other differences between means were not significant.

Table 21

Means and SDs of the Job Satisfaction Scores of Teachers Classified According to their Sex and Level and the Results of the 't' Test on Factor-3 (Physical Facilities)

	Men	Women	
Juniors	N = 120 Mean = 14.91 SD = 3.30	N = 120 Mean = 14.75 SD = 4.52	t = 0.31@
Seniors	N = 120 Mean = 17.65 SD = 3.44	N = 120 Mean = 15.78 SD = 4.04	t = 3.82***
	t = 6.23***	t = 1.84@	

Note: *** Significant at 0.001 level
@ Not significant at 0.05 level

Among the seniors, men were more satisfied with physical facilities than the women teachers. As explained earlier, women in India are not social, need more privacy and do not mix with men freely. Anything short of women's expectation is a problem for them, especially in the case of toilet facilities, staff rooms, furniture, etc. Similarly, among the juniors, the men teachers obtained higher mean scores than the women on F_3. But the 't' was not significant.

Among men teachers, juniors were less satisfied (14.91) than the seniors (17.65). The obtained 't' value (6.23) was significant at 0.001 level. As explained earlier, many junior colleges did not have their own buildings, library, laboratory, play ground, furniture, etc., for which junior teachers have to depend on high schools. Similarly, among the women teachers, juniors obtained lesser mean (14.75) score than the seniors, though 't' value (1.84) was not significant. This result is in expected direction.

(d) Factor-4 : Self Esteem

The means and SDs of the satisfaction scores of the defferent sub-groups of teachers on factor4 (self esteem) are presented in Table 22.

It may be seen from the table that the mean scores of all subgroups of teachers were well above the ueutral point (21). Further analysis was carried out to find the significance of the differences among the mean scores of the different subgroups of teachers. The results of ANOVA are presented in Table 23.

Table 22
Means and SDs of the Job Satisfaction Scores of Different Subgroups of Teachers on Facor-4 (Self Esteem)

Group	*Mean*	*SD*
Government	28.52	3.18
Private	27.60	3.67
Men	28.44	3.61
Women	27.68	3.27
Seniors	27.74	3.75
Juniors	28.38	3.12

Table 23
Results of ANOVA of the Job Satisfaction Scores of Teachers Classified According to Type of Management, Sex and Level, on Factor-4 (Self Esteem)

Source	*SS*	*df*	*MS*	*F*
Management (M)	101.69	1	101.69	8.76**
Sex (S)	68.25	1	68.25	5.88*
Level (L)	50.06	1	50.06	4.31*
M x S	2.31	1	2.31	0.20@
M x L	23.06	1	23.06	1.99@
S x L	3.50	1	3.50	0.30@
M x S x L	4.50	1	4.50	0.39@
Error	5479.92	472	11.61	
Total	5733.29	479		

Note: ** *Significant at 0.01 level.*
* *Significant at 0.05 level.*
@ *Not significant at 0.05 level.*

Table 23 shows that all the 'F' ratios for the main effects were significant at or above 0.05 level and that none of the interaction effects were significant at 0.05 level.

From the results presented in Tables 22 and 23, we see that in the case of management, teachers working in private colleges obtained a significantly lesser mean score (27.60) than those working in government colleges (28.52).

All government college teachers are Gazetted officers. They have more respect in the society than those working in private colleges. An examination of the responses of the teachers to the different items in this factor indicates that the government college teachers seemed to like their job more, feel important in their job, etc., than the private college teachers. This may be the reason why those in government colleges were more satisfied than those working in private colleges on this factor.

The mean scores of men and women teaches were 28.44 and 27.68 respectively. The obtained 'F' ratio was 5.88, significant at 0.05 level, indicating that men teachers experienced a greater self esteem in their job compared to their women counterparts. It may be because that women teachers may not participate actively in their professional activities in this men dominated society. An observation of the responses of the women teachers to the different items in this factor reveals that they seemed to feel less important in their job than the men teachers, were getting fatigue rather quickly in teaching, etc. Because of these reasons, women may have had less self esteem in their job.

In the case of level, junior teachers (M = 28.38) were significantly more satisfied with the factor-self esteem than the senior teachers (M = 27.74). This result is in the expected direction, because the junior teachers teach intermediate students at +2 level who are fresh from high schools. These students continue to show regard to their teachers as they were showing to the teachers in the high schools. Most of the junior colleges were located in small towns where the junior lecturers got respect and regard from the society. As the student strength of these junior colleges is less, they have a better rapport with the students, they get associated with various activities of the college and feel important in their profession. Under these circumstances, naturally, junior college teachers enjoy greater self esteem than their counterparts in the degree colleges.

(e) Factor-5 : Fringe Benefits

The means and SDs of the satisfaction scores of the different subgroups of teachers on this factor are presented in Table 24.

Table 24

Means and SDs of the Job Satisfaction Scores of Different Subgroups of Teachers on Factor - 5 (Fringe benefits)

Group	*Mean*	*SD*
Government	10.95	2.26
Private	10.49	2.24
Men	10.34	2.57
Women	11.09	1.82
Seniors	11.31	1.93
Juniors	10.32	2.40

Table 24 shows that the mean scores of all the subgroups of teachers were above the neutral point (9).

Table 25

Results of ANOVA of the Job Satisfaction Scores of Teachers Classified According to Type of Management, Sex and Level, on Factor-5 (Fringe Benefits)

Source	*SS*	*df*	*MS*	*F*
Management (M)	25.21	1	25.21	5.67*
Sex (S)	67.50	1	67.50	15.17***
Level (L)	170.41	1	170.41	38.29***
M x S	0.21	1	0.21	0.05@
M x L	14.67	1	14.67	3.30@
S x L	60.21	1	60.21	13.53***
M x S x L	4.80	1	4.80	1.08@
Error	2100.40	472	4.45	
Total	2443.41	479		

Note: *** Significant at 0.001 level.
* Significant at 0.05 level.
@ Not significant at 0.05 level

The results of ANOVA of the scores presented in Table 25 show that the 'F' ratios for all the three main effects viz., management, sex and level, were significant at or above 0.05 level, where as in the case of interaction effects, only S x L interaction effect was significant.

In the case of management, teaches working in government colleges (M = 10.95) were significantly more satisfied with fringe benefits than those working in private colleges (M = 10.49). Government college teachers have provision to claim medical allowances, Gazetted officers' allowance, leave travel allowance, etc., which are not provided to the private college teachers by their managements. This explains the significant difference between the two groups of teachers on this factor.

The 'F' ratio (15.17) for sex was significant at 0.001 level. The mean score of men teachers (M = 10.34) was significantly less than that of the women teachers (M = 11.09). In the Indian context, very often it is the men who are the breadwinners and look after the family. If anything is in short supply and the needs of the family are not satisfied, the blame goes to the men. They have to look after both family and profession with equal responsibility. The provision that exists with regard to pension, casual leave, earned leave, medical leave, etc., may not be sufficient for the men teachers in order to attend to the chores of life and to satisfy the aspirations of their families. Women teachers on the other hand do not worry much about the fringe benefits. They work only to supplement the income of their families or to pass time or to have status in the society. Job for women is of secondary importance. This explains the above result.

Junior lecturers were significantly less satisfied with the fringe benefits than the senior lecturers. The obtained 'F' ratio (38.29) was significant at 0.001 level. As explained earlier, the salaries and other benefits of juniors are less than that of the seniors, though qualifications to teach at both the levels were the same. Under such circumstances the juniors are less satisfied with fringe benefits than the seniors.

These conclusions drawn from the main effects of sex and level are however, limited in view of the significant 'F' ratio for the interaction between the two variables.

The 'F' ratio (13.53) for sex x level interaction was significant at 0.001 level, indicating that the difference between the satisfaction of men and women teachers is not independent of the level of the teachers. To probe into this aspect, the mean scores of the Ss, classified according to sex and level were further analysed.

Table 26
Means and SDs of the Job Satisfaction Scores of Teachers Classified According to their Management and Level, and the Results of the 't' Test, on Factor - 5 (Fringe Benefits)

	Men	Women	
Juniors	N = 120 Mean = 9.39 SD = 2.53	N = 120 Mean = 10.85 SD = 1.91	t = 5.26***
Seniors	N = 120 Mean = 11.29 SD = 2.17	N = 120 Mean = 11.33 SD = 1.65	t = 0.17@
	t 6.79***	t = 2.18*	

Note: *** Significant at 0.001 level
* Significant at 0.05 level.
@ Not significant at 0.05 level.

It could be seen from Table 26 that among men as well as women, seniors were more satisfied than juniors with regard to fringe benefits. Comparing the mean scores of men and women teachers, there was significant difference between the two sexes in the case of junior teachers only, women getting a higher mean score than their men counterparts.

Among the senior teachers also, women obtained higher mean (11.33) score than the men (11.29), but the difference between the means of these two groups was not significant. The possible reasons for the lesser satisfaction of men teachers compared to women teachers with regard to fringe benefits, were discussed in the earlier paragraphs.

(f) Factor-6 : Entertainment, Prestige and Courses

The means and SDs of the satisfaction scores of the different subgroups of teachers on Factor-6 are presented in Table 27.

Table 27
Means and SDs of the Job Satisfaction Scores of Different Subgroups of Teachers on Factor-6 (Entertainment, Prestige and Courses)

Group	*Mean*	*SD*
Government	8.94	2.53
Private	9.55	2.50
Men	9.06	2.58
Women	9.43	2.47
Seniors	9.74	2.37
Juniors	8.75	2.59

It could be seen from the Table 27 that the mean satisfaction scores of the government college teachers and junior teachers were below the neutral point (9), whereas the other subgroups of teachers obtained the mean satisfaction scores above the neutral point.

The results of ANOVA presented in Table 28 show that the 'F' ratios for management and level were significant at or above 0.01 level. The 'F' ratio (2.73) for sex was not significant at 0.05 level.

The mean scores of teacher working in government colleges and private colleges were 8.94 and 9.55 respectively. The obtained 'F' ratio (7.43) was significant at 0.01 level, indicating that teachers working in private colleges were significantly more satisfied than those working in government colleges. This may be because private colleges will be permitted to start only when adequate physical facilities which include play ground, and other facilities for entertainment exist. Moreover, private managements offer a variety of vocational courses to student which in turn satisfy the teachers and enhance the image of the management in the public.

Table 28
Results of ANOVA of the Job Satisfaction Scores of Teachers Classified According to Type of Management, Sex and Level on Factor-6 (Entertainment, Prestige and Courses)

Source	*SS*	*df*	*MS*	*F*
Management (M)	45.04	1	45.14	7.43**
Sex (S)	16.52	1	16.52	2.73@
Level (L)	119.02	1	119.02	19.64***
M x S	1.09	1	1.09	0.18@
M x L	5.84	1	5.84	0.96@
S x L	8.79	1	8.79	1.45@
M x S x L	7.25	1	7.25	1.20@
Error	2860.32	472	6.06	
Total	3063.87	479		

Note: *** Significant at 0.001 level.
** Significant at 0.01 level.
@ Not significant at 0.05 level.

As mentioned earlier, situation in government colleges more often than not is entirely different even with regard to physical facilities like accommodation, lab, etc., not to speak of facilities for entertainment. Probably, that is why private college teachers were more satisfied with this factor than their counterparts in government colleges.

In the case of level, juniors were significantly less satisfied with entertainment, prestige and courses offered in their colleges than the seniors. As already explained many of the junior colleges did not have their own buildings. In such cases, the junior teachers need not think of entertainment/recreational facilities and new courses in their college. Equally qualifies as seniors, the juniors sometimes hesitate to say that they are "Junior lecturers". Under the above circumstances it is but natural that the junior teachers were significantly less satisfied with Factor-6 viz., entertainment, prestige and courses.

(g) Factor-7 : Academic Policies

The mean satisfaction scores of the different subgroups of teachers on academic policies are presented in Table 29.

It could be seen from the table that the mean satisfaction scores of all subgroups of teachers were below the neutral point (15).

Table 29
Means and SDs of the Job Satisfaction Scores of Different Subgroups of Teachers on Factor-7 (Academic Policies)

Group	*Mean*	*SD*
Government	14.15	3.54
Private	14.71	3.48
Men	14.37	3.78
Women	14.50	3.24
Seniors	14.79	3.45
Juniors	14.08	3.55

Table 30
Results of ANOVA of the Job Satisfaction Scores of Teachers Classified According to Type of Management, Sex and Level on Factor-7 (Academic Policies)

Source	*SS*	*df*	*MS*	*F*
Management (M)	37.44	1	37.44	3.09@
Sex (S)	1.88	1	1.88	0.15@
Level (L)	60.19	1	60.19	4.96*
M x S	67.50	1	67.50	5.56*
M x L	0.00	1	0.00	0.00@
S x L	14.75	1	14.75	1.22@
M x S x L	18.31	1	18.31	1.51@
Error	5725.36	472	12.13	
Total	5925.43	479		

Note: * Significant at 0.05 level.
@ Not significant at 0.05 level.

The results of further analysis using analysis of variance show that the 'F' ratios for management and sex were not significant at 0.05 level, while the 'F' ratio (4.96) for the other main effect viz., level, was significant at 0.05 level (Table 30).

The mean scores of juniors and seniors were 14.08 and 14.79 respectively, indicating that the juniors were less satisfied with academic policies than the seniors. In the State of Andhra Pradesh, the +2 stage i.e., Junior Colleges come under the control of state government, where as the Degree colleges come under the universities so far as academic matters are concerned. In service programmes, Faculty Improvement Programmes (FIP) and such other facilities to improve their academic calibre are more liberally available to the Degree college teachers i.e., seniors. The juniors, though equally qualified as the seniors, have less access to these facilities. That may be the reason for the lesser satisfaction exhibited by the juniors on this factor, viz., academic policies.

Among the interaction effects, only that between management and sex was significant. This indicates that the difference between the satisfaction of teachers working under the two managements is not independent of their sex. To probe deep into this aspect, the mean scores of the Ss, classified according to management and sex, were further analysed applying 't' test as in the earlier cases.

Table 31

Means and SDs of the Job Satisfaction Scores of Teachers Classified According to their Management and Sex, and the Results of the 't' Test on Factor-7 (Academic Policies).

	Government	Private	
Men	N = 120 Mean = 13.72 SD = 3.63	N = 120 Mean = 15.03 SD = 3.72	t = 2.73***
Women	N = 120 Mean = 14.60 SD = 3.33	N = 120 Mean = 14.40 SD = 3.10	t = 0.49@
	t = 1.96@	t = 1.40@	

Note: *** Significant at 0.001 level.
@ Not significant at 0.05 level.

It could be seen from Table 31 that the 't' values (1.96 and 1.40) were not significant between the mean scores of men and women teachers working in government and private colleges, indicating that men and women teachers did not differ from each other on this factor-academic policies.

Men teachers working in private colleges obtained a significantly ('t' = 2.73) higher mean score (15.03) than their counterparts working in government colleges (m = 13.72). An examination of the responses of the teachers to the different items in this factor indicates that the men teacher working in private colleges had freedom to take initiative in organizing projects, felt satisfied with the availability of inservice training programmes, FIP facilities and such other things.

None of the other interaction effects viz., Management and level; Sex and Level; and Management x Sex x level were not significant at 0.05 level.

(h) Factor-8 : Co-teachers

The mean satisfaction scores of the different subgroups of teachers on Factor-8 presented in Table 32 show that all the mean scores were below the neutral point (9).

Table 32
Means and SDs of the Job Satisfaction Scores of Different Subgroups of Teachers on Factor-8 (Co-teachers)

Group	*Mean*	*SD*
Government	8.29	2.41
Private	8.65	2.29
Men	8.32	2.39
Women	8.61	2.32
Seniors	8.64	2.42
Juniors	8.30	2.27

From the results of ANOVA presented in Table 33, it could be seen that none of the 'F' ratios for the main effects or for the interaction effects were significant at 0.05 level, indicating that the different subgroups of teachers did not differ significantly in the level of their satisfaction with their co-teachers' attitudes and their activities.

Table 33
Results of ANOVA of the Job Satisfaction Scores of Teachers Classified According to Type of Management, Sex and Level, on Factor-8 (Co-teachers)

Source	*SS*	*df*	*MS*	*F*
Management (M)	15.41	1	15.41	2.80@
Sex (S)	10.21	1	10.21	1.85@
Level (L)	14.01	1	14.01	2.54@
M x S	3.33	1	3.33	0.60@
M x L	0.84	1	0.84	0.15@
S x L	2.13	1	2.13	0.39@
M x S x L	7.01	1	7.01	1.27@
Error	2600.72	472	5.51	
Total	2653.66	479		

Note: @ Not significant at 0.05 level

(i) Factor-9 : Girl Students, Personal Activities and Place of Work

The means and SDs of the scores of the different sub-groups of teachers on Factor-9 presented in Table 34 show that the mean scores of all the subgroups of teachers were above the neutral point (9).

Table 34
Means and SDs of the Job Satisfaction Scores of Different Subgroups of Teachers on Factor-9 (Girl Students, Personal Activities and Place of Work)

Group	*Mean*	*SD*
Government	10.20	2.24
Private	10.44	2.33
Men	10.71	2.26
Women	9.93	2.25
Seniors	10.25	2.21
Juniors	10.38	2.35

Analysis of Variance was applied to see the significance of the difference between the means of different subgroups of teachers and the results are presented in Table 35.

Table 35
Results of ANOVA of the Job Satisfaction scores of Teachers Classified According to Type of Management, Sex and Level on Factor-9 (Girl Students, Personal Activities and Place of Work)

Source	*SS*	*df*	*MS*	*F*
Management (M)	6.77	1	6.77	1.35@
Sex (S)	72.86	1	72.86	14.51***
Level (L)	2.00	1	2.00	0.40@
M x S	0.25	1	0.25	0.05@
M x L	0.46	1	0.46	0.09@
S x L	9.35	1	9.35	1.86@
M x S x L	35.76	1	35.76	7.12**
Error	2369.44	472	5.02	
Total	2496.89	479		

Note: *** Significant at 0.001 level
** Significant at 0.01 level
@ Not significant at 0.05 level

It could be seen from the table that the 'F' ratios for management and level were not significant at 0.05 level, while the 'F' ratio (14.51) was significant at 0.001 level for sex.

The mean scores of men and women teachers were 10.71 and 9.93 respectively. This shows that women teachers were significantly less satisfied than their men counterparts on this factor.

An examination of the repsonses of men and women teachers showed that the women teachers were dissatisfied with the girl students who were more marriage oriented than education oriented, they were not able to devote sufficient time to their profession because they have to look after their household work also. More important than these, they had problem when they are required to work far away from their native places. Probably, this explains the significant difference between men and women teachers on this factor.

None of the first order interaction effects was significant at 0.05 level.

But, the M x S x L interaction was significant at 0.001 level. The interaction between any two variables taken at a time is not independent of the level of the third variable.

3. Attitude Towards Teaching Vs. Job Satisfaction

Does the attitude of the teacher towards teaching affect his job satisfaction ? To probe into this, the sample of teachers were classified into Low, Middle and High attitude groups on the basis of their attitude toward teaching and their job satisfaction scores were analysed. Those who scored less than M - 1SD were treated as low attitude group, while those who scored above M + 1SD were treated as high attitude group. Others were treated as middle attitude group.

The job satisfaction scores of the three groups of teachers were analysed and the results of this analysis are presented in the following pages.

It could be seen from Table 36 that the mean overall job satisfaction scores of the low, middle and high attitude groups were 137.61. 147.42 and 154.88 respectively (See Fig. 5). All the above mean scores were above the neutral point (132), indicating that irrespective of the level of attitude towards teaching, the teachers were satisfied with their job. It may also be seen that as the level of the attitude increased the level of job satisfaction also increased. The same trend could be seen in the case of scores on different job factors also.

The job satisfaction scores of the three groups of Ss were further analysed applying one way ANOVA to find whether there was any significant difference between the three groups. The results of ANOVA of the overall job satisfaction and job factor scores of the teachers classified according to their level of attitude towards teaching, are presented in Table 37 in a summary form without loss of essential information.

It may be seen from the table that the 'F' ratios were significant at or above 0.05 level for the overall job satisfaction and also for factors : 1, 2, 4, 6, and 9. The 'F' ratios were not significant for the remaining factors, viz., 3, 5, 7 and 8 at 0.05 level for 2 and 477 df.

Table 36

Means and Sds of Overall Job Satisfaction and Job Factor Scores of Teachers Classified According to their Level of Attitude Towards Teaching.

	Low atitude (N = 76)		*Middle attitude (N = 337)*		*High attitude (N = 67)*	
	Mean	*SD*	*Mean*	*SD*	*Mean*	*SD*
Overall	137.61	15.32	147.42	14.47	154.88	19.32
F_1	37.26	7.23	40.21	6.20	41.48	8.28
F_2	9.13	3.05	10.00	3.16	11.15	4.13
F_3	15.87	3.99	15.78	4.46	15.60	4.33
F_4	25.34	3.65	28.11	3.02	30.91	2.95
F_5	10.29	2.36	10.77	2.17	10.94	2.52
F_6	8.11	2.45	9.34	2.50	10.04	2.37
F_7	14.21	4.06	14.33	3.30	15.19	3.77
F_8	7.95	2.08	8.58	2.22	8.49	3.12
F_9	9.55	2.47	10.32	2.15	11.18	2.44

Table 37

Results of ANOVA of the Overall Job Satisfaction and Job Factor Scores of the Teachers Classified According to the Level of their Attitude Towards Teaching.

	SS		*MS*		*F(df. 2,477)*
	Between	*Within*	*Between*	*Within*	
Overall	10932.00	112559.00	5466.00	235.97	23.16***
F_1	726.88	21348.94	363.44	44.76	8.12***
F_2	145.57	5179.19	72.79	10.86	6.70**
F_3	2.81	9122.00	1.41	19.12	0.07@
F_4	1106.56	4628.69	553.28	9.70	57.02***
F_5	18.13	2423.34	9.06	5.08	1.78@
F_6	144.72	2919.78	72.36	6.12	11.82***
F_7	45.94	5879.94	22.97	12.33	1.86@
F_8	24.76	2628.70	12.38	5.51	2.28@
F_9	94.20	2404.03	47.10	5.04	9.35***

Note: *** Significant at 0.001 level.
** Significant at 0.01 level.
@ Not significant at 0.05 level.

This shows that difference in attitude towards teaching did not have any bearing on the job satisfaction of teachers with regard to factors: physical facilities, fringe benefits, academic policies and co-teachers, while level of attitude towards teaching had a significant effect on the job satisfaction with regard to the factors: Principal; Parents and students; self esteem; entertainment, prestige and courses; and Girl students, personal activities and place of work.

Wherever the 'F' ratio was significant, to find out which of the three groups of Ss differed significantly from the others in the level of their job satisfaction, the mean scores of the three groups of Ss were further analysed by applying 't' test.

Table 38

Means Job Satisfaction Scores of Different Subgroups of the Teachers Classified According to their Level of Attitude Towards Teaching and the Results of 't' Test on Overall Job Satisfaction and Job Factors 1, 2, 4, 6, and 9

	L	M	H
Overall	137.61	147.42	154.88
F_1	37.26	40.21	41.48
F_2	9.13	10.00	11.15
F_4	25.34	28.11	30.91
F_6	8.11	9.34	10.04
F_9	9.55	10.32	11.18

L = Low Attitude group.
M = Middle attitude group.
H = High attitude group.

Note :- 1. The means are arranged in ascending order from left to right.
2. Any two means not underscored by the same line are significantly different at or above 0.05 level.
3. Any two means underscored by the same line are not significantly different at 0.05 level.

The results of the 't' test presented in Table 38 show that with reference to oveall job satisfaction and factors : 2, 4, 6 and 9 (Parents and students; self esteem; entertainment, prestige and courses; and girl students, personal activities and place of work), each mean differed significantly form the others.

In the case of job factor-1, i.e., satisfaction with the principal, teachers who had the lowest attitude towards teaching exhibited least satisfaction with the principals' behaviour than the other two groups which did not differ significantly between themselves.

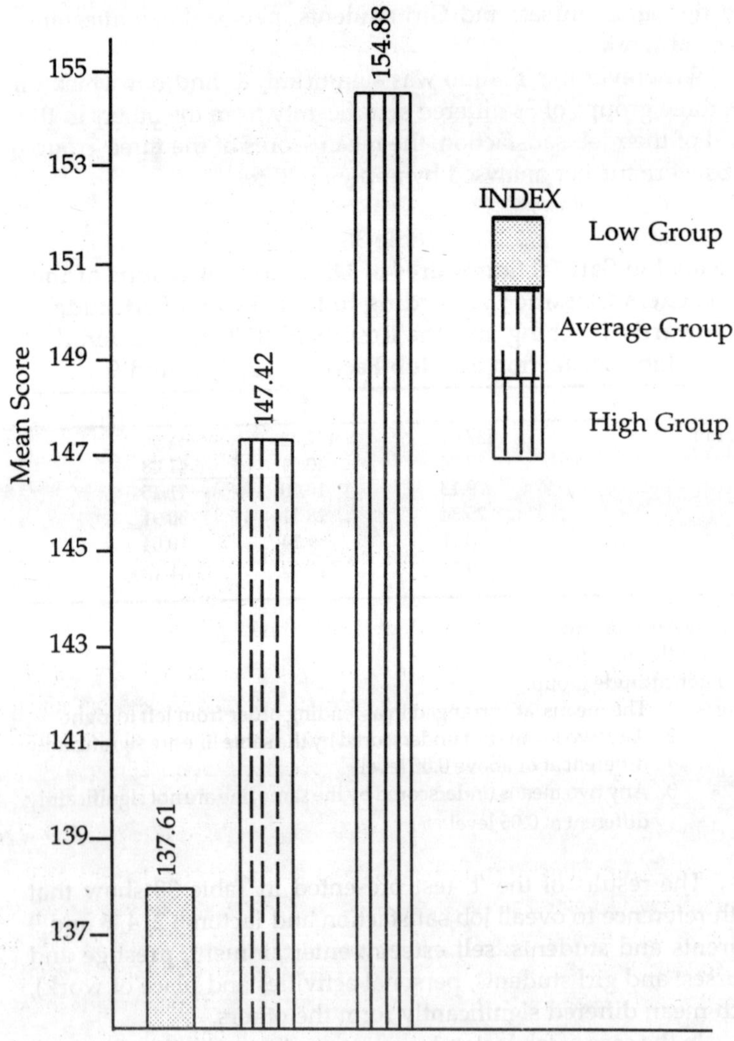

Fig. 5 : Mean Job Satisfaction Scores of Teachers Classified According to their Attitude Towards Teaching as those Having Low, Average and High Attitude

The low attitude groups exhibited less satisfaction while the high attitude group had a higher level of job satisfaction on the whole and also on the above job factors. These results are in line with those obtained by Ramakrishnaiah (1980). It is but natural that those who have a better attitude towards any work are likely to derive more satisfaction than those who are not favourably inclined to that work.

Hence, the hypothesis that 'Differences in attitude towards teaching contribute to differences in job satisfaction; was accepted with reference to overall job satisfaction and satisfaction on the factors: Principal; parents and students; self esteem; entertainment, prestige and courses; and girl students, personal activities and place of work.

4. Qualification Vs. Job Satisfaction

Would there be a significant difference in the level of job satisfaction of teachers who have the minimum qualification and those who have more than the minimum qualification ? To prove into this, the Ss were classified into two groups as (1) those who have the minimum qualification (P.G. Degree in the subject) and (2) Those who have extra qualification (like B.Ed./M.Ed./B.L./ B.G.L.I./ B.L.I.Sc./M.L.I.Sc./another P.G. degree/M.Phil./Ph.D./any other degree or diploma). 354 of the 480 teachers had the minimum qualification only, while the remaining 126 had extra qualifications. The means, SDs and 't' values of the job satisfaction scores of the two groups of Ss are presented in Table 39.

It could be seen from the table that the mean overall job satisfaction scores (147.56 and 145.08) of the two groups were above the neutral point (132). Similarly, the mean satisfaction scores of the two groups of teachers on factors : 1,3, 4, 5, and 9 were above the neutral points : 33, 15, 21, 9, and 9 respectively, but on factors : 2, 7 and 8, the mean satisfaction scores of the teachers were less than the neutral points (12, 15 and 9 respectively). On factor-6, the mean score of the teachers who had only the minimum qualification was above the neutral point (9), where as the mean satisfaction score of the teachers who had other extra qualifications was less than the neutral point (9).

't' test was applied to examine the significance of the difference between the mean scores of the two groups of teachers. The 't' values presented in the last column of Table 39 show that the two groups of teachers differed significantly only on Factor-7

(Academic policies). Teachers who had extra qualifications were significantly less satisfied with academic policies than those who had only the minimum required qualifications.

Therefore, the hypothesis that 'There would be a significant difference between the level of job satisfaction of the teacherswho have the minimum required qualification and those who have more than the required qualification' was accepted only in the case of Factor-7, viz., Academic policies.

Table 39
Means and SDs of Overall Job Satisfaction and Job Factor Scores of Teachers Classified According to their Educational Qualifications and the Results of 't' Test

	Minimum qualification		*Extra qualification*		*'t'*
	Mean	*SD*	*Mean*	*SD*	*(df.478)*
Overall	147.56	16.13	145.08	15.76	1.49@
F_1	39.79	6.95	40.29	6.31	0.71@
F_2	10.20	3.30	9.53	3.38	1.93@
F_3	15.86	4.34	15.52	4.43	0.74@
F_4	28.04	3.49	28.11	3.39	0.19@
F_5	10.74	2.26	10.64	2.26	0.43@
F_6	9.33	2.48	8.99	2.65	1.30@
F_7	14.71	3.57	13.66	3.25	2.90**
F_8	8.48	2.43	8.42	2.12	0.26@
F_9	10.41	2.32	10.06	2.18	1.51@

Note: ** Significant at 0.01 level.
@ Not significant at 0.05 level.

5. Marital Status Vs. Job Satisfaction

Has marital status anything to do with job satisfaction ? The few studies that have been carried out to investigate into this aspect, reported contradictory results. For example, Inlow (1951), NEA (1957) and Venkatarami Reddy and Babjan (1980) found that married teachers were more satisfied than unmarried teachers. Sinha and Nair (1965) Neerja Dwivedi and Pestonjee (1975) and Chen (1977) also obtained similar results on factory workers, whole Butler (1961) found that unmarried beginning teachers were more satisfied than their married counterparts. However, AVA (1948), Redfer (1964), Venkatarami Reddy and Krishna Reddy (1978) and Ramakrishnaiah (1980) reported no relationship between the two variables.

Among the teachers who served as Ss for this study, there were 405 who were married, while 75 were unmarried.

Table 40
Means and SDs of Overall Job Satisfaction and Job Factor Scores of Teachers Classified According to their Marital Status and the Results of 't' Test

	Married (N = 405)		*Unmarried (N = 75)*		*'t'(df. 478)*
	Mean	*SD*	*Mean*	*SD*	
Overall	146.83	16.24	147.31	15.14	0.23@
F_1	39.69	6.94	41.15	5.82	1.71@
F_2	10.00	3.36	10.13	3.20	0.31@
F_3	15.70	4.35	16.16	4.78	0.84@
F_4	28.15	3.38	27.56	3.85	1.36@
F_5	10.80	2.24	10.29	2.34	1.77@
F_6	9.30	2.55	8.93	2.42	1.56@
F_7	14.41	3.57	14.57	3.26	0.37@
F_8	8.50	2.35	8.31	2.37	0.64@
F_9	10.34	2.30	10.19	2.20	0.54@

It could be seen from Table 40 that the mean overall job satisfaction scores of married and unmarried teachers (146.83 and 147.31 respectively) were above the neutral point (132). With regard to factors: 2, 7 and 8, both married and unmarried teachers obtained lesser mean scores than the neutral points (12, 15 and 9 respectively). On Factor-6 the mean score of married teachers was slightly higher than the neutral point (9), where as the mean score of unmarried teachers was slightly lesser than the neutral point (9). On other factors, the mean scores of the married and unmarried teachers were above the respective neutral points.

As in the earlier case, 't' test was applied to see whether there was any significant difference between the mean scores of the two subgroups of teachers. The 't' values presented in the last column of Table 40 show that none of the 't' values were significant at 0.05 level, indicating that married and unmarried teachers did not differ significantly from each other in the level of their job satisfaction. This was true for overall job satisfaction and also for all the nine job factors.

This result is in line with the results of AVA (1948), Redfer (1964) Venkatarami Reddy and Krishna Reddy (1978) and Ramakrishnaiah (1980) who also reported no difference between the job satisfaction of married and unmarried teachers.

Therefore, the hypothesis that 'The level of job satisfaction of married teachers would not be significantly different from that of unmarried teacher', was accepted.

6. Experience Vs. Job Satisfaction

Length of experience may be one of the significant variables which can influence the level of job satisfaction of the employees. Therefore, the total sample of 480 college teachers was divided into three groups on the basis of their experience as low, middle and high groups. Teaches with 5 years or less experience were put in the low group (N = 161), while those with 6-15 years of experience were put in the middle group (N = 201) and those who had more than 15 years of experience were categorised as high group (N = 118). The means and SDs of the job satisfaction scores of the three groups are presented in Table 41.

Table 41
Means and SDs of Overall Job Satisfaction and Job Factor Scores of Teachers Classified According to the Level of their Experience

	Low Experienced (N = 161)		*Middle Experienced (N = 201)*		*High Experienced (N = 118)*	
	Mean	*SD*	*Mean*	*SD*	*Mean*	*SD*
Overall	146.82	15.81	145.60	16.31	149.20	15.83
F_1	39.59	6.44	39.60	7.14	40.92	6.59
F_2	10.40	3.09	9.86	3.49	9.78	3.36
F_3	15.77	4.32	15.87	4.62	15.61	3.99
F_4	28.07	3.46	27.81	3.45	28.48	3.47
F_5	10.35	2.13	10.75	2.31	11.15	2.27
F_6	9.32	2.44	8.99	2.50	9.58	2.67
F_7	14.75	3.48	13.97	3.46	14.79	3.61
F_8	8.27	2.33	8.52	2.46	8.64	2.19
F_9	10.32	2.38	10.23	2.24	10.47	2.24

It could be seen from the table that the mean overall job satisfaction scores of all the three groups of Ss were above the neutral point (132), indicating that all teachers irrespective of their length of experience, were satisfied with their job. Similarly, the mean satisfaction scores of the three groups of teachers were above the neutral points on factors : 1, 3, 4, 5 and 9, but below the neutral points on factors : 2, 7 and 8. In the case of Factor-6, the mean satisfaction scores of low and high experienced teachers were above the neutral point (9), while the mean satisfaction score of the middle group was slightly below the neutral point.

The job satisfaction scores of the three groups of teachers were analysed applying ANOVA as in the earlier cases to see whether there was any significant difference between the three groups with regard to their job satisfaction.

Table 42 shows that the 'F' ratios for overall job satisfaction and for 7 of the 9 job factors (viz., Principal parents and students; physical facilities; self esteem; entertainment, prestige and courses; co-teachers; and girl students, personal activities and place of work) were not significant at 0.05 level. Rao (1970), Anand (1977) and Ramakrishnaiah (1980) in their studies, also, pointed out that the years of experience possessed by teachers had no role to play in the determination of job satisfaction.

Table 42
Results of ANOVA of the Overall Job Satisfaction and Job Factor Scores of the Teachers Classified According to the Level of their Experience

	SS		MS		F
	Between	Within	Between	Within	(df. 2477)
Overall	972.00	122519.00	486.60	256.85	1.89@
F_1	155.31	21920.50	77.66	45.95	1.69@
F_2	35.64	5289.13	17.82	11.09	1.31@
F_3	4.88	9119.94	2.44	19.12	0.13@
F_4	34.06	5701.19	17.03	11.95	1.42@
F_5	43.83	2397.64	21.91	5.03	4.36*
F_6	26.86	3037.64	13.43	6.37	2.11@
F_7	74.31	5851.56	37.16	12.27	3.03
F_8	10.01	2643.46	5.00	5.54	0.90@
F_9	4.20	2494.04	2.10	5.23	0.41@

Note: * Significant at 0.05 level
@ Not significant at 0.05 level

However, experience of the teachers seems to have a significant effect on the level of their satisfaction on two job factors viz., fringe benefits and academic policies, as indicated by the 'F' ratios of 4.36 and 3.03 respectively, which are significant at 0.05 level. To examine which of the three groups differed significantly from the others on these two job factors, 't' test was applied.

It could be seen form Table 43 that with regard to Factor 5, high experienced group got the highest mean score and differed significantly from the least experienced group who got the lowest mean score. The low experienced teachers who are naturally young, will have high aspirations in their life, they have chances

Table 43
Mean Job Satisfaction Scores of Teachers with Different Levels of Experience and the Results of 't' Test on Factors 5 and 7

	L	*M*	*H*
F_5	10.35	10.75	11.15
	M	L	H
F_7	13.97	14.97	14.79

L : Low Experienced group.
M : Meddle Experienced group.
H : High Experienced group.
Note :- 1. The means are arranged i ascending order from left to right.
2. Any two means not underscored by the same line are significantly different at or above 0.05 level.
3. Any two means underscored by the same line are not significantly different at 0.05 level.

to jump into more attractive jobs, they compare the fringe benefits in their job with the benefits available in others jobs and tend to feel dissatisfied. As they gain experience and become old, the teachers try to adjust and reconcile with the existing benefits.

In the case of Factor-7 viz., academic policies, the middle group was the least satisfied compared to the other two groups. The reason may be that low experienced teachers who might have joined the profession recently, may take time to understand the merits and demerits of the existing policies. So, the question of dissatisfaction with the academic policies does not arise with them. The middle experienced teachers after knowing the loop holes of the policies, might have made attempts to bring changes in the educational system and settled down with dissatisfaction, whereas the high group who are naturally old, might have got themselves adjusted to the existing system of education.

Hence, the hypothesis that 'Teachers with different levels of experience differ in the level of their job satisfaction', was accepted in the case of job Factors 5 and 7 viz., fringe benefits and academic policies.

7. Age Vs. Job Satisfaction

The sample of college teachers was classified into three groups on the basis of their age: (1) Young (30 years or less), (2) Middle (31 to 40 years) (3) Old (41 years or above). The means and SDs of the overall job satisfaction and job factor scores of the teachers of the three age groups are presented in Table 44.

Table 44
Means and SDs of Overall Job Satisfaction and Job Factor Scores of Different Age Groups of Teachers.

	Young (N = 154)		*Middle (N = 205)*		*Old (N = 121)*	
	Mean	*SD*	*Mean*	*SD*	*Mean*	*SD*
Overall	146.64	16.27	145.65	15.86	149.37	15.97
F_1	39.58	6.91	39.30	6.84	41.39	6.37
F_2	10.31	3.08	10.07	3.38	9.58	3.55
F_3	15.61	4.59	15.74	1.62	16.02	3.58
F_4	28.25	3.18	27.65	3.54	28.51	3.61
F_5	10.32	2.20	10.92	2.20	10.88	2.38
F_6	9.20	2.41	9.20	2.55	9.38	2.66
F_7	14.69	3.33	14.07	3.55	14.72	3.67
F_8	8.32	2.28	8.55	2.39	8.50	2.39
F_9	10.37	2.28	10.19	2.25	10.48	2.35

It could be seen from the table that the mean overall job satisfaction scores of all the three groups of teachers were above the neutral point (132). An examination of the factor wise mean scores shows that the mean scores of the three groups of teachers were less than the respective neutral points (12, 15 and 9 respectively) in the case of factors: 2, 7 and 8. On all other factors, the mean scores were above the respective neutral points.

The mean scores of the teachers indicates that old teachers were the most satisfied group, followed by young and middle aged teachers. The same trend can be observed in the case of factors: 1, 4, 6, 7 and 9. Young teachers obtained highest mean scores on factors: 5 and 8 seem to give more satisfaction to middle aged teachers and least satisfaction to the youngsters. To examine the significance of the differences between the mean scores of the three groups, one way ANOVA was applied and the results were presented in Table 45.

The obtained 'F' ratio (2.10) for the overall job satisfaction scores of three groups of teachers was not significant at 0.05 level for 2 and 477 df. This shows that differences in the age of teachers had no significant effect on their overall job satisfaction. This result is supported by other studies conducted by Rao (1970), Pestonjee and Singh (1973), and Anand (1977) who reported that there was no significant relationship between age and job satisfaction of workers.

Considering the different job factors, the 'F' ratios were significant in the case of only two factors, viz., 1 and 5 (Principal and Fringe benefits). To find out which of the three groups of Ss differed significantly from the others in the case of these two factors, 't' test was applied

Table 45
Results of ANOVA of the Job Satisfaction and Job Factor Scores of Different Age Groups of Teachers

	SS		MS		F
	Between	Within	Between	Within	(df. 2,477)
Overall	1076.00	122415.00	538.00	256.64	2.10@
F_1	356.44	21719.38	178.22	45.53	3.91*
F_2	35.73	5289.04	17.86	11.09	1.61@
F_3	11.94	9112.88	5.97	19.10	0.31@
F_4	65.19	5670.06	32.59	11.89	2.74@
F_5	34.97	2406.49	17.48	5.05	3.47*
F_6	3.04	3061.47	1.52	6.42	0.24@
F_7	46.50	5879.38	23.25	12.33	1.89@
F_8	4.74	2648.72	2.37	5.55	0.43@
F_9	7.18	2491.06	3.59	5.22	0.69@

Note: * Significant at 0.05 level
@ Not significant at 0.05 level

Table 46
Mean Job Satisfaction Scores of Different Age Groups of Teachers and the Results of 't' Test on Factors 1 and 5

	M	Y	O
F_1	39.30	39.58	41.39
	Y	O	M
F_5	10.32	10.88	10.92

Y : Young age group.
M : Middle age group.
O : Old age group.

Note : 1. The means are arranged in ascending order from left to right.
2. Any two means not underscored by the same line are significantly different at or above 0.05 level.
3. Any two means underscored by the same line are not significantly different at 0.05 level.

The results of the 't' test presented in Table 46 show that in the case of factor-1 i.e., principal, the old group got the highest mean score and differed significantly from the young and middle aged teachers, indicating that the old aged teachers were more satisfied with the principal than the young and middle aged teachers. It seems that older generation can easily get on with others compared to the younger generation who confront with others for petty things. This attitude is no exception to teachers.

In the case of fringe benefits, young group got a significantly lower mean score than the other two groups. Teachers whose age was 30 years or less as explained earlier, have chances to jump into other professions which offer higher salaries, quarters, car, health insurance, power, challenging tasks, etc. There is a chance for younger teachers to compare themselves with their counterparts in other professions which enjoy high status in the society. Whereas older teachers have no other option except to continue in the teaching profession because of the age factor. They are forced to reconcile, adjust, compromise and feel satisfied with the fringe benefits that are available in their job. This explains the above result.

Hence, the hypothesis that 'Teachers belonging to different age groups differ in the level of their job satisfaction', was accepted in the case of job Factors 1 and 5, and rejected in the case of overall job satisfaction and other factors.

8. Size of the Family Vs. Job Satisfaction

The teachers were classified on the basis of the size of their family into three groups: (1) Small family, (2) Medium family and (3) Large family, in order to examine the relation between the size of the family and job satisfaction. For the purpose of analysis, families with 4 or less members were treated as small families, families with 5 members were treated as medium sized families while families with 6 or more members were considered as large families. The means and SDs of satisfaction scores of three groups of teachers are presented in Table 47.

Table 47 shows that the mean overall job satisfaction scores of all the three groups of teachers were above the neutral point (132). Considering the mean scores on the different factors, it may be seen that the mean scores of the three groups of teachers were less than the respective neutral points with regard to factors: 2, 7 and 8. On factor-6, the mean satisfaction score of the teachers with large families was below the neutral point (9), whereas the mean scores of the other two groups were above the neutral point. On other factors, the mean satisfaction scores of all the three groups of teachers were above the respective neutral points.

One way ANOVA was applied to findout whether there was any significant difference between the three groups with regard to their job satisfaction. The results of this analysis are presented in Table 48.

Table 47
Means and SDs of Overall Job Satisfaction and Job Factor Scores of the Teachers Classified According to the Size of their Families

	Small (N = 268)		*Medium (N = 110)*		*Large (N = 102)*	
	Mean	*SD*	*Mean*	*SD*	*Mean*	*SD*
Overall	145.65	15.59	149.16	17.84	147.77	15.05
F_1	39.06	6.90	40.94	6.57	41.07	6.47
F_2	10.08	3.19	9.93	3.37	9.98	3.68
F_3	15.75	4.34	15.75	4.24	15.83	4.60
F_4	27.82	3.40	28.13	4.12	28.62	2.73
F_5	10.56	2.26	10.93	2.35	10.91	2.14
F_6	9.22	2.56	9.59	2.63	8.92	2.29
F_7	14.41	3.28	14.65	4.06	14.27	3.51
F_8	8.47	2.27	8.51	2.64	8.40	2.27
F_9	10.30	2.27	10.65	2.32	10.00	2.25

It may be seen from the table that the 'F' ratio (2.07) for overall job satisfaction was not significant. Similarly the 'F' ratios for different job factors, except for factor 1, were also not significant at 0.05 level for 2 and 477 df. This result was supported by Ramakrishnaiah (1980) who also found that the size of the family did not have any bearing on the job satisfaction of teachers.

Table 48
Results of ANOVA of the Overall Job Satisfaction and Job Factor Scores of the Teachers Classified According to the Size of their Families.

	SS		*MS*		*F*
	Between	*Within*	*Between*	*Within*	*(df . 2,477)*
Overall	1064.00	122427.00	532.00	256.66	2.07@
F_1	444.69	21631.12	222.34	45.35	4.90**
F_2	2.03	5322.73	1.02	11.16	0.09@
F_3	0.50	9124.31	0.25	19.13	0.01@
F_4	47.63	5687.63	23.81	11.92	2.00@
F_5	15.68	2425.76	7.84	5.09	1.54@
F_6	23.97	3040.53	11.99	6.37	1.88@
F_7	7.75	5918.13	3.88	12.41	0.31@
F_8	0.64	2652.83	0.32	5.56	0.06@
F_9	22.84	2475.39	11.42	5.19	2.20@

Note: ** Significant at 0.01 level
@ Not significant at 0.05 level

To find out which of the three groups of Ss differed

significantly from the others in the level of their satisfaction on Factor-1, viz., Principal, 't' test was employed.

Table 49
Mean Job Satisfaction Scores of Different Subgroups of Teachers Classified According to the Size of their Families and the Results of 't' Test on Factor-1.

	S	M	L
F_1	39.06	40.94	41.07

S : Small family group
M : Medium family group
L : Large family group.

Note : 1. The means are arranged in ascending order from left to right.
2. Any two means not underscored by the same line are significantly different at or above 0.05 level.
3. Any two means underscored by the same line are not significantly different at 0.05 level.

The results of the analysis presented in Table 49 shows that the mean score of teachers with small families was the least and it differed significantly from the other two means. This indicates that teachers with small families were relatively less satisfied on this factor than those with medium and large families. As any one can expect, the teachers with medium and large families usually develop greater capacity to adjust than those with small families where the situation is different. This may be the reason why teachers from demium and large families were more satisfied and at home with their principals.

Hence the hypothesis that 'The size of the family of the teachers would have a significant bearing on their job satisfaction' was accepted in the case of job factor-1, viz., Principal.

9. Personality Characteristics Vs. Job Satisfaction

Raw scores on each of the 16 personality factors derived from the 16PF questionnaire were converted into stern values. As recommended by Cattell et.al., (1970), on the basis of the stern values on each of the 16 factors, the teachers were divided into 3 groups. Those whose stern values were 1 to 4 were grouped as low scorers, while those who got stern scores of 5 or 6 were treated as average scorers. Those whose stern score was 7 or above were considered as high scorers. The mean overall job satisfaction scores of the three groups of Ss thus classified were presented in Table 50.

The mean overall job satisfaction scores of the three groups of teachers, classified as low, middle and high on the basis of their scores on factor A were 146.53, 146.32 and 147.85 respectively. It may be seen that all the above mean scores are above the neutral point 132, showing that all the three groups of teachers irrespective of their score on personality factor A, were satisfied with their job. Similar trend of results can be seen in the case of all the other personality factors: B, C, E, F, G, H, I, L, M, N, O, Q_1, Q_2, Q_3, and Q_4. The overall job satisfaction scores of the three groups of Ss were further analysed applying ANOVA as in the earlier cases and the results of the same are presented in Table 51.

Table 50

Means and SDs of Overall Job Satisfaction Scores of Teachers Classified as Low, Middle and High Groups Based Upon their Scores on Different Personality Factors.

Personality factors	*Low*			*Middle*			*High*		
	N	*Mean*	*SD*	*N*	*Mean*	*SD*	*N*	*Mean*	*SD*
A	145	146.53	16.13	171	146.32	13.26	164	147.85	18.52
B	116	148.39	15.84	235	147.32	16.08	129	144.82	16.12
C	127	144.00	15.74	229	146.89	15.96	124	149.93	16.13
E	129	147.35	15.29	238	147.52	15.63	113	145.12	17.73
F	177	146.05	15.98	175	147.46	15.01	128	147.34	17.55
G	161	147.30	15.57	183	146.65	16.30	136	146.79	16.40
H	180	147.29	15.76	127	145.91	15.80	173	147.25	16.60
I	149	146.97	17.42	184	146.62	15.43	147	147.21	15.49
L	193	150.02	15.71	120	146.17	15.51	167	143.84	16.28
M	186	146.09	16.44	164	148.90	15.58	130	145.58	14.64
N	168	147.48	17.57	189	147.15	16.08	123	145.75	13.77
O	166	148.48	14.99	147	148.20	15.33	167	144.22	17.39
Q_1	119	146.57	15.66	255	146.62	16.81	106	147.97	14.67
Q_2	174	147.51	16.48	180	147.92	15.04	126	144.64	16.77
Q_3	168	146.52	16.29	167	147.55	15.34	145	146.61	16.67
Q_4	167	148.06	16.55	155	146.14	15.34	158	146.44	16.24

It could be seen from Table 51 that the 'F' ratios for the factors: C, L and O were significant and for all other factors the 'F' ratios were not significant at 0.05 level.

In the case of these three factors: C, L and O, 't' test was applied to find out which of the three groups of Ss differed significantly from the others in the level of their satisfaction. These results are presented in Table 52.

Table 51

Results of ANOVA of the Overall Job Satisfaction Scores of Teachers Classified as Low, Middle and High Groups Based Upon their Scores on Different Personality Factors

Perso-nality factors	*SS*		*MS*		*F*
	Between	*Within*	*Between*	*Within*	*(df. 2,477)*
A	233.00	123258.00	116.50	258.40	0.45@
B	864.00	122627.000	432.00	257.08	1.68@
C	2212.00	121279.00	1106.00	254.25	4.35*
E	480.00	123011.00	240.00	257.88	0.93@
F	218.00	123273.00	109.00	258.43	0.42@
G	46.00	123445.00	23.00	258.79	0.09@
H	182.00	123309.00	91.00	258.51	0.35@
I	35.00	123456.00	17.50	258.82	0.07@
L	3511.00	119980.00	1755.50	251.53	6.98**
M	1009.00	122482.00	504.50	256.78	1.96@
N	238.00	123253.00	119.00	258.39	0.46@
O	1870.00	121621.00	935.00	254.97	3.67*
Q_1	162.00	123329.00	81.00	258.55	0.31@
Q_2	897.00	122594.00	448.50	257.01	1.75@
Q_3	113.00	123378.00	56.50	258.65	0.22@
Q_4	355.00	123136 00	177.50	258.15	0.69@

Note: ** Significant at 0.01 level.
* Significant at 0.05 level.
@ Not significant at 0.05 level.
(The above notation for indicating level of significance/of 't' or 'F' value is used in all the tables that follow.)

Table 52

Mean Overall Job Satisfaction Scores of Teachers Classified as Low, Middle and High According to their Personality Scores and the Results of 't' Test on Personality Factors C, L and O.

	L	*M*	*H*
C	144.00	146.89	149.93
	H	M	L
L	143.84	146.17	150.02
O	144.22	148.20	143.48

L : Low group
M : Middle group
H : High group

Note :- 1. The means are arranged i ascending order from left to right.

2. Any two means not underscored by the same line are significantly different at or above 0.05 level.

3. Any two means underscored by the same line are not significantly different at 0.05 level.

Factor-C describes the emotional stability of an individual. The mean job satisfaction scores of emotionally less stable (C-), average (C) and emotionally more stable (C+) Ss were 144.00, 146.89 and 149.93 respectively. It may be seen from Table 52 that emotionally more stable teachers were significantly more satisfied in their job then the emotionally less stable teachers. Thus factor-C which differentiates teachers as emotionally unstable and emotionally stable, proved to be a significant variable in affecting the level of satisfaction of the teachers with their job.

With regard to factor-L, teachers who were low (L-) on this personality factor obtained a significantly greater mean job satisfaction score than the teachers who were high (L+) or moderate (L). The qualities of those who fall under L-, are 'trusting, accepting conditions, conciliatory, etc. ' while the qualities of those who fall under L+ are 'suspecting, jealous, irritable, etc.' It is not surprising that the low group (L-) are more satisfied than the other groups. Therefore it could be concluded that factor L was another important factor affecting the job satisfaction of the teachers.

The group of teachers who scored high on factor O obtained the lowest job satisfaction score and differed significantly from the other two groups. Those who are O+ are 'depressed, moody, worried, troubled, insecure, anxious and lonely;, while those who are O-, are 'self-confident, cheerful, placid and important'. This explains the significant difference between the job satisfaction of teachers who are low and high on this personality factor.

Thus out of the 16 personality factors only 3 factors viz., factors: C, L and O, significantly influenced the level of job satisfaction of the teachers. C+, L- and O- were significantly associated with greater satisfaction on the job. A careful examination of the mean scores of the three groups of Ss on 7 factors shows a rend of association among A+, B-, G-, I+, N-, Q1+, and Q_4- with greater job satisfaction.

Hence, the hypothesis that 'Differences in the personality characteristics of the teaches would contribute to differences in the level of their job satisfaction' was accepted only in the case of personality factors:C, L and O.

10. Neuroticism Vs. Job Satisfaction.

The college teachers were divided into three groups: low, average and high, on the basis of their neuroticism scores. Those who obtained less than M - ISD, were treated as low neuroticism group, while those whose score was M + 1SD were treated as high group. Those scoring between M - 1SD and M + 1SD were treated as average group and their job satisfaction scores were analysed. The mean job satisfaction scores of the three groups of subjects were presented in Table 53.

Table 53
Means and SDs of Overall Job Satisfaction Scores of Teachers Classified as Low, Middle and High Groups — According to their Score on Neuroticism Scale

	Low	*Middle*	*High*
N	84	319	77
Mean	147.73	146.39	148.17
SD	17.68	15.52	16.49

The mean scores of the three groups (low, average and high) were 147.73, 146.39 and 148.17 respectively. They were above the neutral point (132), indicating that all the three groups of teaches irrespective of their scores on neuroticism, were satisfied with their job, One way ANOVA was carried out to find out whether there was any significant difference between the level of job satisfaction of the three groups of Ss.

The results of this analysis presented in Table 54 show that the 'F' ratio was not significant at 0.05 level for 2 and 477 df, indicating no significant difference between the job satisfaction of the three groups. In other words, level of neuroticism of the teachers did not have any effect on their job satisfaction.

Table 54
Results of ANOVA of the Overall Job Satisfaction Scores of Teachers Classified According to their Score on the Neuroticism Scale.

Source	*SS*	*df*	*MS*	*F*
Between groups	271	2	135.50	0.52@
Within groups	123220	477	258.32	
Total	123491	479		

Fisher and Hanna (1931), Mehdi and Sinha (1971) and Anand (1977) found that job satisfaction and neuroticism were negatively correlated. The results of this study do not fall in line with those of the above studies.

11. Personality Profiles of Satisfied and Dissatisfied Teachers

what would be the nature of the personality profiles of satisfied and dissatisfied teachers ? Will their be any significant dissimilarity between them or would they be similar ? To examine this, the teachers were divided into two extreme groups as satisfied and dissatisfied on the basis of their overall job satisfaction scores. The personality scores of these two groups on the 16 personality factors were calculated and compared.

For this purpose, teachers whose job satisfaction scores were above M + 1SD were treated as satisfied, while those whose scores were below M — 1SD were treated as dissatisfied. Among the 480 college teachers who participated, 69 teachers were identified as satisfied, while 67 belonged to the dissatisfied group. The personality scores of these two groups, converted into stens, were analysed.

Personality profiles of these two groups of satisfied and dissatisfied teachers were prepared and the Profile Similarity Coefficient (r_p) (Cattel, et.al., 1970) was calculated to examine the similarity/dissimilarity of the personality of these two groups.*

The r_p thus obtained was 0.77, far behind the table value of r_p at 0.01 level. It indicates that the overall personality pattern of the satisfied and dissatisfied teachers was similar (See Fig. 6).

Therefore the hypothesis that 'There would be a significant difference between the personality profiles of satisfied and dissatisfied teachers' was rejected.

---

*The formula used in the computation of personality similarity coefficient was

$$r^p = \frac{4k - Wd^2}{4k + Wd^2}$$

Where k = The median of the chi-square distribution with degrees of freedom equal to the number of factors used, W = Weight given to each factor, and d = defference of the means of satisfied and dissatisfied groups for each factor.

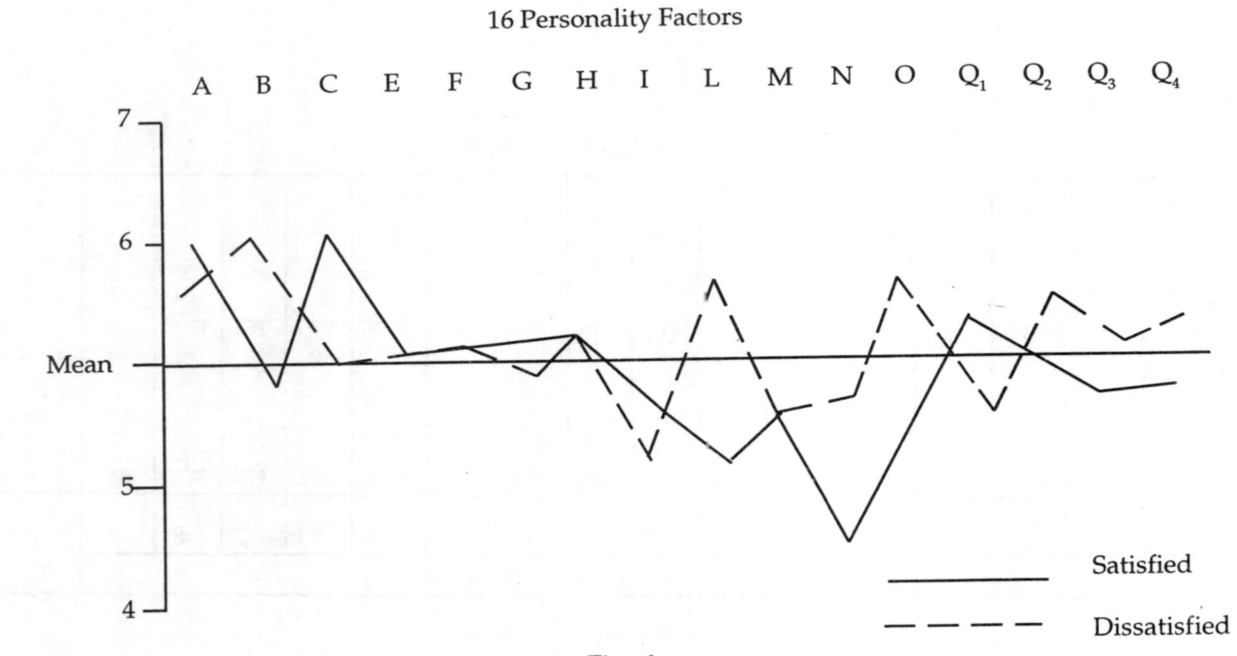

Fig.: 6
Personality profiles of teachers who were (1) Satisfied (ISD above mean score) and (ii) Dissatisfied (ISD below mean score)

Table 55
Comparison of Personality Profiles of Satisfied and Dissatisfied Teachers

Group	*16 Personality Factors*															
	A	*B*	*C*	*E*	*F*	*G*	*H*	*I*	*L*	*M*	*N*	*O*	Q_1	Q_2	Q_3	Q_4
Satisfied (N = 69) (Means in Stens)	6.00	5.26	6.14	5.51	5.64	5.61	5.55	5.32	5.14	5.39	4.65	5.07	5.58	5.42	5.19	5.26
Dissatis-fied (N = 67) (Means in Stens)	5.79	6.03	5.54	5.63	5.64	5.43	5.61	5.03	6.13	5.37	5.39	6.13	5.28	5.67	5.63	5.67

r_p = 0.77**

**Significant at 0.01 level.

SECTION : B
ATTITUDE OF TEACHERS TOWARDS TEACHING

1. Type of Management, Sex and Level of Teaching

How do the different variables like management, sex, level, age, experience, etc., affect the teacher's attitude towards teaching ? This section deals with this aspect.

As mentioned earlier, attitude towards teaching was treated as dependent variable in this section and the effect of different independent variables on this variable viz., attitude towards teaching, was analysed. The college teachers were divided into different categories as in the earlier case, as those working in government colleges and those working in private colleges on the basis of the type of management to which the college in which working belonged; as men and women depending on their sex, and as seniors and juniors depending upon whether they were working in degree or junior colleges.

As mentioned earlier, the attitude of the teachers towards teaching was measured by an attitude scale developed for the purpose. The attitude scale contained 50 items, with the score on any item ranging between 1 and 5. Hence, the attitude scores of the Ss could range between 50 and 250 with 150 as the neutral point (Shaw and Wright, 1967).

Table 56
Means and SDs of the Attitude Scores of the Teachers Classified According to the Type of Management, Sex and Level of Teaching and the Results of the 't' Test

Group	Mean	SD	t
Government	182.88	17.38	29.30***
Private	181.82	17.74	27.79***
Men	181.48	19.30	25.27***
Women	183.21	15.60	32.97***
Seniors	181.65	17.51	28.00***
Juniors	183.05	17.60	29.09***

Note: *** Significant at 0.001 level

Table 56 shows the mean attitude scores and SDs of the different subgroups of teachers. It may be seen from the table that all the mean scores were above the neutral point. 't' test was applied to see whether the difference between the mean score and the neutral point was significant.

The results of the 't' test presented in the last column of Table 56 show that all the subgroups of teachers had a significantly positive attitude towards teaching. Thus it may be concluded that on the whole the college teachers have a favourable attitude towards teaching.

Hence, the hypothesis that 'College teachers in general have a favourable attitude towards teaching' was accepted. The attitude scores of the teachers were further analysed using ANOVA of 2x2x2 factorial design to findout the effect of management, sex and level on the attitude.

Table 57
Results of ANOVA of the Attitude Scores of the Teachers Classified According to the Type of Management, Sex and Level of Teaching

Source	*SS*	*df*	*MS*	*F*
Management (M)	134.41	1	134.41	0.43@
Sex (S)	357.08	1	357.08	1.15@
Level (L)	235.20	1	235.20	0.76@
M x S	31.01	1	31.01	0.10@
M x L	800.83	1	800.83	2.58@
S x L	168.03	1	168.03	0.54@
M x S x L	154.13	1	154.13	0.50@
Error	128177.00	472	310.36	
Total	147544.00	479		

Note: @ Not significant at 0.05 level

It may be seen from Table 57 that the 'F' ratios for management, sex and level were not significant at 0.05 level for 1 and 472 df. Thus neither management, nor sex nor level of the teachers had any bearing on the attitude of the teachers towards teaching. In other words, the environment in terms of the management in which the teacher works had no significant influence on his attitude towards teaching. Similarly, whether one is working as a senior lecturer or junior lecturer also did not have any significant bearing on one's attitude towards teaching. One comes to the teaching profession with a certain disposition towards teaching as a career, and the differences in the circumstances in which one works, or the sex or level to which one belongs seem to have no bearing on one's attitude.

Ramakrishnaiah (1980) reported that women teachers had a significantly more favourable attitude towards teaching than their men counterparts. The results of the present investigation are not in line with the above. With regard to the relation between level of teaching and attitude towards teaching, the present results are supported by Ramakrishnaiah (1980) who found that whether one is working as a junior lecturer or a senior lecturer had no significant relation with one's attitude towards teaching. However, Wandt (1954), Beamer and Ledbetter (1957), Lindgreen and Pattan (1958), and Ryans (1960) reported that the attitudes of elementary school teachers towards pupils, administrators, fellow teachers and non-administrative personnel were markedly more favourable than were similar attitudes of secondary school teachers.

The 'F' ratios for the different two factor and three factor interaction effects between management, sex and level of teaching were also not significant at 0.05 level showing that the effect of each of the three variables on attitude towards teaching was independent of the level of the others.

Hence, the three hypotheses that :

1. 'There would not be any significant difference in the attitude of teachers working in government and private colleges',
2. 'Men and women teachers would not differ significantly in their attitude towards teaching' and
3. 'Degree college teachers and junior college teachers would not differ in their attitude towards teaching'were accepted.

2. Qualification Vs. Attitude Towards Teaching

An attempt was made to see whether the college teachers who had the minimum required qualifications and those who had more than the required qualifications differ in their attitude towards teaching. For this purpose, the subjects were classified into two groups: (1) Those who had the minimum required qualifications and (2) those who had extra qualifications. 354 of the 480 teachers who served as Ss for the study, had the required qualifications while 126 had extra qualifications. Mean attitude scores and SDs of the two groups of Ss are presented in Table 58.

Table 58
Means and SDs of the Attitude Scores of the Teachers Classified According to their Educational Qualifications and the Results of the 't' Test

Group	*N*	*Mean*	*SD*	*t*
Minimum qualifications	354	182.83	18.02	1.01@
Extra qualifications	126	180.99	16.14	

@ 't' not significant at 0.05 level.

The mean attitude score (180.99) of the teachers who had extra qualification was somewhat less than the mean attitude score (182.83) of those who had only the minimum required qualification. 't' test was employed to see whether this difference was significant. The 't' value (1.01), however was not significant at 0.05 level. This shows that there was no significant difference in the attitude of the two groups of teachers towards teaching.

Therefore, the hypothesis that 'Teachers who have the minimum required qualification and those who have more than the required qualification differ in their attitude towards teaching', was rejected.

3. Marital Status Vs. Attitude Towards Teaching

Among the teachers who served as Ss for this investigation, there were 405 married teachers and 75 unmarried teachers. Does the marital status influence the attitude of teachers towards teaching? An attempt was made to investigate into this aspect.

Table 59 shows the mean attitude scores of the two groups of teachers. The mean attitude score (184.59) of unmarried teachers was somewhat higher than the mean score (181.93) of married teachers. 't' test was applied to see whether the difference between the two groups was significant.

Table 59
Means and SDs of Attitude Scores of Teachers Classified According to their Marital Status and the Results of 't' test

Group	*N*	*Mean*	*SD*	*t*
Married	405	181.93	17.47	
Unmarried	75	184.59	17.91	1.20@

@ 't' not significant at 0.05 level.

The obtained 't' value (1.20) was not significant at 0.05 level. It may be concluded therefore that married and unmarried teachers did not differ in the level of their attitude towards teaching. Ryans (1960) and Ramakrishnaiah (1980) reported that the unmarried teachers had a significantly more favourable attitude towards teaching than their married counterparts. The results of the present study do not support the above findings.

From the results of the present investigation the hypothesis: 'Married and unmarried college teachers would not differ significantly with regard to their attitude towards teaching', was accepted.

4. Experience Vs. Attitude Towards Teaching

The total sample of 480 teachers was divided into three groups — low, middle and high — on the basis of their length of experience to findout the effect of experience on their attitude. Those who had an experience of 5 years or less, were categorised as low group, while those who had an experience of 6-15 years were put in the middle group. Those who had more than 15 years of experience were categorised as high group. The attitude scores of the teachers categorised thus, were analysed to know the effect of experience on attitude towards teaching. The means and SDs of the attitude scores of the 3 groups of teachers are presented in Table 60.

Table 60
Means and SDs of the Attitude Scores of Teachers Classified According to the Length of their Experience

Experience	*N*	*Mean*	*SD*
Low	161	183.35	17.85
Middle	201	181.27	17.18
High	118	182.81	17.81

The mean attitude scores of the three groups were low: 183.35, middle: 181.27 and high: 182.81. The mean scores do not indicate much difference between the attitude of the three groups.

The results of further analysis of attitude scores by ANOVA are presented in Table 61. It may be seen that the obtained 'F' ratio of 0.69 was not significant at 0.05 level. This shows that experience of the teachers did not have any effect on their attitude towards teaching. Ramakrishnaiah (1980) also found that differences in teaching experience did not have any significant effect of attitude towards teaching.

Table 61
Results of ANOVA of the Attitude Scores of the Teachers Classified According to the Length of their Experience

Source	*SS*	*df*	*MS*	*F*
Between groups	424.00	2	212.00	0.69@
Within groups	147120.00	477	308.43	
Total	147544.00	479		

@ 'F' not significant at 0.05 level

So, the hypothesis that 'Experience would not have any significant bearing on the attitude of the college teachers towards teaching' was accepted.

5. Age Vs. Attitude Towards Teaching

As in the case of analysis of job satisfaction scores, the teachers were categorised into three groups, viz., (1) young (30 years or less), (2) middle aged (between 31-40 years) and (3) old (41 years or above). Means and SDs of the attitude scores of these three groups are presented in Table 62.

Table 62
Means and SDs of the Attitude Scores of Different Age Groups of Teachers

Group	*N*	*Mean*	*SD*
Young	154	185.83	16.71
Middle	205	180.10	17.15
Old	121	181.71	18.68

The mean scores of the young teachers was 185.83 while those of the middle aged and old groups were 180.10 and 181.71 respectively. The younger group seems to have a more favourable attitude towards teaching (See Fig. 7).

Further analysis of the attitude scores of the Ss was carried out by one way ANOVA to find out whether the difference between the attitude of the three groups was significant.

It may be seen from Table 63 that the obtained 'F' ratio (4.88) was significant at 0.01 level for 2 and 477 df. This indicates that differences in the age of teachers had a significant effect on their attitude towards teaching.

Table 63
Results of ANOVA of the Attitude Scores of Different Age Groups of Teachers.

Source	*SS*	*df*	*MS*	*F*
Between groups	2957.00	2	1478.50	4.88**
Within groups	144587.00	477	303.12	
Total	145744.00	479		

**Significant at 0.01 level.

To find out which of the three groups of Ss differed significantly from the others in the level of their attitude, 't' test was applied.

Table 64
Mean Attitude Scores of Different Age Groups of Teachers and the Results of 't' test.

M	O	Y
180.10	181.71	185.83

Y = Young, M = Middle, O = Old

Note :- 1. The means are arranged in ascending order from left to right.
2. Any two means not underscored by the same line are significantly different at or above 0.05 level.
3. Any two means underscored by the same line are not significantly different at 0.05 level.

The results of the 't' test presented in Table 64, show that the young group differed significantly from the middle aged group. No other differences between means was significant.

It is possible that young teachers, when they enter the profession, may be bubling with enthusiasm expecting to contribute their might to the job, especially as the teaching profession is considered as the noblest of all professions. But as they pass through the years, they fell unhappy with the drudgery of the work, lack of interest on the part of the students, low salary, lack of social prestige, etc., and their attitude towards the profession might have changed.

Based upon the above results, the hypothesis: 'Teachers of different age groups differ in their attitude towards teaching' was accepted.

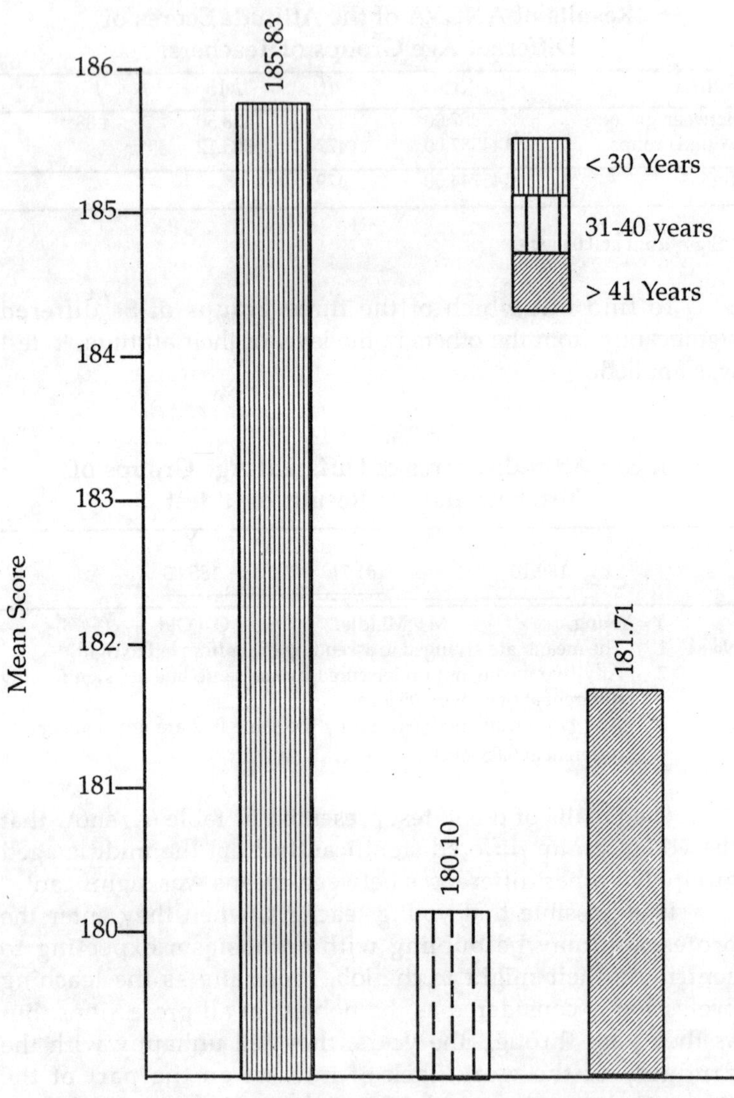

Fig. : 7 Mean attitude scores of different sub groups of teachers classifed according to their age

6. Size of the Family Vs. Attitude Towards Teaching

As explained earlier, the teachers were classified on the basis of the size of their families into three groups, viz., teachers with (1) small family consisting of 4 or less members, (2) medium family consisting of 5 members and (3) large family with 6 or more members, to find out the effect of the size of the family on attitude of the teachers towards teaching.

Table 65
Means and SDs of the Attitude Scores of the Teachers Classified According to the Size of their Families

Size of the Family	*N*	*Mean*	*SD*
Small	268	181.76	17.15
Medium	110	185.14	19.41
Large	102	180.88	16.27

Mean attitude scores and SDs of the three groups of teachers are presented in Table 65. The mean scores of the three groups were — small family : 181.76, Medium sized family: 185.14; and large family: 180.88.

Table 66
Results of ANOVA of the Attitude Scores of the Teachers Classified According to the Size of their Families

Source	*SS*	*df*	*MS*	*F*
Between groups	1174.00	2	587.00	1.91@
Within groups	146370.00	477	306.86	
Total	147544.00	479		

@ 'F' not significant at 0.05

The results of ANOVA of the attitude scores presented in Table 66 show that the 'F' ratio of 1.91 was not significant at 0.05 level for 2 and 477 df., showing that there was no significant difference between the level of the attitude of the three groups of teachers towards teaching.

Therefore, the hypothesis: 'Size of the family of the teachers would not have any significant influence on their attitude towards teaching' also was accepted.

7. Personality Characteristics Vs. Attitude Towards Teaching

As in the case of analysis of job satisfaction scores, the teachers were categorised into 3 groups on the basis of their personality scores on each of the 16 personality factors as measured by the 16 PF test. Those whose sten scores were between 1 and 4 were put in the low group, while those whose score was 5 or 6 were considered as middle group and those getting 7 or above were categorised as high group. The attitude scores of the three groups were analysed applying ANOVA.

The mean attitude scores of the three groups of teachers are presented in Table 67 and the results of ANOVA in Table 68.

It may be seen from Table 68 that the 'F' ratios were significant for factors - A, B, C, G, L, N, O, Q_1 and Q_3. To find out which of the three groups of subjects differed significantly from the others in the level of their attitude towards teaching, 't' test was applied in the case of the above factors.

Table 67

Means and SDs of the Attitude Scores of the Teachers Classified as Low, Middle and High Groups Based Upon their Scores on the Different Personality Factors.

16PF	Low			Middle			High		
	N	Mean	SD	N	Mean	SD	N	Mean	SD
A	145	179.29	18.95	171	181.87	16.39	164	185.55	17.09
B	116	178.82	20.04	235	182.87	16.87	129	184.56	15.96
C	127	177.46	17.80	229	181.36	16.14	124	189.16	16.93
E	129	183.49	18.63	238	183.36	16.14	113	178.91	18.81
F	177	183.05	16.95	175	182.38	17.49	128	181.32	18.50
G	161	178.49	18.29	183	182.74	16.49	136	186.38	17.19
H	180	180.78	16.65	127	181.17	17.53	173	184.83	18.28
I	149	184.31	17.97	184	181.76	15.72	147	181.10	19.17
L	193	186.35	16.96	120	183.61	16.27	167	176.81	17.77
M	186	184.06	17.10	164	181.82	18.91	130	180.55	16.26
N	168	185.79	18.43	189	180.28	16.53	123	180.81	17.26
O	166	185.29	18.66	147	181.44	15.84	167	180.22	17.56
Q_1	119	179.82	17.47	255	181.94	16.45	106	186.15	19.64
Q_2	174	183.93	16.77	180	182.59	16.46	126	179.82	19.84
Q_3	168	178.30	17.51	167	182.34	16.57	145	187.03	17.65
Q_4	167	183.76	16.41	155	182.39	18.59	158	180.81	17.66

Table 68

Results of ANOVA of the Attitude Scores of the Teachers Classified as Low, Middle and High Groups Based Upon their Scores on Different Personality Factors.

Personality factors	*SS*		*MS*		*F*
	Between	*Within*	*Between*	*Within*	*(df. 2,477)*
A	3083.00	144461.00	1541.50	302.85	5.09**
B	2144.00	145400.00	1072.00	304.82	3.52*
C	9012.00	138532.00	4506.00	290.42	15.52***
E	1748.00	145796.00	874.00	305.65	2.86@
F	299.00	147315.00	114.50	308.84	0.37@
G	4637.00	142907.00	2318.50	299.60	7.74***
H	1688.00	145856.00	844.00	305.78	2.76@
I	873.00	146671.00	436.50	307.49	1.42@
L	8416.00	139128.00	4208.00	291.67	14.43***
M	1022.00	146522.00	511.00	307.17	1.66@
N	3094.00	144450.00	1547.00	302.83	5.11**
O	2322.00	145222.00	1161.00	304.45	3.81*
Q_1	2340.00	145204.00	1170.00	301.41	3.81*
Q_2	1256.00	146288.00	628.00	306.68	2.05@
Q_3	5938.00	141606.00	2969.00	296.87	10.00***
Q_4	712.00	146832.00	356.00	307.82	1.16@

Note: *** Significant at 0.001 level.
** Significant at 0.01 level.
*Significant at 0.05 level.
@Not significant at 0.05 level.

The results of the the 't' test presented in Table 69 show that with regard to Factor A, the high group got a significantly higher attitude score than the low and middle personality groups. In other words, high score on Factor A indicates that teachers who are warm hearted, outgoing, easygoing and participating (A+), had a more favourable attitude towards teaching than those who are reserved, detached, critical and aloof (A-).

Factor-B deals with the intelligence of an individual. The mean attitude score of the more intelligent teachers (B+) was 184.56. They differed significantly from the low and middle intelligent groups with regard to their attitude towards teaching. This shows that teachers who have more intelligence, had more favourable attitude towards teaching than those who have less intelligence.

Table 69

Mean Attitude Scores of Teachers Classified as Low, Middle and High Groups According to their Personality Scores and the Results of the 't' test on Factors A, B, C, G, L, N, O, Q_1, and Q_3.

	L	M	H
A	179.29	181.87	185.55
B	178.82	182.87	184.56
C	177.46	181.36	189.16
G	178.49	182.74	186.38
	H	M	L
L	176.31	183.61	186.35
	M	H	L
N	180.28	180.81	185.79
	H	M	L
O	180.22	181.44	185.29
	L	M	H
Q_1	179.82	181.94	186.15
Q_3	178.30	182.34	187.03

L = Low group, M = Middle group, H = High group.

Note :- 1. The means are arranged i ascending order from left to right.
2. Any two means not underscored by the same line are significantly different at or above 0.05 level.
3. Any two means underscored by the same line are not significantly different at 0.05 level.

Low score on Factor-C indicates emotional instability while high score indicates emotional stability. The mean attitude scores of C+ and C- groups of teachers were 189.16 and 177.46 respectively, while the middle group got a mean score of 181.36 Each of the means differed significantly from the others. This shows that emotionally stable teachers had a more favourable attitude towards teaching than emotionally less stable teachers.

Ss who scored low (L-) on Factor-L are supposed to be trusting, conciliatory and accepting conditions whereas high score (L+) on this factor indicates suspecting, jealous and irritable characters. L+ group of teachers obtained a significantly lesser mean attitude score than the L- and middle groups of teachers, indicating that teachers who scored low on this factor, had a more favourable attitude towards teaching than those who scored high on the factor-L.

Teachers with forthright, natural and unpretentious personality characteristics (N-) obtained a significantly higher attitude score than those who are polished, worldly and shrewed (N+).

Low score on Factor-O indicates self-assured, placid, secure and complacent, and high score reveals apprehensive, self-reproaching, insecure and worrying characteristics of an individual. O-group of teachers obtained a mean attitude score of 185.29 and O+ group got a mean score of 180.22. The mean of the middle group was 181.44. O-group significantly differed in their attitude from the other two groups. Thus it may be concluded that O- is associated with more favourable attitude towards teaching.

Teachers who scored low on Factor-Q_1, tend to be conservative, are reluctant to any change and inclined to go along with traditions. This group of (Q_1-1) teachers obtained a low attitude score (179.82) while the Q_1+ group got a mean score of 186.15 and differed significantly from the Q_1- group. Q_1+ indicates experimenting, liberal, analytical and free thinking nature. This shows that teachers with free thinking, liberal and analytical personality, had more favourable attitude towards teaching than those who are conservative and traditional.

Low score on Factor-Q_3 indicates uncontrolled and careless behaviour and high score reveals controlled, socially precise, compulsive, behaviour. The mean scores of low, middle and high groups were 178.30, 182.34 and 187.03 respectively. Each of the means differed significantly from the others. It is evident that Q_3+ is associated with high favourable attitude towards teaching.

It may be concluded that A+, B+, C+, G+, L-, N-, O-, Q_1+ and Q_3+ Personality factors are associated with more favourable attitude towards teaching. The factors: E, F, H, I, M, Q_2, and Q_4 did not show any significant effect on the attitude of the teachers towards teaching.

Hence, the hypothesis that 'Teachers differing in their personality characteristics differ in their attitude towards teaching' was accepted only in the case of the personality factors: A, B, C, G, L, N, O, Q_1 and Q_3.

8. Neuroticism Vs. Attitude Towards Teaching

The college teachers were divided into three groups — low, middle and high, on the basis of neuroticism score to analyse the relation between neuroticism and attitude towards teaching. Those who scored less than M - 1SD on the NSQ were treated as low group, while those whose neuroticism score was between M - 1SD and M + 1SD, were treated as middle group. Those who scored above M + 1SD were categorised as high group.

The attitude scores of the three groups of Ss thus classified were analysed by applying ANOVA to examine the relation between neuroticism and attitude towards teaching.

Table 70

Means and SDs of the Attitude Scores of Teachers Classified as Low, Middle and High Groups — According to their Score on the Neuroticism Scale

Group	*N*	*Mean*	*SD*
Low	84	184.85	18.96
Middle	319	182.02	17.85
High	77	180.97	14.39

The mean attitude scores of the three groups of Ss are presented in Table 70, while the results of ANOVA are shown in Table 71. The mean attitude scores of the three groups of teachers were - low: 184.85, Middle: 182.02, and High: 180.97.

Table 71

Results of ANOVA of the Attitude Scores of Teachers Classified According to their Score on the Neuroticism Scale

Source	*SS*	*df*	*MS*	*F*
Between groups	709	2	354.50	1.15@
Within groups	146835	477	307.83	
Total	147544	479		

@ 'F' not significant at 0.05 level.

The results of ANOVA (Table 71) show that the 'F' ratio (1.15) was not significant at 0.05 level for 2 and 477 df. It may be concluded that differences in the level of neuroticism of the teachers did not have any effect on their attitude towards teaching.

9. Personality Profiles of Teachers who had a More Favourable Attitude and those who had a Less Favourable Attitude Towards Teaching

What would be the nature of the personality profiles of teachers who have a highly favourable attitude and those who have less favourable attitude towards teaching ? Will there be any significant dissimilarity between them or would they be similar ? To examine this, the teachers were divided into two extreme groups as those

Table 72

Comparison of Personality Profiles of Teachers who had a more Favourable Attitude and those who had a Less Favourable Attitude Towards Teaching

Group	*16 Personality Factors*															
	A	*B*	*C*	*E*	*F*	*G*	*H*	*I*	*L*	*M*	*N*	*O*	Q_1	Q_2	Q_3	Q_4
More Favourable Attitude (N = 67) (Means in stens)	5.93	5.79	6.34	5.30	5.40	5.79	5.99	5.15	4.88	5.40	4.66	5.04	5.91	5.36	6.04	5.28
Less Favourbale Attitude (N = 76) (Means in Stens)	4.91	4.67	4.86	6.08	5.72	4.53	5.36	5.67	6.50	5.61	5.57	5.99	5.08	6.00	4.75	5.42

$r_p = 0.35^*$

* Significant at 0.05 level.

who had a more favourable attitude and those who had less favourable attitude towards teaching, on the basis of their attitude scores. The personality scores of those two groups on the 16 personality factors were calculated and compared.

Teachers whose attitude scores were above M + 1SD were treated as those having a more favourable attitude towards teaching, while those whose scores were below M - 1SD were treated as those having a less favourable attitude towards teaching. Among the 480 Ss who participated in the investigation, 67 teachers had a more favourable attitude while 76 teachers had a less favourable attitude towards teaching. The personality scores of these two groups of Ss were converted into stens and analysed.

Personality profiles of teachers who had a more favourable and those who had a less favourable attitude towards teaching, were prepared and the profile similarity coefficient (r_p) (Cattell, et al., 1970) was calculated to examine the similarity/dissimilarity of the personality of these two groups.

The r_p thus obtained was 0.35, significant at 0.05 level, indicating that the two groups of teachers — those who had a more favourable attitude and those who had a less favourable attitude towards teaching, had similar personality profiles (See Fig. 8). Therefore, the hypothesis that 'Teachers with more favourable attitude and those with less favourable attitude towards teaching, differ in their personality profiles' was rejected.

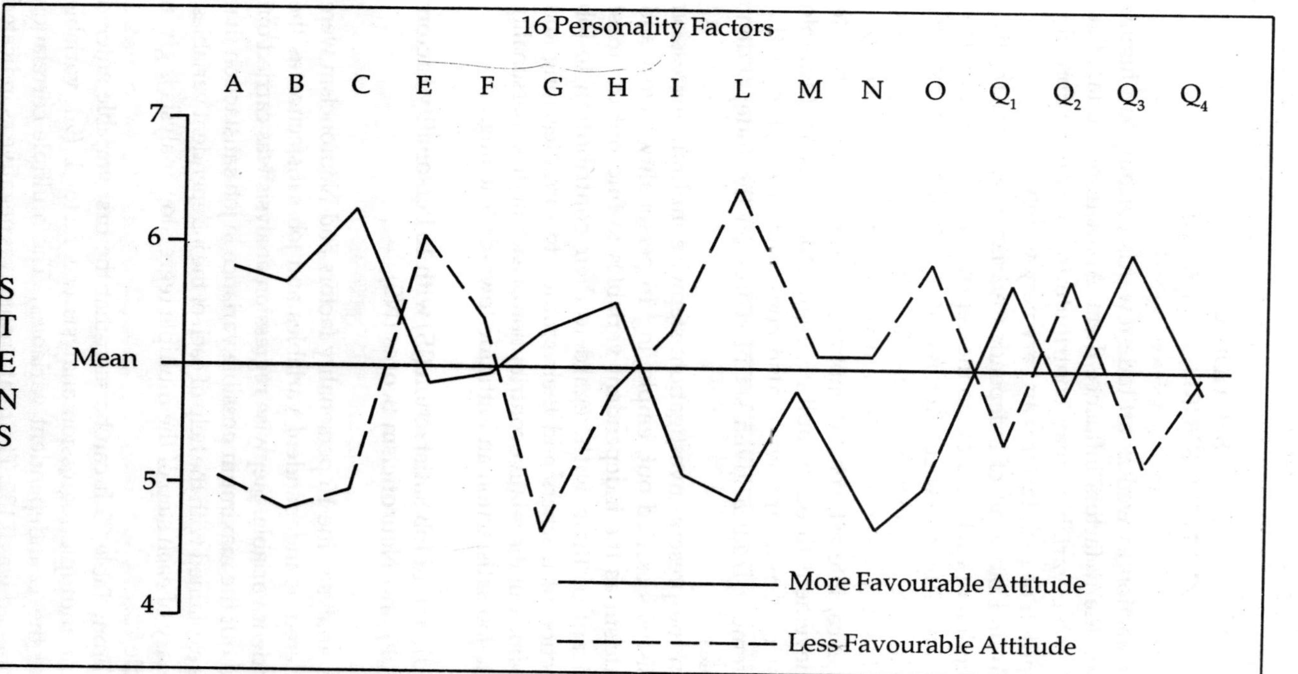

Fig.: 8 Personality profiles of teachers who have (i) more favourable attitude (ISD above mean score). and (ii) Less favourable attitude (ISD below mean score) towards teaching.

SECTION C
MULTIPLE REGRESSION ANALYSIS

Job Satisfaction as well as attitude towards teaching are highly complex. Many factors influence them. Apart from the fact that innumerable variables may contribute to job satisfaction, the contribution of each factor may vary very widely.

To find out a set of independent variables and the relative contribution of each of them to the dependent variable, multiple regression analysis has been successfully employed in educational research. Investigations on scholastic achievement, for example, could identify a set of significant independent variables like intelligence, interest, socio-economic status, etc., that contribute to achievement through multiple regression analysis. Multiple regression equations were also constructed to predict the achievement from a given set of scores on the independent variables.

In the present investigation, stepwise multiple regression analysis was carried out, employing 16 personality factors and neuroticism as the independent variables to find out the most significant of them with regard to their contribution to job satisfaction of teachers and their attitude towards teaching and also to find out the relative contribution of each of these personality traits to job satisfaction and attitude towards teaching.

1. Prediction of Job Satisfaction (JS) with 16 Personality Factors (16PF) and Neuroticism Scores (NS)

In this analysis, the 16 personality factors and Neuroticism were considered as independent variables and job satisfaction as the dependent variable. Stepwise regression analysis was carried out to find out the maximum possible variance in job satisfaction that can be explained with the help of each of the independent variables. Summary of each step of the multiple regression analysis is given in Table 73.

From Table 73 it can be seen that the first variable entered into the multiple regression analysis was factor L (9th variable among the 17 independent variables). The multiple correlation (R) obtained was 0.182. The relationship was negative as indicated by the negative value of 'b', the partial regression coefficient. This

Table 73
Multiple (Stepwise) Regression Analysis
Dependent Variable : Job Satisfaction (JS)
Independent Variables : 16 Personality Factors (16PF), Neuroticism Scores (NS)

Step No.	IV	R	'F' Value for R	R^2	SE of R	b	'F' Value for b	Constant	B	r	% of $ Variance
1	2	3	4	5	6	7	8	9	10	11	12
1	L (9)	0.182	16.414***	0.033	15.804	-1.337 (9)	16.414***	154.272	-0.182	-0.182	3.31
			(1,478)								
2	0 (12)	0.211	11.053***	0.045	15.729	-1.170 (9)	12.116***	157.811	-0.159	-0.141	2.89
			(2,477)			-0.807 (12)	5.536**		-0.108		1.52
3	B (2)	0.224	8.406***	0.050	15.696	-1.81 (9)	12.394***	161.121	-0.161	-0.076	2.93
			(3,476)			-0.799 (12)	5.461***		-0.107		1.51
						-0.591 (2)	3.020*		-0.078		0.59
4	Q_2 (14)	0.237	7.059***	0.056	15.665	-1.135 (9)	11.421***	164.213	-0.155	-0.090	2.82
			(4,475)			-0.793 (12)	5.387***		-0.106		1.49
						-0.609 (2)	3.220*		-0.080		0.61
						-0.605 (14)	2.917*		-0.076		0.68
5	N((11)	0.244	6.003***	0.060	15.653	-1.136 (9)	11.465***	166.378	-0.155	-0.077	2.82
			(5,474)			-0.714 (12)	4.242***		-0.095		1.34
						-0.656 (2)	3.695**		-0.086		0.65
						-0.589 (14)	2.767*		-0.074		0.66
						-0.469 (11)	1.735@		-0.060		0.46
								Total variance upto Step No. 4 = 5.6%			

Note : As the partial regression coefficients were not significant from the step No. 5, the further details were not given.
***Significant at 0.001.
** Significant at 0.01 level.
* Significant at 0.05 level.
@ Not significant at 0.05 level.
IV : Independent variable; R: Multiple correlation; SE : Standard Error; b: Partial regression Coefficient; B: beta coefficient; r: Simple correlation coefficient with the dependent variable; $: % of variance in the dependent variable explained by each independent variable.
The numbers in the parenthesis in columns 2 and 7, correspond to the serial numbers of the independent variables entered into the regression analysis.

shows that higher the score on factor L, lower was the job satisfaction and vice versa. The value indicated that the strength of the relationship between the two was about 18 per cent. It could also be observed form the table that R was significant at 0.001 level ('F' = 16.414, for 1 and 478 df). The coefficient of multiple R^2 was 0.033. This shows that 3.3 per cent of the variance in job satisfaction was accounted for by factor L.

The standard error of multiple R (SE of R) was 15.804. Thus nearly 68 per cent of the obtained or actual job satisfaction scores would lie within + 15.804 points of the job satisfaction scores predicted with the help of this factor.

The partial regression coefficient or b coefficient presented in column 7 was -1.337. This value indicates that JS changed by -1.337 units for every unit of change in factor L. The 'F' value for b was 16.414 (column 8). The value of the constant that would go into the multiple regression equation that could be constructed to predict job satisfaction at this stage was 154.272.

The general form of the multiple regression equation may be given as :

$$y = A+b_1X_1+b_2X_2+b_3X_3+\dots\dots\dots b_nX_n$$

where y is the predicted score on the dependent variable,

A is a constant,

$b_{1,} b_{2,} b_{3\dots\dots\dots} b_n$ are partial regression coefficients and

$X_{1,} X_{2,} X_{3\dots\dots} X_n$ are the scores on different independent variables.

Thus the multiple regression equation at the end of this step could be written as:

$$JS = 154.272 - 1.337\ L \qquad (1)$$

Factor O was entered into the stepwise regression analysis as the second most significant variable. The multiple correlation (R) between job satisfaction on one side and the two independent variables, viz., factor L and O on the other side was 0.211. Thus the strength of the relationship between job satisfaction and the two independent variables put together was about 21 per cent. R was significant at 0.001 level ('F' = 11.053, df = 2 and 477).

R^2 was equal to 0.045. Hence, the two variables put together could explain about 4.5 per cent of the variance in the dependent variable, viz., job satisfaction. Out of this, 2.89 per cent of the variance was explained by factor L and the remaining 1.52 per cent was accounted for by factor O (column 12). These percentages can be obtained by multiplying the B coefficients or standard partial regression coefficients (column 10) with the corresponding simple correlations between the dependent variable and the respective independent variables given in column 11.

It is evident that by including factor O, the contribution of factor L was brought down from 3.31 per cent to 2.89 per cent due to inter-correlation between the two predictor variables.

The standard error of multiple R was 15.729 (column 6). Hence, 95 per cent of the obtained or actual job satisfaction scores would lie within (+ 15.729 x 1.95) + 30.67 points of predicted scores of job satisfaction.

The partial regression coefficients shown in column 7 show that when both factors L and O of 16 PF were included as predictor variables, then the job satisfaction would change by -1.170 and - 0.807 points for every unit of change in L and O respectively. These partial regression coefficients of L and O were significant at 0.001 and 0.01 levels respectively as shown in column 8. The regression equation to predict job satisfaction with these two factors L and O as predictor variables was:

$$JS = 157.811 - 1.170\ L - 0.807\ O \qquad (2)$$

where 157.811 was the constant to be considered at this step and -1.170 and -0.807 were partial regression coefficients and L and O are the scores on the two factors L and O.

In the third step, factor B of the 16 PF entered as the next most important independent variable. The multiple correlation with the three factors L, O and B was 0.224 which was significant at 0.001 level ('F' = 8.406 for 3 and 476 df). The value of R^2 (0.050) shows that 5 per cent of variance in job satisfaction was explained by these three variables. Out of this variance, 2.93 per cent, 1.51 per cent and 0.59 per cent of the variance were explained by factors L, O and B respectively. It may be observed that by including factor B as one more predictor variable, the variance accounted for by factor L had gone up from 2.89 per cent to 2.93 per cent and the variance accounted for by factor O had come down from 1.52 per cent to 1.51 per cent due to the inter correlations between the three independent variables.

The obtained partial regression coefficients with these three predictor variables indicate that the change in the job satisfaction was by -1.181, 0.779 and -0.591 units for every unit of change in factors L, O and B respectively.

The regression equation at this step was :

$$JS = 161.121 - 1.181 L - 0.799 O -0.591 B \quad (3)$$

Variable Q_2 entered into the step wise regression analysis next. The multiple correlation (0.237) was significant at 0.001 level ('F' = 7.059 for 4 and 475 df). R^2 was equal to 0.056. Thus the 4 factors L, O, B and Q_2 as a combination could explain 5.6% of the variance in the job satisfaction. It may be seen that out of the 5.6 per cent of predictable variance, the contribution of each one of the predictor variables L, O, B and Q_2 were 2.82 per cent, 1.49 per cent, 0.615 and 0.69 per cent respectively. The 'b' coefficients presented in column 7 show that when the four independent variables viz., L, O, B and Q_2 were included in the regression analysis, the job satisfaction would change by -1.135, -0.793, -0.609 and -0.605 units for every unit of change in the four variables respectively.

The regression equation which would predict the job satisfaction of teachers with the 4 variables was :

$$JS = 164.213 - 1.135 L 0.793 O - 0.609 B - 0.605 Q_2 \quad (4)$$

The next variable entered into the step wise regression analysis was factor N. As the partial regression coefficient for this factor (-0.469) was not significant at 0.05 level ('F' = 1.735 for 5 and 474 df.), further regression equations to predict the job satisfaction of teachers were not given. However, the summary of the predicted variance in job satisfaction by all the 14 factors (the other 3 factors: G, I and Q_1 were not considered in the analysis as the 'F' values or tolerance levels were not sufficient for further computations) is shown in Table 74.

7.35 per cent of variance in job satisfaction was predicted by all the factors. Out of which, the factors L, O, B and Q_2 could explain about 5.6 per cent of the variance in the job satisfaction. The remaining variables put together contributed to only 1.75 per cent of the variance in the job satisfaction.

Hence, it could be concluded that equation 4 would be the best equation to predict job satisfaction of college teachers employing the 16 PF and neuroticism as the independent variables.

2. Prediction of Attitude of Teachers Towards Teaching with the Help of 16 Personality Factors and Neuroticism

This part of the section deals with the prediction of Attitude of the Teachers Towards Teaching (ATTT) with the help of personality characteristics. The 17 predictor variables used were the 16 personality factors of Cattell and neuroticism. As in the earlier analysis, stepwise regression analysis was carried out and the results of the analysis are presented in Table 75.

The first factor that entered into the analysis was factor L. The multiple R (0.249) was significant at 0.001 level ('F'= 31.486 for 1 and 478 df). The R^2 was 0.062. Therefore, this factor alone could explain 6.2 per cent of the variances in the attitude of the teachers towards teaching. The partial regression coefficient (-1.994) which was significant at 0.001 level, shows that for every unit of change in this factor, there would be a change of -1.994 units in the attitude of teachers towards teaching (ATTT). The regression equation could be written as :

$$ATTT = 193.328 - 1.994\ L \qquad (1)$$

The second most important factor that entered into the analysis was factor C. The value of the multiple R and multiple R^2 were 0.320 and 0.102 respectively. Thus, the two factors L and C put together could explain 10.2 per cent of the variance in ATTT. The equation with these two predictor variables L and C, would be :

$$ATTT = 181.826 - 1.724\ L + 1.814\ C \qquad (2)$$

In the third step, factor G was taken. The values of R and R^2 were 0.367 and 0.135 respectively. The variance in ATTT that could be explained with these three variables viz., L, C and G, put together was 13.5 per cent. Out of this, 5.20 per cent, 4.54 per cent and 3.73 per cent of variance was explained by factors L, C and G respectively. The partial regression coefficients of these three variables were significant. The prediction equation at this step was :

$$ATTT = 172.872 - 1.681\ L + 1.699\ C + 1.705\ G \qquad (3)$$

Factor A which was entered in the fourth step, increased R from 0.367 to 0.384 and R^2 from 0.135 to 0.148. The multiple R was significant at 0.001 level. All the four variables, viz., L, C, G and A, put together could explain 14.8 per cent of the variance in ATTT. The multiple regression equation could be written as:

Table 74
The Summary of the Multiple Regression Analysis
Dependent Variable : Job Satisfaction
Independent Variable : 16 PF and Neuroticism (NS)

Step No.	*IV*	*R*	*'F' Value for R*	R^2	*SE of R*	*b*	*'F' Value for b*	*Constant*	*B*	*r*	*% of $ Variance*
1	2	3	4	5	6	7	8	9	10	11	12
1	L (16 PF)	0.182	16.414*** (1,478)	0.033	15.804	-1.199	12.249***	168.827	-0.163	-0.182	2.97
2	O (16 PF)	0.211	11.053***	0.045	15.279	-0.676	3.372*		-0.090	-0.141	1.27
3	B (16 PF)	0.224	8.406***	0.050	15.696	-0.615	3.072*		-0.081	-0.076	0.62
4	Q_2 (16 PF)	0.237	7.059***	0.056	15.665	-0.602	2.614*		-0.076	-0.090	0.68
5	N (16 PF)	0.244	6.003***	0.060	15.653	-0.478	1.711@		-0.061	-0.077	0.47
6	E (16 PF)	0.250	5.256***	0.063	15.644	-0.460	1.244@		-0.052	-0.065	0.34
7	Q_3 (16 PF)	0.255	4.697***	0.065	15.639	-0.616	2.343*		-0.076	-0.007	0.05
8	C (16 PF)	0.262	4.321***	0.069	15.628	0.599	2.016*		0.073	0.100	0.73
9	H (16 PF)	0.268	4.049***	0.072	15.615	-0.492	1.622@		-0.062	-0.001	0.01
10	M (16 PF)	0.269	3.671***	0.072	15.626	0.191	0.274@		0.024	0.009	0.02
11	F (16 PF)	0.270	3.343***	0.073	15.641	0.128	0.122@		0.016	0.038	0.06
12	Q_4 (16 PF)	0.270	3.064***	0.073	15.656	-0.105	0.083@		-0.014	-0.064	0.09
13	NS	0.270	2.826***	0.073	15.672	0.029	0.052@		0.011	-0.036	-0.04
14	A (16 PF)	0.270	2.620*** (14,465)	0.073	15.689	0.057	0.024@		0.008	0.038	0.04

Note : Independent variables - G, I and Q_1 of 16 PF were not considered in the analysis as the 'F' values or tolerance levels were not sufficient for further computations.
*Significant at 0.05 level.
*** Significant at 0.001 level.
@ Not significant at 0.05 level.
IV : Independent variable; R: Multiple correlation; SE : Standard Error; b: Partial regression Coefficient; B: beta coefficient; r: Simple correlation coefficient with the dependent variable; $: % of variance in the dependent variable explained by each independent variable.
The numbers in the parenthesis in columns 2 and 7, correspond to the serial numbers of the independent variables entered into the regression analysis.

Table 75
Multiple (Stepwise Regression Analysis
Dependent Variable : Attitude Towards Teaching
Independent Variables : 16 PF and Neuroticism (NS)

Step No.	*IV*	R	*'F' Value for R*	R^2	*SE of R*	*b*	*'F' Value for b*	*Constant*	*B*	*r*	*% of $ Variance*
1	2	3	4	5	6	7	8	9	10	11	12
1	L (9)	0.249	31.486*** (1,478)	0.062	17.017	-1.994 (9)	31.486***	193.328	-0.249	-0.249	6.20
2	C (3)	0.320	27.112*** (2,477)	0.102	16.665	-1.724 (9)	23.862***	181.826	-0.215	0.239	5.35
						1.814 (3)	21.394***		0.203		4.85
3	G (6)	0.367	24.730*** (3,476)	0.135	16.376	-1.681 (9)	23.478***	172.872	-0.209	0.205	5.20
						1.699 (3)	19.324***		0.190		4.54
						1.705 (6)	18.030***		0.182		3.73
4	A (1)	0.384	20.570*** (4,475)	0.148	16.271	-1.657 (9)	23.094***	168.928	-0.207	0.174	5.15
						1.530 (3)	15.468***		0.172		4.11
						1.613 (6)	16.215***		0.172		3.53
						0.941 (1)	7.135***		0.115		2.00
5	B (2)	0.403	18.359*** (5,474)	0.162	16.148	-1.646 (9)	23.142***	163.578	-0.205	0.136	5.10
						1.486 (3)	14.795***		0.167		3.99
						1.523 (6)	14.596***		0.162		3.32
						1.013 (1)	8.344***		0.124		2.16
						1.011 (2)	8.259***		0.121		1.65
6	N (11)	0.414	16.275*** (6,473)	0.171	16.079	-1.628 (9)	22.808***	158.626	-0.203	-0.137	5.05
						1.432 (3)	13.794***		0.161		3.85
						1.503 (6)	14.330***		0.160		3.28
						0.994 (1)	8.095***		0.122		2.12
						0.934 (2)	7.029***		0.112		1.52
						-0.813 (11)	5.067***		-0.095		1.30

7	Q_3 (15)	0.421	14.548*** (7,472)	0.178	16.035	-1.557 (9)	20.728***	166.593	-0.194	0.213	4.83
						1.195 (3)	8.747***		0.134		3.20
						1.462 (6)	13.582***		0.156		3.20
						0.928 (1)	7.027***		0.114		1.98
						0.836 (2)	5.558***		0.100		1.36
						-0.832 (11)	5.321***		-0.097		1.33
						0.769 (15)	3.640***		0.087		1.85
8	I (8)	0.427	13.145*** (8,471)	0.183	16.002	-1.564 (9)	21.022***	170.362	-0.195	-0.079	4.86
						1.193 (3)	8.757***		0.134		3.20
						1.423 (6)	12.890***		0.152		3.12
						0.902 (1)	6.665***		0.111		1.93
						0.881 (2)	6.163***		0.106		1.44
						-0.859 (11)	5.693***		-0.100		1.37
						0.743 (15)	3.413***		0.084		1.79
						-0.615 (8)	2.913**		-0.072		0.57
9	Q_2 (14)	0.431	11.891*** (9,470)	0.186	15.990	-1.534 (9)	20.161***	173.393	-0.191	-0.117	4.76
						1.222 (3)	9.172***		0.137		3.27
						1.465 (6)	13.585***		0.156		3.20
						0.778 (1)	4.613***		0.095		1.65
						0.863 (2)	5.900***		0.104		1.41
						-0.843 (11)	5.487***		-0.099		1.36
						0.697 (15)	2.976**		0.079		1.68

Variance upto step no. 8 = 18.28%

(Contd.)

1	2	3	4	5	6	7	8	9	10	11	12
						-0.603 (8)	2.805**		-0.070		0.55
						-0.493 (14)	1.698@		-0.057		0.67

Note : As the partical regression coefficients were not significant from the step No, 9, the further details were not given.

** Significant at 0.01 level.

*** Significant at 0.001 level.

@ Not significant at 0.05 level.

The numbers in the parenthesis in columns 2 and 7, correspond to the serial numbers of the independent variables entered into the regression analysis.

IV : Independent variable; R: Multiple correlation; SE : Standard Error; b: Partial regression Coefficient; B: beta coefficient; r: Simple correlation coefficient with the dependent variable; $: % of variance in the dependent variable explained by each independent variable.

The numbers in the parenthesis in columns 2 and 7, correspond to the serial numbers of the independent variables entered into the regression analysis.

$$ATTT = 168.928 - 1.657\ L + 1.530\ C + 1.613\ G + 0.941\ A \quad (4)$$

Factor B was entered in the fifth step. R and R^2 at this step were 0.403 and 0.162 respectively. Hence, the amount of variance contributed by these 5 variables was 16.2 per cent. All the five partial regression coefficients were significant at 0.001 level and the multiple regression equation was:

$$ATTT = 163.578 - 1.646\ L + 1.486\ C + 1.523 + G\ 1.013\ A + 1.011B \quad (5)$$

The variable that entered into the sixth step was factor N. The multiple R at this step was 0.414 and R^2 was 0.171. In other words, 17.1 per cent of the variance in ATTT was explained by all the six variables put together. The regression equation at this step was:

$$ATTT = 168.626 - 1.628\ L + 1.432\ C + 1.503\ G + 0.994\ A + 0.934 - 0.813\ N \quad (6)$$

Factor Q_3 entered next into the analysis as the next most important independent variable. The value of R and R_2 at this stage were 0.421 and 0.178 respectively. Thus the 7 predictor variables were able to predict 17.8 per cent of variance in ATTT. The prediction equation with the seven factors could be written as :

$$ATTT = 166.593 - 1.557\ L + 1.195\ C + 1.462\ G + 0.928\ A + 0.836\ B - 0.832\ N + 0.769\ Q_3 \quad (7)$$

The next important variable in the hierarchy was factor I. At this step, the value of R^2 was 0.183 indicating that all the 8 variables that entered in this step, could predict 18.3 per cent of variance in the ATTT. The multiple regression equation for prediction of ATTT with the eight factors was:

$$ATTT = 170.362 - 1.564\ L + 1.193\ C + 1.423\ G + 0.902\ A + 0.881\ B - 0.859\ N + 0.743\ Q_3 - 0.615\ I \quad (8)$$

As the partial regression coefficients of the remaining independent variables, viz., Q_2, Q_1, F, O, NS, H, E, Q_4 and M were not significant event 0.05 level, further equations for prediction of

ATTT were not give. However, the summary of the predicted variance in ATTT by all the 17 factors is shown in Table 76.

The total variance in ATTT predicted by all the factors was 19.27 per cent. Out of which the first 8 factors, namely, L, C, G, A, B, N, Q_3 and I could explain about 18.3 per cent of the variance. The remaining nine variables put together contributed to only 1.42 per cent of the variance in the ATTT.

Therefore, it could be concluded that equation 8 would be the best equation to predict attitude of the teachers towards teaching employing the 16 personality factors and neuroticism as the independent variables.

Table 76

The Summary of the Multiple Regression Analysis
Dependent Variable : Attitude Towards Teaching (ATT)
Independent Variable : 16 PF and Neuroticism (NS)

Step No.	IV	R	'F' Value for R	R^2	SE of R	b	'F' Value for b	Constant	B	r	% of $ Variance
1	2	3	4	5	6	7	8	9	10	11	12
1	L (16 PF)	0.249	31.486*** (1,478)	0.062	17.017	-1.493	18.093***	167.987	-0.186	-0.249	4.63
2	C (16 PF)	0.320	27.112***	0.102	16.665	-1.117	6.688***		0.125	0.239	2.99
3	G (16 PF)	0.367	24.730***	0.135	16.376	1.339	10.789***		0.143	0.205	2.93
4	A (16 PF)	0.384	20.570***	0.148	16.271	0.822	4.783***		0.101	0.174	1.76
5	B (16 PF)	0.403	18.359***	0.162	16.148	0.815	5.135***		0.098	0.136	1.33
6	N (16 PF)	0.414	16.275***	0.171	16.079	-0.827	4.898***		-0.097	-0.137	1.33
7	Q_3 (16 PF)	0.421	14.548***	0.178	16.035	0.678	2.713***		0.077	0.213	1.64
8	I (16PF)	0.427	13.145***	0.183	16.002	-0.650	3.183**		-0.076	-0.079	0.60
9	Q_2 (16 PF)	0.431	11.89***	0.186	15.990	-0.519	1.814@		-0.060	-0.117	0.70
10	Q_1 (16 PF)	0.435	10.943***	0.189	15.971	0.465	1.368@		0.051	0.129	0.66
11	F (16 PF)	0.437	10.042***	0.191	15.970	-0.368	0.959@		-0.043	-0.036	0.15
12	O (16PF)	0.438	9.267***	0.192	15.974	-0.364	0.938@		-0.044	-0.142	0.62
13	NS	0.440	8.614***	0.194	15.977	0.134	1.034@		0.047	-0.043	-0.20
14	H (16PF)	0.442	8.055***	0.195	15.980	0.375	0.880@		0.043	0.120	0.52
15	E (16PF)	0.443	7.547***	0.197	15.988	-0.302	0.509@		-0.032	-0.105	0.34
16	Q_4 (16 PF)	0.444	7.098***	0.197	15.977	0.261	0.496@		0.032	-0.171	-0.23
17	M (16 PF)	0.444	6.668***	0.197	16.013	0.060	0.025@		0.007	-0.072	-0.05

Total variance = 19.72

Note ** Significant at 0.01 level.
*** Significant at 0.001 level.
@ Not significant at 0.05 level.
IV : Independent variable; R: Multiple correlation; SE : Standard Error; b: Partial regression Coefficient; B: beta coefficient; r: Simple correlation coefficient with the dependent variable; $: % of variance in the dependent variable explained by each independent variable.
The numbers in the parenthesis in columns 2 and 7, correspond to the serial numbers of the independent variables entered into the regression analysis.

7

SUMMARY AND CONCLUSIONS

1. Summary

In ancient India when the 'Gurukula' system of education prevailed, the teacher was given the utmost respect in the society. But the Indian teacher today finds himself in a new era entirely different from that of the teacher of the olden days. After Independence and the establishment of democratic form of government, the teachers have a new set of ideals before them.

It is the teacher that moulds the most precious material of the land, viz., the boys and girls, in their most impressionable periods of development, into required shapes. Saiyidain (1950) makes the role of the teacher quite illustrative when he says that the teacher has to patiently cut out form, from a crude and unshaped stone.

Choice of a job emerges as a result of the interplay of a multiplicity of factors. It is mainly the result of an interaction between factors pertaining to the job and those that characterise the chooser. Parsons, the father of vocational guidance movement, said that vocational guidance, in its simplest form, is matching the man and machine. Great vocational psychologists like Burnstein, Hollender, Super and many others consider occupational choice as a developmental process over a period of years that ends in a compromise between interests, capacities, values, etc., of the individual on the one hand and the opportunities on the other.

However, many are said to be taking up teaching profession as a career not because they are interested in it but because they are not able to get any better employment. If one has to be happy in his life, he must be satisfied and happy in his occupation. To get satisfaction in his job, in turn, he must choose it wisely.

Prestige, power, salary, leisure and other features of a job are no doubt important. But these features become meaningful only to those who value them. The value given by an individual to a particular feature of a job is in turn determined by his personality, and social and psychological background. This is implied in the proposition of Thompson (1947) that jobs differ in their attractiveness from person to person depending upon the need pattern or value system of the individual.

Much has been said about the need for maintenance of equality of pay in professions requiring similar qualification and skill. Yet, it is unfortunate that the teachers are in no way comparable to others like doctors, lawyers, engineers, etc. The facilities and incentives offered in this profession are so meagre that many of the talented do not think of becoming teaches but seek positions elsewhere in the world of work.

It is opined that many who have taken up teaching, repent over their choice and would be too willing to change their job in favour of some other lucrative ones, if any opportunities are available. A dissatisfied teacher is lost not only to himself but also to the entire society and spells disaster to the country's future. Dissatisfaction of the individuals, whatever may be the occupation in which they are engaged, results in professional stagnation and deterioration. Dissatisfaction among the workers is undesirable and dangerous in any profession, it is just suicidal if it occurs in the teaching profession.

Every profession has got certain aspects conducive for job satisfaction. At the same time, it has other aspects that lead to dissatisfaction. Teaching profession is no exception. Lack of public recognition of the teachers in this country is a very sore point. The teachers of today suffer from neglect, indifference and insecurity. We always expect a lot from the teacher, but with so little recognition and insufficient facilities.

In Andhra Pradesh and some other states in India, under the 10+2+3 pattern, the +2 stage has been separated from the schools and also from the colleges and a separate institution, called the junior college, has been created. Though the qualifications of teachers employed in degree colleges and junior colleges are the same , there is a vast difference in their pay structure and also in their service conditions. What is the effect of the above on their job satisfaction ?

Further, the colleges in Andhra Pradesh are controlled by two types of managements — Government and Private. Does the type of management under which the teachers work affect their job satisfaction ?

Similarly, is there any significant difference between the job satisfaction of men and women teachers ? Is it related to attitude towards teaching ? What are the other correlates of job satisfaction?

Vroom (1964) asserts that explanation of satisfaction requires the use of both work role and personality variables. Satisfied teachers showed fewer indications of emotional maladjustment (Hoppock, 1935). Hence, the personality characteristics of the teachers were analysed to understand the causes of satisfaction/dissatisfaction.

An individual's emotional stability is likely to manifest itself in the satisfaction/dissatisfaction in his job. If a teachers was neurotic, he would be emotionally maladjusted and dissatisfied with the job (Hoppock, 1935).

Though it is remarked by many that many teachers are not happy with the teaching profession and would like to quit it and take up some other profession, not many empirical studies have been conducted on the attitude of teachers towards teaching and its relationship with job satisfaction.

Hence, the problem chosen for this study was an investigation into the job satisfaction of college teachers in relation to some variables. The independent variables considered in the study are type of management of the institution, sex, level (junior/senior), marital status, experience, the size of the family, 16 personality factors, and neuroticism, etc.

The study was essentially of a 2^3 factorial design. The sample for the study was 480 college teachers equally distributed between the two managements, the two sexes and the two levels. The sample was selected by a multistage stratified random sampling procedure from the teachers working in 18 degree colleges and 18 junior colleges located in three districts of Andhra Pradesh.

A job satisfaction iverntory with 70 items was administered to 320 teachers and factor analysis was carried out by applying varymax rotation (Overall and Keltt, 1972). On the basis of this analysis, 44 items were selected and the job satisfaction inventory was prepared. Its reliability and validity were established. An attitude scale to measure the attitude of teachers towards teaching was also developed on similar lines. Its reliability and validity were also established.

16 personality traits were measured by adapting Form C of the *16 PF* questionnaire (Cattell et al., 1970), Neuroticism was measured by adapting the instrument developed by Scheier and Cattell (1961).

The data regarding personal and demographic variables was collected with the help of a personal data sheet.

The instruments were administered to the sample of teachers individually. The data thus collected was analysed using relevant statistical techniques like 't' test, 'F' test and regression analysis.

2. Conclusions

From the results of this investigation, the following conclusions were drawn:

(A) Job Satisfaction

1. The mean job satisfaction score of the sample of teachers was significantly above the neutral point.

Therefore, the hypothesis, 'In general college teachers are satisfied with their job', was accepted.

2. Teachers were satisfied with six of the nine job factors, viz., Principal; Physical facilities; self esteem; fringe benefits; entertainment, prestige and courses; and girl students, personal activities and place of work.

Therefore, the hypothesis, 'The different job factors would contribute to the satisfaction of the teachers' was accepted in the case of the above factors and rejected in the case of the other three job factors, viz., parents and students; academic policies; and co-teachers which were found to be causing dissatisfaction to the teachers.

3. The teachers working in government colleges and private colleges did not differ in the level of their job satisfaction.

Hence, the third hypothesis 'Teachers working in government and private colleges do not differ significantly in the level of their job satisfaction' was accepted.

4. Similarly, men and women teachers did not differ significantly in their job satisfaction.

Therefore, the fourth hypothesis, 'There would not be any significant difference between the level of job satisfaction of men and women teachers' was accepted.

5. The next hypothesis viz., 'Teachers working in junior colleges would be less satisfied with their job than those working in degree colleges', was accepted because it was found that teachers working in junior colleges were less satisfied with their job than those working in degree colleges.

6. Factorwise analysis of the job satisfaction scores of the sample of teachers seem to warrant the following conclusions:

(a) *Principal*: Teachers working in government junior colleges were more satisfied with their principal than the seniors working in government degree colleges. Among the seniors, teachers working in private colleges, were more satisfied with their principal than their counterparts in government colleges.

(b) *Parents and students*: Men teachers were less satisfied with the attitude of students and their parents towards education than women teachers.

(c) *Physical facilities*: Teachers working in private colleges were significantly more satisfied with physical facilities than those working in government colleges.

Women teachers were less satisfied with physical facilities than their men counterparts.

In the case of level, seniors were more satisfied with physical facilities than the juniors.

(d) *Self esteem* : Government college teachers seemed to like their job more, feel important in their job, etc., than the private college teachers.

Men teachers experienced a greater self esteem in their job compared to their women counterparts.

In the case of level, junior teachers were significantly more satisfied with this factor i.e. self-esteem, than the senior teachers.

(e)*Fringe benefits* : Teachers working in government colleges were more satisfied with fringe benefits than those working in private colleges.

Men teachers were significantly less satisfied with fringe benefits than their women counterparts.

Similarly, junior teachers were less satsified with the existing fringe benefits than the senior teachers.

Among the junior teachers, men teachers were less satisfied with the fringe benefits than the women teachers. However, among the senior teachers, men and women teachers did not differ from each other. As mentioned earlier, junior teachers were less satisfied with fringe benefits than the seniors among men and women teachers.

(f) *Entertainment, prestige and courses* : With regard to thifactor, teachers working in private colleges were more satisfied than teachers working in government colleges.

In the case of level, juniors were significantly less satisfied with entertainment, prestige and courses offered in their college than the seniors.

(g) *Academic policies*: Senior teachers were more satisfied with academic policies than the juniors. Among the men, teachers working in government colleges were less satisfied with academic policies than those working in private colleges.

(h) *Co-teachers* : The different subgroups of teachers did not differ significantly in the level of their satisfaction with their co-teachers' attitude and their activities.

(i) *Girl students, personal activities and place of work* : Women teachers were more dissatisfied with the attitude of girl students, personal activities and place of work, than their men counterparts.

7. Teachers who had less favourable attitude towards teaching exhibited least satisfaction with their job, while teachers with more favourable attitude towards teaching exhibited the highest satisfaction in their job.

Therefore, the hypothesis 'Teachers differing in their attitude towards teaching, differ in their job satisfaction' was accepted.

Considering factorwise, it was found that : teachers differing in their attitude towards teaching, did not differ significantly in their satisfaction with factors: physical facilities; fringe benefits; academic policies; and co-teachers. So, the above hypothesis was rejected in the case of the above factors and accepted in the case of the factors: Principal; parents and students; self esteem; entertainment, prestige and courses; and girl students, personal activities and place of work.

8. Teachers who had more than the required qualifications did not differ from those who had only the minimum required qualifications, in their overall job satisfaction.

Hence, the hypothesis 'There would be a significant difference in the level of job satisfaction of teachers who have the minimum required qualifications and those who have more than the required qualifications' was rejected.

However, with regard to one job factor, i.e., academic policies, teachers who had extra qualifications were less satisfied than those who had only the minimum required qualifications. So, the above hypothesis was accepted only in the case of the above factor and rejected in others.

9. The hypothesis that, 'The level of job satisfaction of married teachers would not be significantly different from that of unmarried teachers', was accepted as there was no significant difference between married and unmarried teachers either with regard to their overall job satisfaction or on different job factors.

10. Experience of the teachers did not have any effect on their overall job satisfaction.

So, the hypothesis that 'Teachers differing in their experience differ in the level of their job satisfaction' was rejected with regard to overall job satisfaction.

However, teachers differing in their experience, differed significantly on the following two job factors: Fringe benefits and academic policies. Teachers who have 5 years or less experience, were less satisfied with fringe benefits than those whose experience was 16 years or above. Teachers with 6 to 15 years of experience were the least satisfied with the academic policies and differed significantly from the other two groups. Hence, the above hypothesis was accepted with regard to the above two factors and rejected in the case of other factors.

11. The hypothesis, 'Teachers belonging to different age groups differ in the level of their job satisfaction', was rejected as the teachers belonging to different age groups did not differ significantly in their overall job satisfaction.

However, teachers whose age was 41 years or above were more satisfied with their principal than those whose age was 40 years or less. In the case of fringe benefits, teachers 30 years or below were less satisfied than those whose age was 31 years or more. Therefore, the above hypothesis was accepted in the case of the two factors: principal and fringe benefits and rejected in the case of the other job factors.

12. The size of the family of the teachers did not have any effect on their overall job satisfaction.

So, the hypothesis 'The size of the family of the teachers would have a significant bearing on their job satisfaction' was rejected with regard to overall job satisfaction.

However, the hypothesis was accepted in the case of only one job factor i.e., principal, since teachers with small families were relatively less satisfied with the principal than those with medium and large families.

13. The analysis of job satisfaction in relation to the 16 personality factors showed that emotionally less stable teaches were less satisfied on their job than emotionally more stable teachers (factor C).

Teachers who were trusting, accepting conditions, conciliatory etc., were more satisfied with their job than those who were suspecting, jealous, irritable (factor L).

Similarly, teachers who were self confident, cheerful, placid and impenitent were more satisfied than those who were depressed, moody, worried, troubled, insecure, anxious and lonely (factor O).

Hence, the hypothesis 'Teachers differing in their personality characteristics differ in the level of their job satisfaction was accepted in the case of personality factors: C, L and O and rejected in the case of the remaining personality factors and neuroticism.

14. A comparison of the personality profiles of satisfied and dissatisfied teachers by computing the profile similarity coefficient 'r_p' showed that the two groups of teachers viz., satisfied and dissatisfied, had similar personality profiles.

Therefore, the hypothesis 'There would not be any significant difference between the personality profiles of satisfied and dissatisfied teachers', was accepted.

(B) Attitude of Teachers Towards Teaching :

1. In general, college teachers were found to have a favourable attitude towards teaching.

Hence, the hypothesis 'College teachers in general have a favourable attitude towards teaching' was accepted.

2. The environment in terms of the management in which the teachers work, had no significant influence on their attitude towards teaching.

Therefore, the hypothesis 'There would be a significant difference in the attitude of teachers working in government and private colleges', was rejected.

3. Similarly, the hypothesis that 'Men and women teachers would differ significantly in their attitude towards teaching' was also rejected, since there was no significant difference between the attitude of men and women teachers.

4. The hypothesis, 'Senior and junior college teachers would not differ in their attitude towards teaching', was accepted because the level of the teachers (senior or junior) did not have any bearing on their attitude towards teaching.

5. Teachers who had the required qualifications and those who had extra qualifications, did not differ in the level of their attitude towards teaching.

Therefore, the hypothesis 'Teachers who differ in their qualifications, differ in their attitude towards teaching', was rejected.

6. Married and unmarried teachers did not differ in the level of their attitude towards teaching.

As such, the hypothesis that 'Married and unmarried college teachers would not differ significantly with regard to their attitude towards teaching' was accepted.

7. Teachers differing in their teaching experience did not differ significantly in the level of their attitude towards teaching.

Therefore, the hypothesis that 'Experience would not have any significant bearing on the teachers' attitude towards teaching', was accepted.

8. The hypothesis, 'Teachers of different age groups differ in their attitude towards teaching' was accepted because young teachers whose age was 30 years or below, had a more favourable attitude towards teaching than middle aged and old teachers.

9. The hypothesis that 'Size of the family of the teachers would not have any significant influence on their attitude towards teaching', was accepted since the teachers differing in the size of their family did not differ in their attitude towards teaching.

10. Personality factors : A+, B+, C+, G+, L-, N-, O-, Q_1+ and Q_3+ were associated with more favourable attitude towards teaching while factors: E, F, H, I, M, Q_2 and Q_4 did not show any significant effect on the attitude of the teachers towards teaching.

Hence, the hypothesis that 'Teachers differing in their personality characteristics, differ in their attitude towards teaching' was accepted in the case of the personality factors: A, B, C, G, L, N, O, Q_1 and Q_3; and rejected in the case of other personality factors, viz., E, F, H, I, M, Q_2 and Q_4; and neuroticism.

11. The two groups of teachers - those who had a more favourable attitude and those who had a less favourable attitude towards teaching, had similar personality profiles. Therefore, the hypothesis that 'Teachers with more favourable attitude and those with less factorable attitude towards teaching, differ in their personality profiles' was rejected.

(C) Multiple Regression Analysis

1. *Prediction of the Job Satisfaction*: 7.35 per cent of variance in job satisfaction was predicted by the 13 personality factors and Neuroticism (the other 3 factors: G, I and Q_1 were not considered in the analysis as the 'F' values or tolerance levels were not sufficient for further computations). Out of which, the factors: L, O, B and Q_2 could explain about 5.6 per cent of the variance in the job satisfaction. The remaining variables put together contributed to only 1.75 per cent of the variance in the job satisfaction.

2. *Prediction of Attitude of Teachers Towards Teaching*: The total variance in ATTT predicted by all the factors was 19.72 per cent. Out of which the first 8 factors viz., L, C, G, A, B, N, Q_3 and I could explain about 18.3 per cent of the variance in the attitude of teachers towards teaching. The remaining 9 variables put together contributed to only 1.42 per cent of the variance in the ATTT.

8

EDUCATIONAL IMPLICATIONS, LIMITATIONS AND SUGGESTIONS FOR FURTHER RESEARCH

1. Education Implications

There is no gainsaying that the destiny of the Nation is shaped in her class rooms, because it is in the classrooms that the future citizens acquire the required knowledge and skills to lead a useful and fruitful life and contribute their might to the welfare of the Nation. It is there that their personality characteristics and their value system are shaped. The pivot in this process is undoubtedly the teacher. The role of the teacher is exceedingly crucial today, more than ever before in the process of bringing about a social change and rebuilding India. Therefore it is the bounden duty of the managements of the Institutions and the government to see that the teachers are happy and satisfied.

A satisfied and happy teacher is very likely to exert himself, work with enthusiasm and deliver the goods more efficiently and there by make his pupils efficient, satisfied, enthusiastic and happy. Likewise a dissatisfied teacher is likely to make his pupils also dissatisfied in several respects. Dissatisfaction is like a contagious disease as is maladjustment. Hence, the welfare of the teacher should be of supreme concern to the educational administrators, the government and the society. Though the government has been doing moderately good work to enhance the prestige of the teacher by increasing the salaries, much remains yet to be done, as shown by the results of this investigation.

Though, in general, the college teachers were satisfied with their job, they were not satisfied on certain job factors like academic policies, co-teachers, lack of interest on the part of the parents in their children's education, poor quality of the students, etc.

Establishment of a parent teacher associations in the colleges may be thought of a solution to the apathy of the parents with regard to the education of their wards. Parent teacher associations, especially, parent conferences have been found to be extremely helpful on such situations.

Teachers expressed dissatisfaction with insufficient in service training programmes, lack of adequate Faculty Improvement Programmes (FIP), lack of freedom to take initiative in organising projects, lack of advance information about the changes that are going to take place in academic matters, etc. Such problems can be solved by the government by proper planning of the academic programmes and by allocating necessary funds for the in service training programmes. Any government worth the name should see that there are adquate facilities for the academic growth of the faculty lest there can not be any improvement in the standards may, standards may even go down if the teachers are not conversant with the latest developments in their subjects.

Problems like lack of freedom to take initiative in organizing projects, can be solved without any difficulty if only the heads of the institutions are real heads. One may not like (it may not be desirable also) to give full freedom to his subordinates in all respects, but if he does not give freedom to his colleagues in 'academic matters' he is probably unfit to be the head of an educational institution.

In Andhra Pradesh, at the school level a system called non-detention system is in vogue. According to this system any student will be automatically promoted to the next higher class irrespective of his achievement provided he puts in the required percentage of attendance. However he may be detained at the VII an X class levels if he does not get the required minimum marks in the common examinations conducted at the end of these two classes. In all other classes he is automatically promoted whatever may be his academic progress. From informal discussion with the teachers, the investigator was given to understand that the above system of automatic promotions was the main cause for the deterioration of standards at colleges and for the students' unrest and indiscipline which is rampant. It may be well that the government of Andhra Pradesh evaluates the non-detention system, and revamp it if not abolish the same.

Further, teachers were not happy with the groupism, casteism, political afiliations, etc., among the teachers. Political affiliations, casteism and regionalism have been dominating the teachers and polluting the academic atmosphere of the colleges and universities to the maximum possible extent. Political affiliations among teachers are rampant in recent years, when small regional parties with the support of immature youth with doubtful merit and calibre have entered the political field. To curb this, a code of conduct must be evolved and strictly implemented. This is probably a very urgent need. Unhealthy atmosphere among the teachers is undesirable. The proverb 'So are the teachers as are the students' holds good in this context more than anywhere else.

Junior lecturers were less satisfied with their job than the senior lecturers. Though qualifications are equal for both juniors and seniors, the later get a higher pay and enjoy a higher status. The juniors have been demanding parity of pay scales with the seniors. Under the above circumstances it would be well if the government evolves a suitable policy and sees that the dissatisfaction among the juniors is eliminated.

Seniors felt that principals give contradictory orders from time to time, are not sympathetic to grievances the teachers, partial and do not trust their colleagues. It may be because of the fact that in big institutions where the staff strength is too large, principals can not maintain close relationship and intimacy with their subordinates and may not also find time to maintain relationships with all the colleagues.

Maintaining close relationship between the 'boss' and all the colleagues in big institutions is a problem because of sheer numbers, very few can, indeed, enter into the so called inner circle of the principals. This problem can, however, be mitigated at least in government colleges by reducing the frequency of transfers, though as a policy the government does not allow any of its officers to be kept permanently in any one place. Necessity and importance of close association between the principal and the colleagues need no emphasis because once there is mutual understanding between them they can work easily, enthusiastically and happily for the development of the institution.

Another source of dissatisfaction to the teachers working in government collages, was lack of physical facilities like furniture, play grounds, staff rooms, toilet etc. In fact, many of the junior colleges did not have buildings of their own. The government should allot more funds and provide more working facilities to the colleges in general and junior colleges in particular.

Teachers who had a more favourable attitude towards teaching were found to be satisfied with their job. Similarly, those who obtained a high score on personality factor C and low scores on factors L and O had the highest job satisfaction. Further, teachers with high scores on factors: A, B, C, G, Q_1 and Q_3 and low score on factors L, N and O, had a more favourable attitude towards teaching. If these results are confirmed on other samples of teachers, it would be well for the administrators to use attitude and personality measures in the process of selection of teachers.

2. Limitations and Suggestions for Further Research

This study was limited to junior and degree college teachers working in Andhra Pradesh only.

A more intensive study including teachers working in the universities, professional colleges, secondary and primary schools on a larger population, will throw more light on different issues related to job satisfaction.

An in-depth investigation on satisfied and dissatisfied teachers may be of an immense practical utility to the educational administrators and it can also have some theoretical value as it could throw light on Herzberg's Two Factor Theory.

BIBLIOGRAPHY

Adams, J.S., 1963, Toward an understanding of inequity., *Journal of Abnormal Psychology*, 67, 422-436.

Adler, S., 1980,. Self-Esteem and causal attributions for job satisfaction and dissatisfaction, *Journal of Applied Psychology*, 65, 3 327-332.

Ahmed, S.H., 1984, A study of personal and job facets as determinants of job satisfaction for public senior high school teachers in the common wealth of Pennsylvania. Dissertation Abstracts International, 45, 5, 1580-A.

Ahuja, D.C., 1976, Mental health hazards among school teachers, *The Educational Review*, 8, 155-157.

Alexander, T., 1951, Certain characteristics of the self as related to affection, *Child Development*, 22, 285-290.

Al-Khaldi, A.M., 1983, Job content and context factors related to satisfaction and dissatisfaction in three occupational levels of the publec sector in Saudi Arabia, *Dissertaion Abstracts International*, 44, 5, 1917-A.

Allport, G.W. ,1929, The composition of political attitudes, *American Journal of Sociology*, 35, 220-238.

Allport, G.W., 1937, *Personality : A psychological Interpretation*, Hort, New York.

Altekar, A.S., 1951, *Education in Ancient India,* Nandkishore and Bros., Banaras, 48.

Altimus, C.A., and Tersine, R.J., 1973, Chronological age and job satisfaction : The young blue-collar worker. *Academy of Management Journal,* 16, 1, 53-66.

American Academy of Family Physicians, 1979, Lifestyle / Personal health care in different occupations : A study of attitudes and practices. Kansas city, Mo. : The Academy. (In) Mitzel, H.E. (Ed.) 1982, *Encyclopedia of Educational Research,* 4, 1903-1908.

Anand, S.P., 1971, *Study of Teacher-pupil Relationship in Higher Secondary Classes in Delhi,* Unpublished Ph.D. Thesis, University of Delhi.

Anand, S.P., 1972, School teachers and job satisfaction, *Teacher Education,* 7, 1, 16-23.

Anand, S.P., 1977, School teachers : Job satisfaction Vs. Extraversion and uroticism, *Indian Educational Review,* 12, 2, 68-78.

Anand S.P., 1986, Attitude of teachers towards pupils and their job-satisfaction, *Indian Educational Review,* Vol. XXI, 3, 38-50.

Anjaneyulu, B.S.R., 1968, A study of job satisfaction in the secondary school teachers and its impact on the education of pupils with special reference to the state of Andhra Pradesh. (In) *'A Survey of Research in Education'*, (Ed.) Buch. M.B. Centre of Advanced Study in Education, M.S. University, Baroda.

Anjaneyulu, B.S.R., 1970, Teaching Profession and Job Satisfaction. *Educational India,* 37, 6, 185-188.

Anjaneyulu, B.S.R., 1971, Teaching Profession and Job Satisfaction, *Educational India,* 37, 10, 340-342.

Apte, D.G., 1961, Our Educational heritage, Acharya Book Depot., Baroda, 145.

Armstrong, T.B., 1971, Job content and context factors related to satisfaction for different occupational levles, *Journal of Applied Psychology*, 55, 1, 57-65.

Arora, R.K., 1986, Teachers' anxiety at different levlels of job satisfaction, *Indian Educational Review*, Vol. XXI, 1, 151-157.

Arvey, R.D., Dewhirst, H.D. and Boling, J.C., 1976, Relationships between goal clarity, participation in good setting, and personality characteristics on job satisfaction in a scientific organisation, *Journal of Applied Psychology*, 61, 1, 103-105.

Arvey, R.D., and Mussio, S.J., 1974, Job expectations and valences of job rewards for culturally disadvantaged and advantaged clerical exployees, *Journal of Applied Psychology*, 59, 2, 230-232.

Ash, P., 1954, The SRA Employees Inventory - A statistical analysis, *Personnel Psychology*, 7, 337-364.

Askar, A.G., 1981, A study of teacher job satisfaction in Kuwait, *Dissertation Abstracts International*, 42, 2, 466-A.

Atteberry, M.G., 1977, The relationship between emotional stability and job satisfaction of elementary school principals. *Dissertation Abstracts International*, 37, 1, 6163-A.

Austin, A.N., 1985, A study of the attitudes of teachers and principals toward mainstreaming practices at selected elementary schools in the district of Columbia, *Dissertation Abstracts International*, 45, 8, 2315-A.

AVA., 1948, American Vocational Association research bulletin No. 3, *Fators Affecting the Satisfaction of Home Economics Teachers*, Committee on research publications, AVA Inc., Washington, D.C.

Balasubramaniyam, S., and Narayanan, S., 1977, Effect of personality on job satisfaction among college teachers, *Journal of Educational Research and Extension*, 13, 191-194.

Baldwin, J.M., 1905, *Dictionary of Philosophy and Psychology*. Macmillan, New York.

Bange, E.J., 1944, How to learn what workers think of job and boss, *Factory Management and Maintenance*, 102, 5, 101-104.

Beamer, G.C., and Ledbetter, E.W., 1957, The relation between teacher attitudes and the social service interest, *Journal of Educational Research*, 50, 655-666.

Belasco, J.A., and Alutto, J.A., 1972, Decisional participation and teacher satisfaction, *Educational Administration Quarterly*, 8, 1, 44-58.

Bentzen, M.M., Williams, R.C. and Heckman, P., 1980, A study of schopling : Adult experiences in schools, *Phi Delta Kappan*, 61, 394-397.

Bernard, N. and Kulandaivel, K., 1976, A study of job satisfaction among graduate teachers in Coimbatore, *Journal of Educational Research and Extension*, 13, 2, 120-124.

Best, J.W., 1948, *Research in Education*, Prentice-Hall International Inc., Englewood Cliffs. N.J.

Bidwell, C.E., 1959, The administration and teaching satifaction, *Phi Delta Kapan*, 37, 258-288.

Birmingham, J.A., 1985, Job satisfaction and burnout among Minnesota teachers, *Dissertation Abstracts International*, 45, 8, 2318-A.

Bizman, Y., 1976, Effects of relative magnitude of reward and type of need on satisfaction, *Journal of Applied Psychology*, 61, 303-304.

Blai, Jr.B., 1982, Predicting job satisfaction. From ERIC Vol. 17(5). Document Reproduction Service No. ED 210582.

Blair, B., 1964, An occupational study of job satisfaction and need satisfaction, *Journal of Experimental Education*, 32, 383-388.

Blau, P.M., and Scott, W.R., 1962, *Formal Organizations : A Comparative Approach*, San Francisco : Chandler, Intext.

Bloch, A., 1978, Combat neurosis in innercity schools, *American Journal of Psychiatry*, 135, 1189-1192.

Bloland, P.A.; and Selby, T.J., 1980, Factors associated with career change among secondary school teachers : A review of the literature, *Educational Research Quarterly*, 5, 3, B-24.

Blood, M.R. and Hulin, C.L., 1967, Alineation, environmental characteristics and worker responses, *Journal of Applied Psychology*, 51, 284-290.

Blum, M.L., 1952, *Readings in Experimental Industrial Psychology*, Prentice Hall, Inc. Englewood Cliffs, New Jersy. p. 107-110.

Blum, M.L., 1956, *Industrial Psychology and its Social Foundations*, Harper and Row, New York.

Blum, M.L., and Naylor, J.C., 1968, *Industrial Psychology*, Harper and Row, New York, 364-386.

Blum, S.M., 1961, The desire for security, *Journal of Educational Psychology*, 52, 317-321.

Bogardus, E.W., 1941, *Fundamental Social Psychology*, Century, New York, 62.

Bradburn, N.H., 1969, *The Structure of Psychological Well-being*, Aldine, Chicago, 147-179.

Brayfield, M.L., 1957, Inter-relationship between measures of job satisfaction and general satisfaction, *Journal of Applied Psychology*, 14, 201-205.

Brayfield, M.L., and Crockett, W.H., 1955, employee attitudes and employee performance, *Psychological Bulletin*, 52, 392-424.

Brown, D.R., 1960, Non-intelective qualities and the perception of the ideal student by college faculty, *Journal of Educational Sociology*, 33, 369-378.

Brown, F., 1973, The job satisfaction of administrators within a multi-ethnic steeing, *ERIC*, Vol. 8., Document Reproduction Service No. ED 90645.

Browning, C., 1963, How to tackle the problem of teacher turnover? *Social Management*, 7, 80-82.

Bryson, R., Bryson, J.B., and Johnson, M.F., 1978, Family size, satisfaction, and productivity in dual-career couples, *Psychology of Women Quarterly*, 3, 1, 67-77.

Butler, T.M., 1961, Satisfaction of beginning teachers, *Clearing House*, 36, 11-13.

Caldwell, D.F., and O'Reilly III, C.A., 1982, Task perceptions and Job satisfaction : A question of causality, *Journal of Applied Psychology*, 67, 3, 361-369.

Caplan, R.D., Cobb, S., French, J.R.P. (Jr), Van Harrison, R. and Pinneau, S.R. (Jr)., 1975, Job demands and worker health : Main effects and occupational differences. (HEW publication No. N10SH). Washington, D.C. : U.S. Government Printing Office. (In) Hendrix, W.H., Ovalle, 2d, N.K. and Troxler, R.G., 1985, Behavioural and physiological consequences of stress and its antecedent factors, *Journal of Applied Psychology*, 70, 1, 188-201.

Carrell, M.R. and Elbert, N.F., 1974, Some personal and organizational determinants of job satisfaction of postal clerks, *Academy of Management Journal*, 17, 2, 368-372.

Cattell, R.B., 1946, *The Description and Measurement of Personality*, World, New York.

Cattell, R.B., 1950, The main personality factors in questionnaire, self-estimated material, *Journal of Social Psychology*, 31, 3-38.

Cattell, R.B., 1956, Validation and intensification of the Sixteen Personality Factor Questionnaire, *Journal of Clinical Psychology*, 12, 205-214.

Cattell, R.B., 1957, *Personality and Motivation Structure and Measurement*, New york : World Bank.

Cattell R.B., 1961, Theory of situational, instrument, second order and refraction factors in personality structure research, *Psychological Bulletin*, 58, 160-174.

Cattell R.B., 1964, Validity and Reliability : A proposed more Basic set of concepts, *Journal of Educational Psychology*, 55, 1-22.

Cattell R.B., Eber, H.W. and Tatsuoka, M.M., 1970, *Hand book for the Sixteen Personality Factor Questionnaire (16PF)*, Institute for Personality and ability testing Champaign, Illinois, U.S.A.

Chase, F., 1951, Factors for satisfaction in teaching, *Phi Delta Kappan*, 33, 127-132.

Cheloha, R.S. and Farr, J.L., 1980, Absenteeism, job involvement and job satisfaction in an organizational setting, *Journal of Applied Psychology*, 65, 4, 467-473.

Chen, W.S., 1977, The job satisfaction of school teachers in the Republic of China as related to personal and organisational characteristics, *Dissertation abstracts international* 38, 6, 3167-A.

Chopra, R.K., 1986, Institutional climate and teacher job satisfaction, *Indian Educational Review*, Vol. XXI, 2, 33-45.

Chu, D.C., 1964, How can teachers' prestige be raised ? *Journal of Experimental Education*, 32, 4, 333-346.

Cichon, D.J., and Koff, R., 1980, Stress and teaching. National Association of Secondary School Principals Bulletin, 64 (434), 91-103. (In) Mitzel, H.E. (Ed)., 1982, *Encyclopedia of Educational Research*, 4, 1903-1908.

Clarke, R.L., 1977, Sources of teacher Job satisfaction and dissatisfaction for senior high school teachers. *Dissertation Abstracts International*, 37, 9, 5471-A.

Cohen, M.A., 1977, The job consciousness of public school teachers : A case study of work ideology in Newton, Massachusetts, *Dissertation Abstracts International*, 37, 9, 5471-A.

Cohen, M.A., 1977, The job consciousness of public school teachers : A case study of work ideology in Newton, Massachusetts, *Dissertation Abstracts International*, 38, 5, 3017-A.

Coladarci, A.P., 1958, Educational Psychology, *Annual Review of Psychology*, 9, 189-212.

Cook, D.H., 1979, Teacher Morale : Symptoms, diagnosis and Prescription, *Clearing House*, 52, 355-358.

Cook W.W. Kearney, N.C., Rocchio, P.D. and Thompson, A., 1956, Significant factors in teachers' classroom attitudes, *Journal of Teacher Education*, 7, 274-279.

Cook W.W., Leeds, C.H. and Callis, R., 1951, *The Minnesota Teacher Attitude Inventory*, Psychological corposation, New York.

Cooper, C., and Marshall, J., 1976, Occupational sourcess of stress : A review of the literature relating to coronary heart disease and mental ill health, *Journal of Occupational Psychology*, 49, 11-28.

Corwin, R.G., 1965, Professional persons in public organizations, *Educational Administration Quarterly*, 1, 3, 1-15.

Counts, G.E., 1978, Senior teachers : An endangered species. *ERIC*, Vol. 13. Document Reproduction Service No. ED 159132.

Crites, J.O., 1961, Factor analytic definitions of vocational motivation, *Journal of Applied Psychology*, 45, 330-337.

Cruickshank, D.R., 1982, Five areas of teacher concern, *Phi Delta Kappan*, 63, 7, 460.

Daly, R.E., 1981, A causal analysis of satisfaction, performance, Work environment and leadrship in selected secondary schools. *Dissertation Abstracts International*, 42, 2, 472-A.

Davis, F.G.T., 1981, Secondary teacher satisfaction - dissatisfaction : a symbolic interactionist analysis. *Dissertation Abstracts International*, 42, 2, 645-A.

Deasi., 1968, (In) Paliwal, M.B. and Paliwal, K.M., 1974, A study of need importance in relation to personal characteristics of industrial employees, *Psychological Studies*, 19, 2, 118-126.

Desai, M., 1977, President and P.M. Great teachers, *The Hindu*, 5th September, 1977, 1.

DeYoung, A.J., 1980, Professionalism and Politics : Toward a more realistic assessment of the issue, *Clearing House*, 53, 268-270.

Dobge, J.M., 1983, Perceived organizational and personal factors related to job satisfaction in public school teachers, *Dissertation Abstracts International*, 44, 5, 1730-A.

Domian, D.J., 1981, Impact of job stress on job satisfaction of iowa high school principals, *Dissertation Abstracts International*, 42, 1, 32-A.

Dunnette, M.D., 1965, Factor structures of unusually satisfying and unusually dissatisfying job situations for six occupational groups. Paper presented at Midwestern Psychological Association meeting, Chicago. (In) cage, N.L. 1963. Handbook of research on Teaching. Rand McNally & Co., Chicago.

Eckert, R.E., Stecklein, J.E., and Sagan, H.B., 1959, College faculty members view their jobs, *Association of University Professors Bulletin*, 45, 513-528.

Educational Research Service, 1980, Employee Absenteeism : A summary of research. (In) Mitzel, H.E. (Ed). 1982, *Encyclopedia of Educational Research*, 4, 1903-1908.

Education Commission, 1966, The Report of the Education Commission (1964-1966). Ministry of Education, Government of India.

Edwards, A.L., 1968, *Experimental Design in Psychological Research*, Amerind Publishing Co., Pvt. Ltd., New Delhi.

Edwards, A.L., 1969, *Techniques of Attitude Scale Construction*, Vakils, Feffer & Simons, Bombay.

Edwards A.L. and Kilpatrick, F.P., 1948, A technique for the construction of attitude scales, *Journal of Applied Psychology*, 32, 374-384.

Encyclopedia of Educational Research., 1982, The Free Press, A Division of Macmillan Publishing Co., Inc., New York, Fifth Edition, Vol. 4, 1903-1908.

Englhardt, V., 1973, Teachers' job satisfaction in schools of different levels. Journal of psychologic in Enziehung and Untirricht, (In) *Psychologic Abstracts*, 52, 11974.

Etzioni, A., 1964, *Modern Organizations.*Englewood Cliffs, N.J. : Prentice-Hall.

Ewen, R.B., 1964, Some determinants of job satisfaction : A study of the generality of Herzberg's theory, *Journal of Applied Psychology*, 48, 161-163.

Fager, R.E., 1958, Student and faculty conceptions of the 'successful student', *Journal of Counselling Psychology*, 5, 98-103.

Faris, J.P., 1977, A study of the determinants of job satisfaction. *Dissertation Abstracts International*, 37 (10), 6163-A.

Festinger, L., 1957, *A Theory of Congnitive Dissonance*, Evanston, Ill.: Row, Peterson.

Fisher, V.E., and Hanna, J.V., 1931, *The Dissatisfied Worker*, Macmillan & Co., New York.

Foa, U.G., 1957, Relation of worker's expectatopm to satisfaction with supervisor, *Personnel Psychology*, 10, 161-168.

Ford, R.N., 1969, Motivation through the work itself. American Asociation, New York. (In) Wanous, J.P. 1974. Individual differences and reactions to job characteristics, *Journal of Applied Psychology*, 59, 5, 616-622.

Fortune, 1947, (June). The Fortune Survey, pp. 5-10.

Fox, W.H., and Richey, R.W., 1948, An analysis of various factors associated with selection of teaching as a vocation, *Indiana University School of Education Bulletin*, 24, 1-58.

Freeman, F.S., 1967, *Theory and Practice of Psychological Testing*, Oxford and IBH Publishing Company, New Delhi, 108-116.

Friedlander, F., 1963, Underlying sources of job satisfaction, *Journal of Applied Psychology*, 47, 4, 246-250.

Friedlander, F., 1964, Job characteristics as satisfiers and dissatisfiers, *Journal of Applied Psychology*, 48, 388-392.

Friedlander, F., 1966, Importance of work Vs. Non work among socially and occupationally satisfied groups, *Journal of Applied Psychology*, 50, 437-441.

Fuller, R. and Miskel, C., 1972, Work attachments and job satisfaction among public school educators. Paper presented at the annual meeting of the American Educational Research Association, Chicago. (In) Mitzel, H.E., (Ed)., 1982, *Encyclopedia of Educational Research*, 4, 1903-1908.

Gandhi, K.A., 1982, Personality characteristics of teaching staff and organizational climate of schools. *Experiments in Education*, 10, 6, 110-116.

Gangappa, M.A., 1969, Professional status of a teacher, *Educational India*, 36, 188-190.

Ganguli, 1954, (In) Paliwal, M.B. and Paliwal, K.M. 1974. A study of need importance in relation to personal characteristics of industrial employees, *Psychological Studies*, 19, 2, 118-126.

Ganguli, H.C., 1964, *Structure Processes of Organisation*, Asia Publishing House, Bombay-89.

Gellmon, W., 1939, The components of vocational adjustment, *Personnel Guidance Journal*, 31.

Gilmer, B.V.H., 1966, *Industrial Psychology*, McGraw-Hill Book Company, New York.

Girdano, D.E., and Everly, G.S., 1979, *Controlling Stress and Tension*, Englewood Cliffs, N.J.: Prentice-Hall.

Glass, G.V., Cahen, L.S., Smith, M.L. and Filby, N.N., 1979, Class size and learning new interpretations of the research literature, *Today's Education*, 68, 2, 42-44.

Glicken, M.D., 1977, A regional study of the job satisfaction of social workers, *Dissertation Abstracts International*, 38, 3, 1658-A.

Goble, J.W., 1977, Relationships between job satisfaction, demographic factors, absenteeism and tenure of workers in a Delmarva broiler processing plant, *Dissertation Abstracts International*, 38, 4, 1820-A.

Godkin, R.L., 1982, Anticipated job satisfaction : Attitudinal bias among university female business majors, *Disertation Abstracts International*, 43, 1, 211-A.

Gordon, J.E., 1963, Review of R.B. Cattell's Personality and Social Psychology, Contemporary Psychology, 11, 236-238.

Gordon, P.A., 1981, A validation study of the theory of work adjustment : The prediction of teacher satisfaction, *Dissertation Abstracts International*, 42, 1, 34-A.

Gowin, R., 1975, Innovation in organisation : the case of schools, *Sociology of Education*, 48, 1-37.

Greene, C.N., 1973, Causal connections among managers' merit pay job satisfaction and performance, *Journal of Applied Psychology*, 58, 1, 95-100.

Gronlund, N.E., 1953, Relationship between the sociometric status of pupils and teachers' preferences for or against having them in class, *Scociometry*, 16, 142-150.

Guilford, J.P., 1954, Psychometric methods. Tata MacGraw-Hill Publishing Company, Faridabad, Haryana, India.

Gupta, A., 1973, Teachers — their changing roles, *N.I.E. Journal*, 4, 48-50.

Gupta, R.N., 1977, A study of the personality traits of primary school teachers, *Journal of Applied Psychology*, 55, 3, 259-286.

Gutman, L., 1947, A basis for scaling qualitative data, *American Social Review*, 9, 139-150.

Hackman, J.R. and Lawler III, E.E., 1971, Employee reactions to job characteristics, *Journal of Applied Psychology*, 55, 3, 259-286.

Hackman, J.R. and Oldham, G.R., 1976, Development of the job diagnostic survey, *Journal of Applied Psychology*, 60, 2, 159-170.

Halpern, G., 1966, Relative contributions of motivator and hygiene factors to overall job satisfaction, *Journal of Applied Psychology*, 50, 198-200.

Hansen, O.W., and Stanley, G.M., 1969, A study of the motivation of high school teahcers. Unpublished doctoral idssertation, University of Southern California. (In) Padmanabhaiah, S., 1984, *Job Satisfaction and Teaching Effectiveness of Secondary School Teachers,* Unpublished Doctoral Dissertation, S.V. Univeraity, Tirupati.

Harring, N.G., Stern, G.G., and Cruickshank, W.M., 1958, *Attitudes of Educators Towards Exceptional Children*, Syracuse University Press : Syracuse, New York.

Garvey, O.J., White, B.J., Prather, M., Alter, R.D. and Hoffameister, J.K., 1966, Teachers' belief systems and preschool atmospheres, *Journal of Educational Psychology*, 57, 373-381.

Hayeslip, D.W., 1977, Pupil control ideology — pupil control behaviour congruence and the job satisfaction of public school teachers, *Dissertation Abstracts International*, 37, 11, 6871-A.

Herzberg, F., Mausner, B., Peterson, R.O. and Capell, D.F., 1957, *Job Attitudes : Review of Research and Opinion*, psychological services of Pittisburgh, Pittisburgh.

Herzberg, F., Mausner, R.R.O. and snyderman, B.B., 1959, *The Motivation to Work,* Wiley, New York, 157.

Hodge, C.M., 1977, An analysis of the attitudes regarding job satisfaction held by negro professors and white professors in selected institutions of higher education desegregated since 1954, *Dissertation Abstracts International,* 37, 11, 6976-A.

Holdaway, E.A., 1978, Fact and overall satisfaction of teachers, *Educational Administration Quarterly,* 14, 1, 30-47.

Holder, C.A., 1985, Principal leadership behaviour and teacher job satisfaction in public elementary schools in Columbus, *Dissertation Abstracts International,* 45, 8, 2330-A.

Hollen, C.J., and Gemmill, G.R., 1976, A comparison of female and male professors on participation in decision making job related tension, job involvement and job dissatisfaction, *Educational Administration Quarterly,* 12, 1, 80-93.

Hooker, A.L., 1977, A study of the perceptions of selected school-based administrators in Florida relative to certain variables in secondary school administration as they relate to job satisfaction, *Dissertation Abstracts International,* 38, 4, 1782-A.

Hoppock, R., 1935, *Job Satisfaction,* Harper and Bros., New York.

Hoppock, R., 1960, A twenty seven year follow up on job satisfaction of employed adults, *Personnel Guidance Journal,* 38, 489-492.

Hornby, A.S., 1985, *Oxford Advanced Learner's Dictonary of Current English,* Oxford University Press, Delhi.

Hornby, A.S., Cowie, A.P., and Lewis, J.W., 1968, *Oxford Advanced Learner's Dictionary of Current English,* The English Language Book Society, Oxford University Press, London.

Houge, H.W., 1980, Personality characteristics and effectiveness of special education teachers, *Dissertation Abstracts International,* 40, 11, 5821-A

Hughes, H.M., 1972, Vocational choice, level and consistency : An investigation of Holland's theory on an employed sample, *Journal of Vocational Behaviour,* 2, 4, 377-388.

Hulin, C.L.,1977, Satisfactions and other job attitudes. (In) Wolman, B.B., (Ed.) 1977, *International Encyclopedia of Psychiatry, Psychology, Psychoanalysis and Neurology,* Vol. 10 (SA-ST). Aesculapius Publishers, Inc., New York.

Hulin, C.L., and Smith, P.C., 1964, Sex differences in job satisfaction, *Journal of Applied Psychology,* 48, 2, 88-92.

Hull, R.L. and Kolstad, A., 1942, Morale on the job (In) Watson, G., (Ed.). 1942, *Civilian Morale,* Reynal and Hitchcock : New York.

Hunter, E.C., 1957, Changes in teachers' attitudes toward children's behaviour over the last thirty years, *Mental Hygiene,* 41, 3-11.

Inlow, G.M., 1951, Job satisfaction of Liveral arts graduates, *Journal of Applied Psychology,* 35, 175-181.

Ivanceivch, J.M., 1974, Effects of the shorter work week on selected satisfaction and performance measures, *Journal of Applied Psychology,* 59, 6, 717-721.

Ivanceivch, J.M. and Matteson, M.T., 1980, *Stress and Work : A Managerical Perspective,* Glenviwe, IL. : Scott-Foresman.

Ivancevich, J.M., and Matteson, M.T., and Preston, C., 1982, Occupational stress, Type a behaviour, and physical well being, *Academy of Management Journal,* 25, 373-391.

Jenkins, D.H. and Lippitt, R., 1951, Interpersonal perceptions of teachers, students and parents. *National Educational Asociation* : Washington, D.C., (In) Gage, N.L., 1963, *Handbook of Research on Teaching,* Rand McNally & Co., Chicago.

Jervis, F.M., and Congdon, R.G., 1958, Student and faculty perceptions of educational values, *American Psychologist,* 13, 464-466.

Johnson, E.D., 1967, An analysis of factors related to teachers' satisfaction and dissatisfaction. Unpbulished doctoral dissertation, Auburon University, (In) *Psychological Abstracts*, 54, 1975, p. 393.

Johnson, G.H., 1955, An instrument for the measurement of job satisfaction, *Personnel Psychology*, 8, 27-37.

Kalanidhi, M.S., 1973, Problems of job satisfaction among women workers in industry, (In) Shanmugam, T.E.(Ed.), *Researches in Personality and Social Problems*, University of Madras, India.

Kapoor, 1967, (In) Paliwal, M.B. and Paliwal, K.M., 1974, A study of need importance in relation to personal characteristics of industrial employees, *Psychological Studies*, 19, 2, 118-126.

Karugu, G.K.,1981, An investigation of job satisfaction — dissatisfaction among elementary school teachers and head teachers in Nairobi, Kenya, and a comparison of their perceptions on fourteen selected job factors from Herzberg's two-factor Theory, *Dissertation Abstracts International*, 42, 1, 38-A.

Kates, S.L., 1950, Rorschach responses, strang blank scales, and job satisfaction among policemen, *Journal of Applied Psychology*, 34, 4, 249-254.

Katti, V.V. and Bennur, C.S., 1971, Attitudes fo secondary school teachers towards the teaching profession, *Journal of the College of Education*, Karnataka University, 2, 1-6.

Katzel, R.A., 1964, Personal values, job satisfaction and job behaviour, 341-363. (In) Borow, H. (Ed.), 1964, *Man in a World at Work*, Houghton Miflin Company: Boston.

Kay, E., et al., 1963, *A Study of the Performance Appraisal Interview*, Employee Relations, General Electric Company, New York, 1-36.

Kearney, N.C. and Rocchio, P.D., 1955, The relation btween the Minnesota teacher attitude inventory and subject matter taught by elementary teachers, *Educational Administration and Supervision*, 41, 358-360.

Kelly, T.L., 1939, A selection of upper and lower group for the validations of test items, *Journal of Educational Psychology*, 30, 17-24.

Kentle, J.V.L., 1985, A follow up study of industrial education doctoral graduates of the period of 1972. through 1982 to investigate the degree of job satisfaction, *Dissertation Abstracts International*, 45, 8, 2421-A.

Kim, J.S. and Hammer, W.C., 1976, Effect of performance, feedback and goal setting on productivity and satisfaction in an organisational setting, *Journal of Applied Psychology*, 61, 1, 48-57.

King, D. and Brass, B., 1970, Leadership, power and influence. Institute for research in the behavioural, economic and management sciences, Herman C., Krannert graduate school of industrial administration, Purdue University (Paper No. 280): Lafayette, Indiana. (In) Slocum, J.W., (Jr) and Strawser, R.H., 1972, Racial differences in job attitudes, *Journal of Applied Psychology*, 56, 1, 28-32.

Kirkpatrick, R.N., 1962, The relationship of job satisfaction to perceived staff promotional policies. (In) Robinson, H.A. and connors, R.P., 1963, Job satisfaction researches of 1962, *Personnel and Guidance Journal*, 42, 136-142.

Klein, S.M. and Maher, J.R., 1966, Education level and satisfaction with pay, *Personnel Psychology*, 19, 195-208.

Klugman, E., Carter, S., and Israel, S., 1979. Too many pieces: A study of teacher fragmentation in the elementary school. (ERIC Document Reproduction Service No. ED 178 515). (In) Mitzel, H.E. (Ed.), 1982, *Encyclopedia of Educational Research*, 4, 1903-1908.

Kohler, W., 1929, *Gestalt Psychology*, Liveright, New York.

Korman, A.K., 1970, Toward a hypothesis of work behaviour, *Journal of Applied Psychology*, 54, 31-41.

Kornhauser, A.W., 1965 *Mental Health of the Industrial Worker,* Wiley, New York.

Kornhauser, A.W., and Sharp, A.A., 1932, Employee attitudes: Suggestions from a study in a factory, *The Personnel Journal,* 10, 393-410.

Krech, D., Crutchfield, R.S., 1948, *Theory and Problems of Social Psychology,* McGraw-Hell, New York.

Krech, D., Crutchfield, R.S., 1948, and Ballachey, E.L. 1962. *Industrial in Society,* McGraw-Hill, New York.

Krishna Reddy, N., 1976, *Job Satisfaction of Teachers in Relation to Some Variables like Sex, Locality, Personality, etc.,* Unpublished M.Ed., dissertation, Sri Venkateswara University, Tirupati.

Kuder, G.F., 1953, *Examiner Manual for the Kuder Preference Record, Vocational Form-C,* Science Research Asociates: Chicago.

Kuhlen, R.G., 1963, Needs, perceived need satisfaction, opportunities, and satisfaction with occupation, *Journal of Applied Psychology,* 47, 56-64.

Kuhn, B.J., 1982, Teacher personality type and job satisfaction, *Dissertation Abstracts International,* 43, 1, 104-A.

Lahiri, and Chowdary, 1966, (In) Paliwal, M.B., and Paliwal, K.M., 1974, A study of need importance in relation to personal characteristics of industrial employees. Psychological studies, 19, 2, 118-126.

Lahiri, D.K., and Srivastava, S., 1967, Determinants of satisfaction in middle-management personnel, *Journal of Applied Psychology,* 51, 3, 254-265.

Latham, G.P., and Yukl, G.A., 1976, Effects of assignied and participative goal setting on performance and job satisfaction. *Journal of Applied Psychology,* 61, 2, 166-171.

Lawler, E.E., 1971, *III Pay and Organisational Effectiveness : A Psychological View,* McGraw-Hill, New York.

Leeds, C.H., 1956, Teacher attitude and temperament as a measure of teacher-pupil rapport, *Journal of Applied Psychology,* 40, 333-337.

Lewis, A.L.F., 1982, Job satisfaction, decisional discrepancy, academic social climate and academic achievement in selected title I elementary schools, *Dissertations Abstracts, International,* 43, 1, 35-A.

Likert, R., 1932, A technique for the measurement of attitudes. Archieves of Psychology, No. 140. (In) Brayfield, A.H. and Rothe, H.F. 1951. An index of job satisfaction, *Journal of Applied Psychology,* 35, 5, 307-311.

Lindgren, H.C., and Patton, G.M., 1958, Attitudes of high school and other teachers toward children and current educational methodology, *California Journal of Educational Research,* 9, 80-85.

Lipham, J., et.al., 1982, The relationship of decision involvement and principals' leadership to teacher job satisfaction in selected secondary schools. Resources in Education, *ERIC,* 17, 2, ED. 207129.

Locke, E.A., 1969, What is job satisfaction ? *Organisational Behaviour And Human Performance,* 4, 309-336.

Locke, E.A., and Whiting, R.J., 1974, sources of satisfaction and dissatisfaction among solid waste management employees, *Journal of Applied Psychology,* 59, 2, 145-156.

Loher, B.T., Noe, R.A. Moeller, N.L., and Fitzgerald, M.P., 1985, A Meta-Analysis of the relation of Job characteristics to Job satisfaction, *Journal of Applied Psychology,* 70, 2, 280,-289.

Lopuch, W.R., 1985, Attitude towards competition in higher education as expressed by faculty members in American Academia, *Dissertation Abstracts International,* 45, 9, 2830-A.

Maddux, C.D., and others, 1982, A Survey of Texas Public School teachers, Resources in Education, *ERIC,* 17.6, ED. 212559.

March, J.G., and Simon, H.A., 1958, *Organisations*, Wiley, New York.

Marr, E., and Mathur, R.K., 1973, Job satisfaction of teacher educators. *Indian Education Review*, 8, 10-20

Marxi, M.H., and Hillix, W.A., 1973, *Systems and Theories in Psychology*, McGraw-Hill Book Company, New York.

Maslach, C., 1978, Job burnout : How people cope, *Public Welfare*, 36, 56-58.

Maslow, A.H., 1943, "A Theory of Human Motivation". Psychological Review, 50, 370-396.

Maslow, A.H., 1954, *Motivation and Personality*, Harper and Row, New York.

Matteson, M.T., & Ivanceich, J.M., 1979, Organizational stressors and heart disease: A research model, *Academy of Management Review*, 4, 347-357.

Mayadeb, 1972, Perceived importance of job-factors in different types of job, *Psychological Studies*, 17, 2, 1-4.

McCanaughy, J.B., and Palmer, J.D., 1969, Personality and performance of federal field executives in South California, *Public Personel Review*, 30, 4, 205-210.

McGowan, J.R., 1981, An investigation of the relationship between certain situatioal variables, personality variables and job satisfaction within the path-goal model of management among public school teachers, *Dissertations Abstracts International*, 42, 2, 485-A.

Mc Grath, J.E., 1964, *Social Psychology: Brief Introduction*, Holt, New York.

McMurry, R.N., 1932, Efficiency, work satisfaction and Neurotic tendency: A study of bank employees, *The personnel Journal*, 11, 201-210.

Mehdi, N.G., and Sinha., I.N., 1971, a study of relationship between Neuroticism and job satisfaction in school teachers, *Indian Journal of Applied Psychology*, 8, 41-47.

Merill-Ii, P.P., 1969, A study concerning the job satisfaction of elementary teachers and principals. Unpublished Doctoral Dissertation, Syracause University. (In) Padmanabhaiah, S., 1984, Job satisfaction and teaching effectiveness of secondary school teachers. Unpublighed Doctoral Dissertation, S.V. University.

Michaels, C.E., and Spector, P.E., 1982, Causes of employee turnover. A test of the Mobley, Griffeth, Hand and Meglino model, *Journal of Applied Psychology*, 67, 53-59.

Miller, F.D., 1934, Construction of an attitude scale toward teaching. (In) Shaw, M.E., and Wright, J.M., 1967, *Scales for Measurement of Attitudes*, McGraw-Hill Book Co., New York, 67-72.

Miller, G.W., 1974, Multi-job holding of Public school teachers, *Public Personnel Managemetn*, 3, 392-402.

Mishra, Y.N., 1972, Stresses and strains of secondary school teachers, Educational India, 38, 218-221.

Miskal, C., 1974, Intrinsic, extrinsic and risk propensity factors in th work attitudes of teachers, educational administrators and business managers, *Journal of Applied Psychology*, 59, 3, 339-343.

Mitchell, J.C., 1943, A study of teachers' and mental hygienists' ratings of certain behaviour problems of children, *Journal of Educational Research*, 36, 292-307.

Mitzel, H.E., (Ed.), 1982, *Encyclopedia of Educational Research*, Vol. 4, 1903-1908, Macmillan Publishing Co., Inc., New York.

Mobley, W.H., Griffeth, R.W., Hand, H.H., and Meglino, B.M., 1979, Review and conceptual analysis of the employee turnover process, *Psychological Bulletin*, 86, 493-522.

Mokry, A-I 1981, Job satisfaction in the education industry: A case study of teachers' interaction whith work conditions in high school, *Dissertation Abstracts International*, 42, 1, 355-A.

Morgan, J.J.B., 1934, Keeping a solid mind, Macmillan, New York.

Morse, N.C., 1953, Satisfactions in White Collar job (Annual report, Michigan Institute for Social Research, University of Michigan). 72.

Morse, N.C., Weiss, R., and Griggs, R., 1954, Attitudes toward work. Unpublished study. Institute for social research, University of Michigan, Ann Arbor. (in) Bum and Maylor (1968), *Industrial Psychology,* Harper & Row, New York.

Mukherji, R.K., 1947, *Ancient Indian Education,* MacMillan & Co., London, 236.

Mukherji S.N., 1957, *Education in India : Today and Tomorrow,* Acharya Book Depot, Baroda, 201-202.

Mukherji, S.N., 1968, *Education of Teacher in India,* S. Chand & Co., India.

Murphy, G., and Likert, A., 1937,. *Public Opinion and the Individual,* Harper: New York.

Myers, M.S., 1964, *Who are Your Motivated Workers ?* Harvard Business Review, 42, 1, 73-88.

Nayyar, S.M., 1967, Students' indiscipline, *The Educational Review,* 73, 4, 83-85.

NEA., 1957, *The Status of American Public School Teacher,* National Education Association Research Bulletin, 35.

Neeraja Dwivedi, 1977, A study of the effect of financial incentives on job satisfaction of blue collar workers, *Indian Educational Review,* 12, 1, 49-76.

Neeraja Dwivedi and Pestonjee, D.M., 1975, Socio-Personal correlates of job satisfaction, *Psychological studies,* 20, 2, 30-49.

New Comb, T.M., Turner, R.H., and Converse, P.E., 1965, *Social Psychology : The Study of Human Interaction,* Holt, New York.

Nielson, A.T., 1985, Attributes of teachers who maintain their teaching position, *Dissertation Abstracts International*, 45, 8, 2475-A

Nixon, M., and Gue, L.R., 1975, Women administrators and Women teachers : A comparative study. Alberta Journal of Educational Research, 21, 3, 196-206, (In) *Psychological Abstracts*, 55, 1976.

Orden, S.R., and Bradburn, N.M., 1968, Dimensions of marriage happiness, *American Journal of Sociology*, 73, 715-732.

Orpen, C., 1981, Effect of flexible working hours on employee satisfaction and performance: A field experiment, *Journal of Applied Psychology*, 66, 1, 113-115.

Orpen, G., 1974, Social desirability as a moderator of the relationship between job satisfaction and personal adjustment, *Personnel Psychology*, 27, 103-108.

Overall, J.E., and Klett, C.J., 1972, *Applied Multivariate Analysis*, MacGraw-Hill, New York.

Padmanabhaiah, S., 1984, Job satisfaction and Teaching effectiveness of secondary school teachers. Unpublished Doctoral Dissertation, S.V. University, Tirupati.

Pagel, S., and Price, J., 1980, Strategies to alleviate teacher stress, *Pointer*, 24, 2, 45-53.

Paliwal, M.B., and Paliwal, K.M., 1974, A study of need importance in relation to personal characteristics of industrial employees, *Psychological Studies*, 19, 2, 118-126.

Parelius, R.J., 1982, The troubles with teaching under graduates: Problems arising from organizational, professional, collegial and client relationships, *ERIC*, 17, 5. Document Reproduction Service No. ED 210985.

Peck, L., 1936, A study of the adjustment difficulties of a group of women teachers, *Journal of Educational Psychology*, 28, 401-416.

Peruman, V., 1969, Teachers' status, *The Education Quarterly*, 21, 15-18.

Pestonjee, D.M., 1971, Effect of financial incentives on job satisfaction, *Indian Journal of Applied Psychology* 8, 47-49.

Pestonjee, D.M., 1973, Organisational structures and job attitudes. (In) Neeraja Dwivedi and Pestonjee, D.M., 1976, off-the-job factors and job satisfaction: Some evidence for the inter actional model, *Psychological Studies*, 21, 2, 11-14.

Pestonjee, D.M., Akhtar, S.S., and Siddiqui, M.M., 1971, Attitudes of different levels of employees towards electronic data processing system. *Psychological Studies*, 16, 1, 9-14.

Pestonjee, D.M., and Singh, A.P., 1972, Authoritarianism and job satisfaction of supervisors in a steel industry, *Journal of the Indian Academy of Applied Psychology*, 9, 2, 54-57.

Pestonjee, D.M., and Singh, A.P., 1973, Morale of first-level supervisors, *Indian Journal of Social Work*, 4, 3, 189-193.

Porter, L.W., 1962, Job attitudes in management. Perceived dificiences in need fulfilment as a function of job level, *Journal of Applied Psychology*, 46, 375-384.

Porter, L.W., 1966, Personal management, *Annual Review of Psychology*, 17, 395-422.

Porter, L.W., and Steers, R.M., 1973, Organisational, work and personal factors in employee turnover and absenteeism, *Psychological Bulletin*, 80, 151-176.

Porter, L.W., Steers, R.M., and Mowday, R.T., 1974, Organisational commitment, job satisfaction, and turnover among psychoatric technicians, *Journal of Applied Psychology*, 595, 603-609.

Quick, J.C., and Quick, J.D., 1979, Reducing stress through preventative management, *Human Resources Management*, 18, 3, 15-22.

Wills, B.R., 1982, Age and sex: The relationship upon perceived job satisfaction among exempt level employees, *Dissertation Abstracts International*, 43, 2, 336-A.

Wolman, B.B., (Ed)., 1977, *International Encyclopedia of Psychiatry, Psychology, Psycho-analysis and Neurology,* Vol. 10. (SA-ST), Aesculapius publishers, Inc., New York.

Woodruff, A.D., 1942, Personal values and the direction of behaviour, *School Review,* 50, 32-42. (In) Zytowski, D.G., 1968, Vocational behaviour : Readings in theory and research. Holt, Rinehent and Winston, Inc.

Wyatt, S., and Langdon, J.L., 1937, *Fatigue and Boredom in Repititive Work,* Industrial Health Research Board, No. 77. His Majesty's Stationary Office, London.

Xydias, N., 1956, Attidue du corps inseignant de vienne (Iserc) vis-a-vis de divers traits de comportement des ecoliers, *Travel Hum* 18, 249-256. (In) Gage, N.L. 1963. *Hand Book of Research on Teaching,* Rand McNally & Co., Chicago.

Young, M.G., 1983, A study of the comparison of job Satisfaction and professional preparation of selected junior and senior high school teachers in colorado, *Dissertation Abstracts International* 44, 5, 1685-A.

Yuskiewics, V.D., and Donaldson, W.S., 1972, Job Satisfaction of the public school teacher: A function of sub culture concensus with respect to pupil control ideology, *ERIC,* Vol. 7, Document Reproduction Service, No. ED 061178, Chicago.

Zytowski, D.G., 1968, *Vocational Behaviour : Readings in Theory and Research.* Holt, Rinehent and Winston, Inc.

Rocchio, P.D., and Kearney, N.C., 1956, Teacher-Pupil attitudes as related to non-promotion of secondary school pupils, *Educational Psychological Measurement*, 16, 244-252.

Roethlisberger, F.W., and Dickson, W.J., 1939, *Management and the Worker*, Hardward University Press, Cambridge.

Roger, D., 1953, A study of the reaction in the elementary schools, *Journal of Social Education*, 4, 120-121.

Rohila, P., 1966, Job satisfaction — a research summary, *Indian Educational Review*, 1.

Rudd, W.G.A., and Wiseman, S., 1962, Sources of dissatisfaction among a group of teachers, *British Journal of Educational Psychology*, 32, 275-291.

Rummel, 1970, (In) Padmanabhaiah, S., 1984, *Job Satsifaction and Teaching Effectiveness of Secondary School Teachers*. Ph.D. Thesis, submitted to S.V. University, Tirupati, India.

Ryans, D.G., 1960, *Characteristics of Teachers*, Sterling Publishers (P.) Ltd., New Delhi.

Saiyidain, K.G., 1950, *Problems of Educational Reconstruction*, Asia Publishing House, Bombay, 297.

Salch, S.D., and Otis, J.L., 1964, Age and level of job satisfaction, *Personnel Psychology*, 17, 425-430.

Sarala, J., 1971, Anxiety and job satisfaction, *Indian Journal of Applied Psychology*, 8, 70-71.

Sarveswaa Rao, G.V., 1972, Intrinsic and extrinsic factors in job satisfaction of male clerical employees, *Psychological Studies*, 17, 1, 45-52.

Savage, R.M., 1967, A study of teacher satisfaction and attitudes: Causes and effects (Doctoral dissertation, Auburn University). (In) Schmidt, G.L., 1976. Job satisfaction among secondary school administrators, *Educational Administration Quarterly*, 12, 2, 68-86.

Schaffer, R.H., 1953, Job satisfaction as related to need satisfaction in work, *Psychological Monograph,* No. 346.

Scheier, I.H., and Cattell, R.B., 1961, *Hand Book for the Neuroticism Scale Questionnaire,* The Institute for Personality & Ability Testing, Champaign, Illinois, U.S.A.

Scherf, G.W.H., 1974, Consumer dissatisfaction as a function of dissatisfaction with interpersonal relationships, *Journal of Applied Psychology,* 59, 4, 465-471.

Schmidt, G.L., 1976, Job satisfaction among secondary school administrators, *Educational Administration Quarterly,* 12, 2, 68-86.

Schneider, B., and Snyder, R.A., 1975, Some relationships between job satisfaction and organisational climate, *Journal of Applied Psychology,* 60, 3, 318-328.

Schuhle, W., 1957, Teachers' understanding of students academic ideals, *Journal of Higher Education,* 28, 388-408.

Schutz, F., 1958, *A Three-Dimensional Theory of International Behaviour* Rinehart and Co., New York.

Schwab, D.P., and Wallace, M.J., 1974, Correlates of employee's satisfaction with pay, *Industrial Relations,* 13, 78-89.

Schwartz, M.M., Jenusaites, E., and Stark, H., 1963, Motivational factors among supervisors in the utility industry, *Personnel Psychology,* 16, 45-53.

Schwerz, et.al., 1966, (In) Paliwal, M.B., and Poliwal, K.M., 1974, A study of need importance in relation to personal characteristics of industrial employees, *Psychological Studies,* 16, 118-126.

Scott, W.E., 1966, "Activation Theory and Task Design", *Organisational Behaviour and Human Performance,* 1, 3-30.

Secondary Education Commission, 1954, *The Report of the Secondary Education Commission,* Ministry of Education, Government of India.

Sergiovanni, T.J., 1975, Financial incentives and teacher accountability: are we paying for the wrong thing ? *Educational Administration Quarterly,* 11, 2, 112-115.

Sharp, G.J., 1984, An analysis of the relationship between job satisfaction and retirement decisions of selected public school prinicpals of a large Midwestern city, *Dissertation Abstracts International*, 45, 5, 1604-A.

Shaver, H.C., 1977, Job satisfaction, career patterns, and job hunting among journalism graduates, *Dissertation Abstracts International*, 37, 11, 6817-A.

Shaw, M.E., and Wright, J.M., 1967, *Scales for the Measurement of Attitudes*, McGraw-Hill Book Co., New York.

Shingwekar, G.K., 1966, Advice to young teachers, *Educational India*, 32, 9, 315.

Siegel, L., 1969, *Industrial Psychology*, Richard, D., Irwin, Inc., Home wood, Illinois, 331-362.

Singh, P.N., and Wherry, R.J., 1963, Ranking of job factors by factory workers, *Personnel Psychology*, 8, 27-37.

Sinha, D., and Nair, R.R., 1965, A study of job satisfactionin factory workers, *Indian Journal of Social Work*, 26, 1-6.

Sinha, D., and Sarma, K.C., 1962, Union attitudes and job satisfaction in Indian Workers. *Journal of Applied Psychology*, 46, 247-251.

Slobertz. F., 1950, Elementary teachers' reactions to school situations, *Journal of Educational Research*, 44, 81-90.

Slobertz, F., 1951, How elementary school teachers meet selected school situations, *Journal of Education Psychology*, 42, 339-356.

Slocum, J.W., (Jr) and Strawser, R.H., 1972, Racial differences in job attitudes, *Journal of Applied Psychology*, 56, 1, 28-32.

Smith, D.B., and Plant, W.T., 1982, Sex differences in the job satisfaction of University Professors, *Journal of Applied Psychology*, 67, 2, 249-251.

Smith, F.D., 1978, A net work analysis of a bureau of Indian affairs school system to determine factors involved in job satisfaction, *Dissertation Abstracts International*, 38, 7, 4085-A.

Smith, H.C., 1945, *Personality Adjustment*, McGraw-Hill, New York.

Smith, H.D., 1982, Teacher voluntary absenteeism and perceptions of the professional environment, job satisfaction and impact of collective bargaining, *Dissertation Abstracts International*, 43, 1, 41-A.

Smith, J.J., 1977, Job satisfaction of Connecticut Public Senior High School Principals as related to school location and school size, *Dissertation Abstracts International*, 37, 9, 5517-A.

Smith, P.C., Kendall, L.M., and Hulin, C.L., 1969, *The Measurement of Satisfaction in Work and Retirement*, Rand McNally, Chicago.

Soliman, H.M., 1970, Motivation-hygiene theory of job attitudes: an emperical investigation and an attempt to reconcile both the one and the two factor theories of job attitudes, *Journal of Applied Psychology*, 54, 5, 452-461.

Sommers, N.L., 1969, *Factors Influencing Teacher Morale in Selected Secondary Schools*, Unpublished Doctoral Dissertation, State University, Kent.

Spector, 1956, (In) Padmanabhaiah, S., 1984, *Job satisfaction and Teaching Effectiveness of Secondary School Teachers*. Ph.D. Thesis, submitted to S.V. University, Tirupati, India.

Spuck, D.W., 1974, Reward structures in the public high school, *Educational Administration Quarterly*, 10, 1, 18-34.

Srivastava, S.K., and Sinha, M.M., 1972, An inquiry into the relationship between job satisfaction and job anxiety. *Journal of Indian Academy of Applied Psychology*, 9, 2, 39-44.

Srole, L., Langer, T., Stanley, M., Marvin, O., and Thomas, R., 1962, *Mental Health in the Metropolis: The Midtown Man Hattan Study*, McGraw-Hill: New York, 177-178.

Stagner, R., Flabee, D.R., and Wood, E.A., 1952, Working on the Railboard: A study of job satisfaction, *Personnel Psychololgy*, 5, 293-306.

Stapleton, J.C., Croft, J.C., and Frankiewicz, R.G., 1979, The relationship between teacher brinkmanship and teacher job satisfaction, *Planning and Changing*, 10, 157-168.

Stern, 1921, (In) Padmanabhaiah, S., 1984, *Job Satisfaction and Teaching Effectiveness of Secondary School Teachers*, Ph.D. Thesis, submitted to S.V. University, Tiruapti, India.

Stern, G.G., Stern, M.I., and Bloom, B.S., 1956, *Methods in personality assessment*, Free Press: Glencoe, III.

Stockford, L.O., and Kunze, K.R., 1950, Psychology and the pay check, *Personnel*, 27, 129-143.

Stouffer, G.A.W., 1956, The attitudes of secondary school teachers towards certain behaviour problems of children, *School Review*, 64, 358-362.

Stouffer, S.A., Suchman, E.A., Devinney, L.C., Star, S.A., and Williams, R.M., Jr. 1949, *The American Soldier: Adjustment During Army Life*, Princeton University Press, Princeton, N.J.

Subrahmanian, K., 1987, "APCHE will be only a stumbling block". *The Hindu*, Dated 7-8-1987. p. 18.

Sucher, J.H., 1962, A study of morale in education utilising incomplete sentences, *Journal of Educational Research*, 56, 75-81.

Suehr, J.C., 1962, A study of morale in education: utilizing incomplete sentences, *Journal of Educational Research*, 56, 75-81.

Super, D.E., 1939, Occupational level and job satisfaction, *Journal of Applied Psychology*, 23, 547-564.

Surbida, M.M., 1984, A study of the job satisfaction of elementary principals, *Dissertation Abstracts International,* 45, 3 1010-A.

Tabatabai, H.A., 1981, A comparative study of job satisfaction and internal-external locus of control in private and public organizations, *Dissertation Abstracts International,* 42, 2, 780-A.

Teacher Opinion Poll: Attacks on teachers, 1980, *Today's Education,* 69, 3, 21, (In) Mitzel, H.E., (Ed.), 1982, *Encyclopedia of Educational Research,* 4, 1903-1908.

Teacher opinion poll : Job satisfaction, 1980, Today's Education, 69, 4, 8, (In), Mitzel, H.E., (Ed.), 1982, *Encyclopedia of educational research,* 4, 1903-1908.

The U.S., Department of Labour, 1949, A career bureau of labour standards hunting.

The University Education Commission, 1948, *The Report of the University Education Commission,* Ministry of Education, Government of India.

Thompson, C.E., 1940, The attitudes of various groups toward behaviour problems of children, *Journal of Abnormal Social Psychology,* 35, 120-125.

Thompson, G, 1947, *Factoral Analysis of Human Ability,* University of Chicago Press: Chicago.

Thurstone, L.L., 1946. Comment. *American Journal of Sociology,* 5, 52.

Travers, R.M.W., and Rabinowitz, W., 1953, A drawing technique for studying certain outcomes of teacher education, Part-II. A quantitative comparison of certain outcomes in tow institutions. (In) Travers, R.M.W., Rabinowitz, W., Page, M.H., Nemovicher, E. and Ventur, P., Explanatory studies in teacher personality, City colleges: Division of education office of research and evaluation (Res. Servies, No. 14., 29-40), New York.

Travers, R.M.W., and Rabinowitz, W., and Nemovicher, W., 1953, The anxieties of a group of student teachers. (In) Travers, R.M.W., Rabinowitz, W., Page, M.H., Nemovicher, E., and Ventur. P., Explorator studies in teacher Personality, City colleges Div. of teacher education, Office of Research and Evaluation (Res. series No. 14, 45-51): New York. (In) Gage, N.L. 1963, *Handbook of Research on Teaching*, Rand McNally & Co., Chicago.

Trier, H.E., 1954, Job satisfaction and occupational status. Unpublished Masters Thesis, Michigan state College. (In) Gage, N.L., 1963, *Handbook of Research on Teaching*, Rand McNally & Co., Chicago.

Umstot, D.D., Bell, C.H., (Jr) and Mitchell, T.R., 1976, Effects of job enrichment and task goals on satisfaction and productivity: Implications for job design, *Journal of Applied Psychology*, 61, 4, 379-393.

Urban teachers report more stress, 1980, *Compact*, 14(1), cl-4. (In) Mitzel, H.E. (Ed), 1982, *Encyclopedia of Educational Research*, 4, 1903-1908.

Vaneist, R.H., 1951, Worker Popularity and job satisfaction, *Personnel Psychology*, 4.

Venkatarami Reddy, A., 1978a, Attitude of post graduate students towards internal assessment, *Indian Educational Review.* 13, 16-32.

Venkatarami Reddy A., 1978b. A two year follow up study on internal assessment, *Journal of Higher Education*, 4, 47-56.

Venkatarami Reddy, 1979, Students' reactions towards english and regional media: A comparative study, *Journal of Higher Education*, 5, 101-108.

Venkatarami Reddy, A., 1980, Do under graduate students want regional medium ? *Indian Psychological Review*, 19, 48-52.

Venkatarami Reddy, A., 1984, Post graduates want a change over to Internal Assessment. *Asian Journal of Psychology and Education*, 13.

Venkatarami Reddy A., and Babjan, O., 1980, Why do teachers working in government and private schools differ in the level of their job satisfaction ? *Journal of Educational Research and Extension,* 17, 65 to 74.

Venkatarami Reddy A., and Krishna Reddy, N., 1978, Job satisfaction of teachers working under different managements, *The Education Quarterly,* 30, 28-29.

Venkatarami Reddy A., and Ramakrishnaiah, D., 1981, Job satisfaction of college teachers, *Journal of Education and Psychology,* Vol. 38, 4, 211-218.

Vernon, P.E., 1963, *Personality Assessment: A Critical Survey,* Methuen & Co. Ltd., London, pp 14-15.

Vickroy, S.C., Shaw, J.B., and Fisher, C.D., 1982, Effects of temperature, Clothing, and task complexity on task performance and satisfaction, *Journal of Applied Psychology,* 67, 1, 97-102.

Vroom V.H., 1964, *Work and Motivation,* Wiley: New York.

Walsh, D., 1979, Classroom stress and teacher burnout, *Phi Delta Kappan,* 61, 253.

Wandt, E., 1954, A comparison of the attitudes of contrasting groups of teachers, *Educational and Psychological Measurement,* 14, 418-422.

Wanous, J.P., and Lawler, E.E.III, 1972, Measurement and Meaning of job satisfaction, *Journal of Applied Psychology,* 56, (2), 95-105.

Warren, H.C., 1934, *Dictionary of Psychology,* Niffillin Co., Houghton, Boston.

Weaver, C.N., 1974, Correlates of job satisfaction: some evidence from the national surveys, *Academy of Management Journal,* 17, 2, 373-375.

Weaver, C.N., 1977, Relationships among pay, race, sex, occupational prestige, supervisory work, autonomy and job satisfaction in a national sample, *Personnel Psychology*, 30, 437-466.

Weiner, A.M., 1981, Sex role preference and job satisfaction among secondary Home Economics teachers, *Dissertation Abstracts International*, 42, 2, 580-A.

Weinroth, E.D., 1977, Motivation, Job satisfaction, and career aspirations of married wome teachers at different career stages, *Dissertation Abstracts International*, 38, 6, 3206-A.

Weiskopf, P.E., 1980, Burnout among teachers of exceptional children, *Exceptional Children*, 47, 1, 18-23.

Weitz, J., and Nuckolos, R.C., 1955, Job Satisfaction and job survival, *Journal of Applied Psychology*, 39, 294-300.

Werner, A., 1980, Support for teachers in stress, *Pointer*, 24, 2, 54-60.

Wernimont, P.F., 1964, Intrinsic and extrinsic factors in job satisfaction. Doctoral Thesis, University of Minnesota, Minneapolis. (In) Gage, N.L. 1963. *Handbook of Research on Teaching*, Rand McNally & Co., Chicago.

Wickman, E.K., 1928, *Children's Behaviour and Teachers' Attitudes*, Common wealth fund: New York, (In) Gage, N.L., 1963, *Handbook of Research on Teaching*. Rand McNally & Co., Chicago.

Wickstrom, R.A., 1971, An investigation into job Satisfaction among teachers. Doctoral disertation, University of Oregon. (In) Schmidt, G.L., 1976, Job satisfaction among secondary school administrators, *Educational Administration Quarterly* 12, 2, 68-86.

Williams, L.K., 1965, Some Correlates of risk taking. *Personnel Psychology*, 18, 297-309.

Wills, B.R., 1982, Age and sex: The relationship upon perceived job satisfaction among exempt level employees, *Dissertation Abstracts International,* 43, 2, 336-A.

Wolman, B.B., (Ed)., 1977, *International Encyclopedia of Psychiatry, Psychology, Psycho-analysis and Neurology,* Vol. 10. (SA-ST), Aesculapius publishers, Inc., New York.

Woodruff, A.D., 1942, Personal values and the direction of behaviour, *School Review,* 50, 32-42. (In) Zytowski, D.G., 1968, Vocational behaviour : Readings in theory and research. Holt, Rinehent and Winston, Inc.

Wyatt, S., and Langdon, J.L., 1937, *Fatigue and Boredom in Repititive Work,* Industrial Health Research Board, No. 77. His Majesty's Stationary Office, London.

Xydias, N., 1956, Attidue du corps inseignant de vienne (Isere) vis-a-vis de divers traits de comportement des ecoliers, *Travel Hum* 18, 249-256. (In) Gage, N.L. 1963. *Hand Book of Research on Teaching,* Rand McNally & Co., Chicago.

Young, M.G., 1983, A study of the comparison of job Satisfaction and professional preparation of selected junior and senior high school teachers in colorado, *Dissertation Abstracts International* 44, 5, 1685-A.

Yuskiewics, V.D., and Donaldson, W.S., 1972, Job Satisfaction of the public school teacher: A function of sub culture concensus with respect to pupil control ideology, *ERIC,* Vol. 7, Document Reproduction Service, No. ED 061178, Chicago.

Zytowski, D.G., 1968, *Vocational Behaviour : Readings in Theory and Research.* Holt, Rinehent and Winston, Inc.

Index